JAY ERSTLING • SAMSON HELFGOTT • T. DAVID REED

THE PRACTITIONER'S GUIDE TO THE PCT

AMERICAN BAR ASSOCIATION
Section of
Intellectual Property Law

Cover by Kelly Book/ABA Publishing.

Printed in the United States of America

17 16 15 14 13 5 4 3 2 1

Library of Congress Cataloging-in-Publication Data

The practitioner's guide to the PCT / by Jay Erstling.—First edition.
pages cm
Includes bibliographical references and index.
ISBN 978-1-62722-014-9 (print : alk. paper)
1. Patent Co-operation Treaty (1970 June 19) 2. Patents (International law) 3. Patent practice. I. Erstling, Jay A., editor.
K1505.P73 2013
346.04'86—dc23

2013012054

CONTENTS

ABOUT THE AUTHORS

Jay Erstling was the Director of the Office of the PCT and Director-Advisor for PCT Matters at the World Intellectual Property Organization in Geneva, Switzerland. His responsibilities included the administration and reform of the PCT legal framework and PCT policy, the maintenance of effective working relations with all PCT member countries, and daily oversight of the PCT system. Since his return to Minnesota, Mr. Erstling has served as a professor of law at William Mitchell College of Law and Of Counsel at the Minneapolis intellectual property firm of Patterson Thuente IP. At William Mitchell, he teaches and publishes primarily in the area of international and comparative patent law. In addition to the PCT, Mr. Esrtling has a particular interest in the patent systems of China, Korea, India, and other emerging countries. At Patterson Thuente IP, he counsels clients on their international intellectual property strategies and advises on changes in intellectual property law and practice. Mr. Erstling was a Fulbright Scholar in Cyprus and Sri Lanka and an Indo-American Fellow in New Delhi and Bangalore, and he has served as a law consultant and speaker in South Asia, the Middle East, Western Africa, and the Caribbean for the United States Agency for International Development, the U.S. State Department, and The Asia Foundation. He earned BS and JD degrees from Cornell University.

Samson Helfgott has practiced for over 40 years in domestic and international patent, trademark, and copyright matters; international patent strategy; and patent and trademark administration before U.S. and foreign patent tribunals. He is a prolific writer and lecturer who is frequently published in the area of international prosecution and litigation pertaining to patents, among others. Mr. Helfgott served as a member of the Council of the American Bar Association (Intellectual Property Law Section), a member of the Board of Directors of AIPLA, a member of the Board of Directors of the New York Patent Law Association, and co-chair of the International Patent Practice Committee of IPO. He was the founder and first Chairman of the U.S. Bar/JPO Liaison Council; Chairman of the U.S. Bar EPO Liaison Council; U.S. Industry Representative to the Trilateral and IP5 meetings; and a member of the Global Dossier Task Force. Mr. Helfgott worked at IBM (1967–1969) as a patent engineer, at Western Electric (1971–1973) as a patent attorney, and at General Electric (1969–1971 and 1973–1986) where he was head of the International Patent Operation. In 1968 he started his own firm of Helfgott & Karas, P.C. that in 2001 merged in KattenMuchinRosenman, LLP, where he currently serves as Director of Patents. He earned a BEE degree from the City College of New York, an MEE degree from New York University, a JD degree from Fordham Law School, and MHL and DHL degrees from Yeshiva University.

T. David Reed is a patent agent registered before the USPTO and the Canadian Intellectual Property Office. He graduated from Northwestern University with a degree in Chemical Engineering and did post-graduate studies at the University of Cincinnati. Mr. Reed became registered before the USPTO in 1988 and spent the last half of his 40-year career at The Procter & Gamble Company (P&G) managing the foreign patent filing function with responsibility for prosecution of applications in Canada, Latin America, and the Asia/Pacific region for most of his tenure. In 1990 he managed the transition of P&G's foreign filing strategy from individual country filings under the Paris Convention to filing under the PCT. Following the transition, P&G became the largest single user of the PCT, holding this distinction for a number of years. In the mid-1990s Mr. Reed was asked by WIPO to share P&G's PCT experience by lecturing in the United States and around the world on the use of the PCT from a user's perspective. Following his retirement from P&G in 2006, he became a consultant for WIPO, teaching the PCT across the United States and Canada. Mr. Reed also operates one of WIPO's two U.S. PCT "help desks" from his home in Cincinnati, Ohio, answering questions on PCT practice for users.

ACKNOWLEDGMENTS

It is a longstanding joke that the letters P-C-T stand not only for Patent Cooperation Treaty, but also for Pretty Complicated Treaty, which is just what the PCT is. While there are good reasons for the treaty's complexity—not least of which is the PCT's need to function properly in all member countries—its opaqueness creates great challenges. Like everyone who uses the PCT system, the three of us have struggled to understand and master it, and we have not been immune to some of its many pitfalls.

The PCT has been the focus of our professional lives. Collectively, we have not only been responsible for countless PCT applications, but we have also been in charge of running the PCT system, lecturing and writing about it, participating in its reform, and attempting to make it more accessible. This guide is the result of almost 100 years of collective experience and acquired wisdom. It is also the result of many years of close collaboration with talented colleagues, mentors, and friends who have informed and honed our knowledge of the treaty. While responsibility for all errors, omissions, and flaws in this guide rests solely with us, we would be remiss if we did not acknowledge some of the individuals who over the years have served as our PCT resources and guides. In no apparent order, we express our gratitude to Marty Kalikow, Louis Maassel, Isabelle Boutillon, Busso Bartels, Phil Thomas, Nicole Bérard, Carol Bidwell, and Mike Neas. To those we have not singled out by name, we both apologize and thank you for the invaluable guidance and assistance you have provided. You have all taught us so much.

Several current and former William Mitchell College of Law students provided vital assistance as researchers, proofreaders, revisers, word processing consultants, and thought provokers. Our great thanks go to Elizabeth Capan, Frederik Struve, Christian Hansen, Rick Nelson, Marissa Dietz, and D.J. Yokom. You are the future of the PCT, and we can rest assured that in hands like yours, the future is bright.

Many thanks to Jeffrey A. Wolfson for the peer review and endorsement of the book.

Last but certainly not least, we thank and express our love and appreciation to our respective spouses, Pixie Martin, Joyce Helfgott, and Heather Reed, whose support, encouragement, and patience know no bounds. We dedicate this guide to you.

Jay Erstling
Sam Helfgott
Dave Reed

CHAPTER 1

An Overview of the PCT System

The Patent Cooperation Treaty (PCT) is the heart of the international patent system. It plays an indispensable role in patent practice and should be considered in every applicant's patent filing strategy. Yet many patent practitioners lack sufficient familiarity with the PCT system. PCT rules are opaque, and PCT terminology is obscure. The combination of the two can easily cause confusion among PCT users, and it makes the system difficult to master. The objective of this guide is to demystify the PCT. The guide is based on the authors' many years of experience with the system, on the numerous PCT seminars and presentations they have given, and on the important lessons they have learned from the mistakes they have made. It is the authors' conviction that the PCT need not be confusing or understood only by a select few, and it is their hope that this guide will allow the broader patent community to take full advantage of all the benefits the PCT has to offer.

1. What the PCT Is

The PCT is a uniquely successful multilateral treaty that provides a unified procedure for filing patent applications in each of its member countries. Instead of having to file a separate patent application in every country where you would like patent protection for your invention, the PCT makes it possible for you to file all of your applications simultaneously with a single "international" PCT application. With 146 countries currently party to the treaty and over two million patent applications filed since its inception, the PCT has come to represent the international patent system.

2. The PCT Framework

2.1 History

The PCT was signed in Washington, D.C., on June 19, 1970, at the conclusion of a diplomatic conference attended by 78 countries. The treaty entered into force on January 24, 1978, and opened its doors to receipt of international applications less than six months later on June 1, 1978. Despite the large number of attendees at the diplomatic conference in 1970, there were only 18 member countries on the first day that applications were received. This number has now increased eight-fold to 146, which, with a few exceptions (Argentina, Saudi Arabia, and Taiwan, in particular), includes the world's major industrialized and emerging countries. The member countries of the PCT are deemed to constitute a Union, and they meet periodically either in committees, working groups, or an all-country Assembly to debate and adopt changes to the system that helps the PCT continue to meet the needs of both applicants and national patent offices.

Country	Date	Country	Date	Country	Date
United Arab Emirates	1999	Côte d'Ivoire	1991	Ghana	1997
Antigua and Barbuda	2000	Chile	2009	Gambia	1997
Albania	1995	Cameroon	1978	Guinea	1991
Armenia	1991	China	1994	Equatorial Guinea	2001
Angola	2007	Colombia	2001	Greece	1990
Austria	1979	Costa Rica	1999	Guatemala	2006
Australia	1980	Cuba	1996	Guinea-Bissau	1997
Azerbaijan	1995	Cyprus	1998	Honduras	2006
Bosnia and Herzegovina	1996	Czech Republic	1993	Croatia	1998
Barbados	1985	Germany	1978	Hungary	1980
Belgium	1981	Denmark	1978	Indonesia	1997
Burkina Faso	1989	Dominica	1999	Ireland	1992
Bulgaria	1984	Dominican Republic	2007	Israel	1996
Bahrain	2007	Algeria	2000	India	1998
Benin	1987	Ecuador	2001	Iceland	1995
Brunei Darussalam	2012	Estonia	1994	Italy	1985
Brazil	1978	Egypt	2003	Japan	1978
Botswana	2003	Spain	1989	Kenya	1994
Belarus	1991	Finland	1980	Kyrgyzstan	1991
Belize	2000	France	1978	Comoros	2005
Canada	1990	Gabon	1978	Saint Kitts and Nevis	2005
Central African Republic	1978	United Kingdom	1978	Rep. of Korea	1980
Congo	1978	Grenada	1998	Republic of Korea	1984
Switzerland	1978	Georgia	1991	Kazakhstan	1991

(continued)

Figure 1.1
Listing of the PCT Member Countries

Country	Date	Country	Date	Country	Date
Lao People's Dem. Rep.	2006	Niger	1993	San Marino	2004
Saint Lucia	1996	Nigeria	2005	Senegal	1978
Liechtenstein	1980	Nicaragua	2003	Sao Tome and Principe	2008
Sri Lanka	1982	Netherlands	1979	El Salvador	2006
Liberia	1994	Norway	1980	Syrian Arab Republic	2003
Lesotho	1995	New Zealand	1992	Swaziland	1994
Lithuania	1994	Oman	2001	Chad	1978
Luxembourg	1978	Panama	2012	Togo	1978
Latvia	1993	Peru	2009	Thailand	2009
Libya	2005	Papua New Guinea	2003	Tajikistan	1991
Morocco	1999	Philippines	2001	Turkmenistan	1991
Monaco	1979	Poland	1990	Tunisia	2001
Republic of Moldova	1991	Portugal	1992	Turkey	1996
Montenegro	2006	Qatar	2011	Trinidad and Tobago	1994
Madagascar	1978	Romania	1979	Tanzania	1999
Macedonia	1995	Serbia	1997	Ukraine	1991
Mali	1984	Russian Federation	1978	Uganda	1995
Mongolia	1991	Rwanda	2011	United States of America	1978
Mauritania	1983	Seychelles	2002	Uzbekistan	1991
Malta	2007	Sudan	1984	Saint Vincent/ Grenadines	2002
Malawi	1978	Sweden	1978	Vietnam	1993
Mexico	1995	Singapore	1995	South Africa	1999
Malaysia	2006	Slovenia	1994	Zambia	2001
Mozambique	2000	Slovakia	1993	Zimbabwe	1997
Namibia	2004	Sierra Leone	1997		

Figure 1.1 *(continued)*

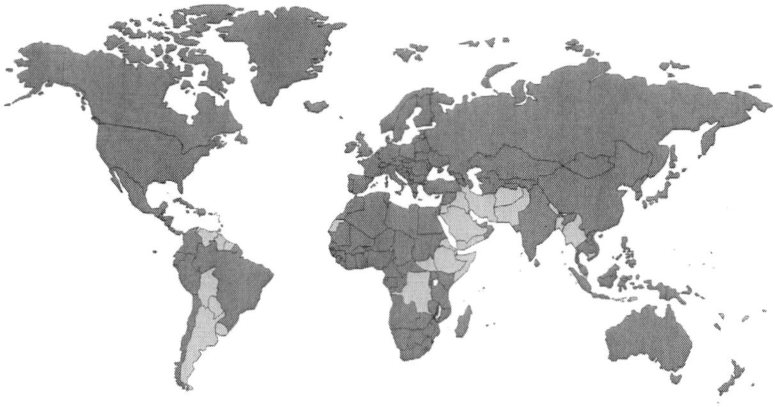

Figure 1.2
World Map of the PCT Member Countries

The PCT has the distinction of being only the second multilateral treaty in the field of patents. The first was the Paris Convention for the Protection of Industrial Property of 1883 (the Paris Convention). The framers of the Paris Convention expressly introduced the right of member countries to enter into special agreements among themselves. The PCT constitutes such an agreement. As a result, a country must be a member of the Paris Convention before it can become a PCT member country.[1]

2.2 Governance

The PCT is administered by the International Bureau (i.e., the secretariat) of the World Intellectual Property Organization (WIPO), a UN specialized agency located in Geneva, Switzerland. The PCT system is governed by a relatively dense legislative framework. In descending hierarchical order, the PCT is governed by (1) the PCT itself; (2) a relatively comprehensive set of regulations; (3) Administrative Instructions,

1. One result of this requirement is that Taiwan, which cannot become a member of the Paris Convention because of the United Nation's "one China policy," cannot join the PCT. See more on non-PCT member countries in Chapter 2, Section 2, "Making an Ineligible Application Eligible: Applicants-of-Convenience."

which mainly deal with technical interactions among national patent offices and WIPO; (4) a series of bilateral agreements that regulate relations between WIPO and the offices that serve as international searching and international preliminary examining authorities; (5) detailed International Search and Preliminary Examination Guidelines, the PCT's equivalent of the Manual of Patent Examining Procedure (MPEP); and (6) the PCT Receiving Office Guidelines, which lay out the administrative responsibilities of national patent offices when applicants file PCT applications with them.

Responsibility for maintenance, oversight, and revision of the PCT legislative framework rests with the PCT Assembly. The Assembly is a legislative body that normally meets annually, is supported by the International Bureau, and is made up of all the members of the PCT Union as well as a handful of nongovernmental organizations—including the American Bar Association and American Intellectual Property Law Association—that participate as observers. Although the member countries form a single Union, the Union does not often speak with one voice. Differing views frequently exist between industrialized and developing countries as well as among countries from different geographic regions. As a result, it may take several years for the Assembly to adopt a PCT proposal that an American user of the system would consider a "no-brainer."

In order to expedite the governing process, the Assembly has authorized the creation of several committees and working groups, which are also supported by the International Bureau and consist of member countries and observers. The Committee for Technical Cooperation, for example, has responsibility for advising the Assembly on the appointment of International Searching and Preliminary Examining Authorities and on the types of patent documents and non-patent literature that should be included among the documents in an international search. The PCT Working Group, which held its fifth session in May 2012, has responsibility for improving the functioning of the PCT and ensuring its future development. In addition, a quasi-ad hoc body of all the International Authorities known as the Meeting of International Authorities (PCT/MIA) meets periodically to update the International Search and Preliminary Examination Guidelines and to review other issues relating to patent documentation, classification, and quality management.

Having a basic understanding of the PCT framework is helpful in understanding how the PCT system works. It also explains some of its complexity.

3. Statistics

In 1978, the first year of PCT operations, applicants worldwide filed fewer than 650 PCT applications. Since then, the number of filings has grown rapidly. It took 26 years (until 2004) for the number of PCT applications to reach one million, but only seven years to reach the second million in 2011. In fact, the only year filings decreased from the previous year was 2009, when applications dropped from 164,000 in 2008 to 155,900 in 2009 (a 4.5 percent decrease), reflecting the global economic downturn. Applications rebounded in 2010 and 2011, however. Applicants filed 164,300 PCT applications in 2010, returning to the 2008 level, and 181,900 applications in 2011, the largest annual number of PCT filings to date and a 10.7 percent increase over 2010. More than half of all foreign applications originate as PCT applications, making the PCT synonymous with foreign filing.

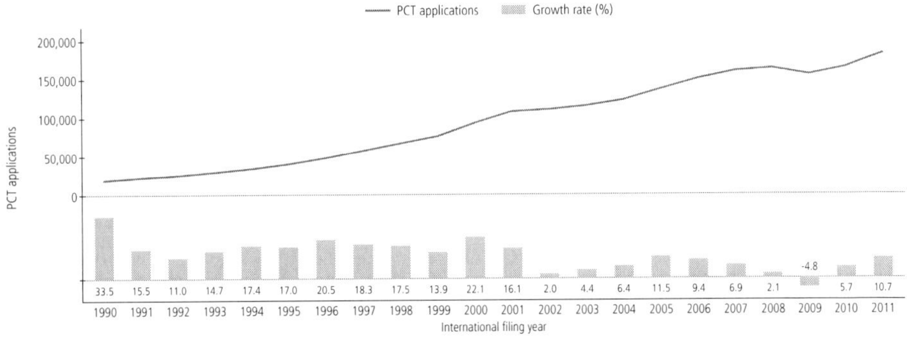

Figure 1.3
PCT Application Filing Growth Rate
Source: WIPO, 2012 PCT Yearly Review

In contrast to a number of Asian countries, including China, South Korea, and India, the number of applications from the United States has grown slowly over the last decade. Nevertheless, the United States remains the world leader in international filings with 48,596 applications in 2011 (representing 26.7 percent of the global share of PCT applications). Japan, Germany, China, and South Korea are the next largest international filers (representing 21.4 percent, 10.2 percent, 9 percent, and 5.7 percent of the global share, respectively). In 2010, Asia became the biggest PCT filing region, overtaking Western Europe, which fell to third place behind North America. Together, applicants from the three regions filed 97 percent of all PCT applications filed in 2011 (the latest year for which PCT filing statistics were available).

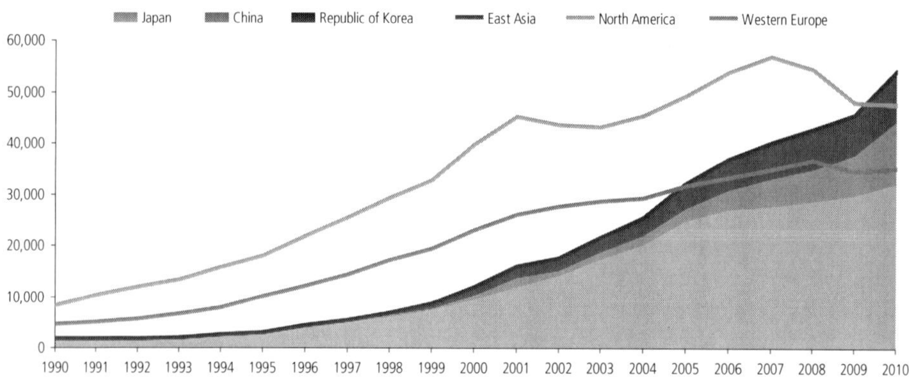

Figure 1.4
PCT Filing Trends
Source: WIPO, 2010 PCT Yearly Review

4. The PCT Time Frame

4.1 The International and National Phases

The PCT process involves two phases: an international phase and a national phase. The international phase is itself divided into three required steps and three optional ones. The required steps are

1. the filing of a PCT application with a Receiving Office (RO);
2. the preparation of an International Search Report (ISR) and Written Opinion on the State of the Art (WO) by an International Searching Authority (ISA); and
3. the publication of the PCT application and ISR by WIPO.

The optional steps are

1. the preparation of one or more Supplementary International Search Reports (SISR) by a different ISA or ISAs;
2. the filing by the applicant of amendments to the claims, or the filing of a demand for international preliminary examination together with amendments to the claims and/or description and/or drawings; and
3. the preparation of an International Preliminary Report on Patentability (IPRP Chapter II) by an International Preliminary Examining Authority (IPEA) on the basis of the demand for international preliminary examination.

The international phase is thus all about filing the PCT application to establish a filing or priority date (if a priority date has not yet been established) and subjecting the application to a standardized level of scrutiny to help determine if the invention is novel, inventive, and industrially applicable. The international phase does not itself result in a patent; for that, you must enter the national phase. You have 30 months at minimum from the date of filing your priority application to complete the requirements for entering the national phase.[2]

You enter the national phase by converting your PCT application into a national or regional application in each of the countries or regions in which you wish to pursue patent rights.[3] For each country or region you have chosen, you must pay the required national fees and, if needed, provide a translation of the application into a language recognized by the national patent office concerned. WIPO then communicates all of the necessary documents in the application file to the chosen offices, which in

2. Some offices, for example the European Patent Office (the EPO), grant applicants 31 months from the priority date. Others are particularly lenient about the deadline and accord applicants even more time against the payment of a fee. For example, Canada permits an additional 12 months and China allows an additional 2 months.

3. Converting your international application into a regional application in a regional patent office, such as the EPO, is referred to as entering the "regional phase." For simplicity's sake, however, we will generally use the term "national phase" to refer to both the national and regional phase.

PCT jargon are referred to as "designated offices."[4] Despite the PCT process, the decision to grant a patent remains solely within the jurisdiction of each national or regional patent office. Because of the fairly rigorous and highly standardized international phase proceedings, however, a growing number of national offices (particularly smaller ones) tend to rely on the search and optional preliminary examination results of the PCT process. Thus, because of the PCT, results can be predicted with a greater level of certainty. In 2011, the PCT system saw approximately 477,500 regional or national phase entries in PCT regional or national offices.

The remaining chapters of this guide are dedicated to explaining in detail the elements of the PCT international and national phases.

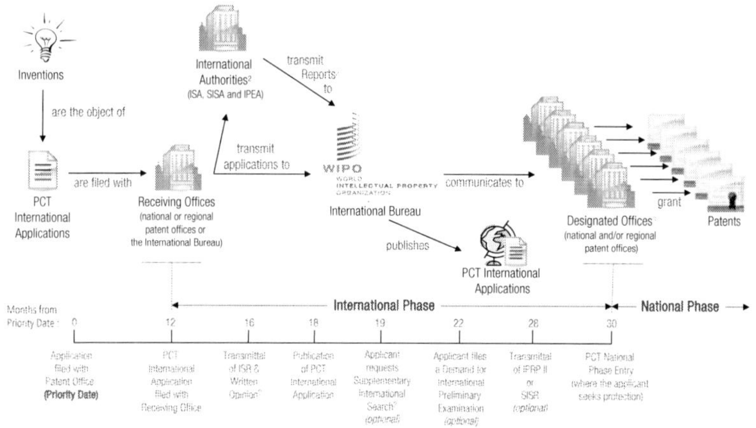

[1] Generally, applicants first file a national or regional patent application with their patent office, and within 12 months from priority date, file a PCT application.
[2] International Searching Authorities (ISA) transmit International Search Reports (ISRs) & Written Opinions/Authorities specified for Supplementary Search (SISA) transmit Supplementary International Search Reports (SISR) / International Preliminary Examining Authorities (IPEA) transmit International Preliminary Reports on Patentability II (IPRP II).
[3] Called elected offices for applicants having filed a demand for international preliminary examination.

Figure 1.5
The PCT Timeline
Source: WIPO

4. As will be explained in Chapter 3, about 10 percent of PCT applicants request optional international preliminary examination under Chapter II of the PCT; when applicants enter the national phase following international preliminary examination, the offices they choose to enter are referred to as "elected offices," not designated ones. This is just one of the many unnecessary complexities of the PCT.

4.2 The PCT Timeline

To set the stage for the remaining chapters, here is a nutshell version of each step in the PCT timeline, together with some corresponding remarks. The timeline is based on the filing of a U.S. application.

- **0 Month:** Applicant files a priority application with the USPTO or other national or regional patent office.
  - A PCT application can constitute the priority application.
  - PCT applications frequently claim priority to U.S. provisional applications.
  - A PCT application can also claim priority to multiple applications.
  - A PCT application can claim priority to another PCT application, in which case the 0-month date is calculated from the first-filed (priority) PCT.
- **12 Months:** Before the end of the priority year, applicant files a PCT application.
  - U.S. applicants can file with either the Receiving Office of the USPTO or the Receiving Office of WIPO. Chapter 2 describes the advantages and disadvantages of each.
  - One of the most important decisions an applicant makes in filing a PCT application is the selection of the ISA. Currently, U.S. applicants have the choice of the following ISAs: USPTO, European Patent Office (EPO), Korean Intellectual Property Office (KIPO), Australian Patent Office (IP Australia), and Russian Patent Office (Rospatent). The choice depends on various factors, not the least of which is the varying amount that each ISA charges for the search fee.
  - There is a technique to drafting a global PCT application that requires less conforming to individual country requirements when the application enters the national phase. Chapter 9 describes that technique.
- **Around 16 Months:**[5] The ISA issues the International Search Report (ISR) and Written Opinion (WO).

---

5. The precise deadline established by Rule 42 of the PCT Regulations is "three months from the receipt of the search copy by the International Searching Authority, or nine months from the priority date, whichever time limit expires later." This formula translates to around 16 months.

- The ISR consists mainly of a listing of references to published patent applications, patents, and technical journal articles that may affect the patentability of the claimed invention, while the WO is a preliminary, nonbinding opinion on whether the invention is novel, inventive, and industrially applicable in light of the search results.
- The ISR is published with the application, but the WO remains confidential until the expiration of 30 months from the priority date.
- The timeliness of the issuance of ISRs and WOs may vary considerably from one ISA to another.
- With a positive WO, an applicant can seek expedited examination in certain cases under the PCT-Patent Prosecution Highway (PCT-PPH).
- Unless an applicant requests international preliminary examination, the WO forms the basis of an international preliminary report on patentability (IPRP Chapter I), which the International Bureau communicates to designated offices.

- **18 Months:** International Bureau publishes the PCT application and the ISR.
    - Publication gives claimed inventions provisional protection in certain countries, including the member countries of the European Patent Organisation and the United States, although the protection may be subject to publication in the national language of the country concerned, as in the case of China and Japan.
    - Published PCT applications are fully searchable on PATENTSCOPE, the WIPO database.
- **18 Months (or Two Months from the Issuance of the ISR):** Applicant *may* file amendments to the claims only under PCT Article 19.
    - Article 19 amendments may be helpful in securing provisional protection or in attempting to overcome prior art

references cited in the ISR in preparation for the national phase examination.
  - Article 19 amendments may not add new matter.
  - Article 19 amendments are published by the International Bureau, but they are not examined in the international phase.
- **19 Months:** Applicant *may* request a supplementary international search.
  - As of July 2011, the Supplementary International Searching Authorities (SISA) are the Austrian Patent Office, EPO, Finnish Patent Office, Nordic Patent Institute, Rospatent, and Swedish Patent Office.
  - A supplementary search may be beneficial for searching claims not searched by the ISA (for example, methods of medical treatment) but searched by the SISA.
  - A supplementary search may also be beneficial if important prior art exists in a language the ISA does not readily search or if the SISA has particularly relevant subject matter expertise.
  - The SISA issues the Supplementary International Search Report (SISR) by the end of the 28th month.
- **22 Months (or Three Months from the Receipt of the ISR):** Applicant *may* file a demand for international preliminary examination under PCT Chapter II.
  - An international preliminary examination may be beneficial to applicants who want to "perfect" their application in the international phase by amending their claims, description, or drawings, and/or responding to the WO pursuant to PCT Article 34.
  - An international preliminary examination is carried out by the ISAs; at this stage, they are called International Preliminary Examining Authorities (IPEAs).
  - The cost of international preliminary examination varies greatly from one IPEA to another.

  - Most applicants who seek international preliminary examination select the IPEA that served as their ISA, but under certain circumstances, it may be useful to choose another.
  - The result of international preliminary examination is the issuance of an IPRP (Chapter II), which the IPEA establishes by the end of the 28th month.
- **28 Months:** Issuance of the IPRP (Chapter II) by the IPEA and/or the SISR by the SISA.
  - The IPRP (II) and SISR are communicated to the applicant and the International Bureau.
- **30 Months:** The International Bureau converts the WO into an IPRP (Chapter I) for applicants who have not sought international preliminary examination.
- **30 (or Sometimes 31 or More) Months:** Applicant enters the national phase in the countries/regions in which protection is desired.
  - Applicant pays the national fees and communicates a translation of the PCT application and any Article 19 and Article 34 amendments, where the application or amendments are not in an accepted national language.
  - For entry into the national phase in the United States, an applicant also submits an inventor's oath or declaration, an application data sheet, and an invention disclosure statement.
  - The International Bureau communicates the PCT application, the ISR, any Article 19 amendments, any declarations,[6] and the IPRP (Chapter I) or (Chapter II) to every designated or elected office.

6. Much more needs to be said about declarations, which are covered in detail in Chapter 2.

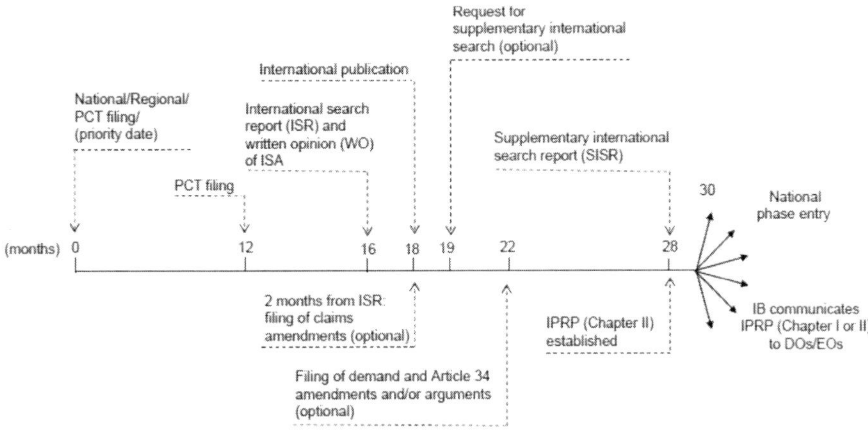

Figure 1.6
PCT Timeline—2
Source: WIPO

5. Benefits of Using the PCT

The PCT provides benefits for applicants, patent offices, and third parties. The remaining chapters of this guide will try to equip applicants with the tools needed to reap those benefits.

5.1 Applicants

Applicants are the primary beneficiaries of the PCT system. In addition to providing a greater level of predictability, filing a PCT application buys applicants time and defers costs compared to the traditional (Paris Convention) route. Under the traditional route, applicants have only one year to make foreign filing decisions, and they have to file an application in every country in which they want protection. In addition to the high cost of foreign filing, including translation costs and attorney and filing fees, one year is rarely enough time to evaluate the importance of an invention and determine where it should be protected. The PCT provides an additional 18 (sometimes 19) months after the priority year (30 or 31 months in total) before having to make foreign filing decisions, and instead of multiple applications, applicants need initially file only one. Moreover, since a PCT application can be filed in English by a U.S. attorney, there are no translation or foreign attorney fees until the national phase. Although a PCT application adds international filing costs, which roughly range from about $2,000 to $5,000, it defers the much more expensive costs of international filing, which can range from $25,000 to more than $50,000.

The ISR and WO that all PCT applicants receive, as well as the optional IPRP (Chapter II) or SISR, not only provide applicants with a better basis for deciding how to proceed in the national phase but also provide evidence of the potential value of the patent, which can prove beneficial when seeking investment. And with the advent of the Patent Prosecution Highway, the PCT has become an important vehicle for obtaining expedited favorable treatment in PPH offices.

5.2 Patent Offices

Patent offices can rely on the valuable information contained in ISRs and IPRPs to help in examination during the national phase. Though smaller offices have always tended to rely heavily on the PCT, the need to deal with application backlogs in the larger offices, the push toward patent office worksharing, and the advent of the Patent Prosecution Highway (PPH) have motivated all offices to look toward the PCT. For example, as of July 2012, the United States had entered into bilateral PCT-PPH agreements with Australia, Austria, China, the EPO, Finland, Japan, Korea, Russia, Spain, and Sweden. Under the terms of those agreements, applicants who receive a "clean" WO or IPRP (Chapter II) as to at least one claim from any one of the PCT-PPH offices, or from the USPTO, can request expedited examination in the other office.[7] The result has been faster and more efficient patent grant. In addition, then-Under Secretary of Commerce and Director of the USPTO David Kappos created a PCT Task Force in the fall of 2009 with the objective of increasing the efficiency and quality of work performed by the USPTO

7. Chapter 9 provides detailed suggestions and strategies for maximum use of PPH. Suffice it here to clarify that expedited national phase examination is limited to the claims that received positive results, and to benefit from PPH, any non-novel or noninventive claims must be canceled or filed in a divisional application.

as an RO, ISA, IPEA, and designated office. The improvement, for the most part, has been dramatic.

5.3 Third Parties

PATENTSCOPE, the WIPO patent application database, provides third parties with rich and valuable information about the activities of competitors as well as about the patent landscape in any area of technology. The database provides machine translation into English for patent applications in other PCT publication languages, fairly extensive national phase entry data, and statistical information relating to each application. It is all free of charge and can be accessed at http://www.wipo.int/patentscope/search/en/search.jsf. In addition, the introduction of a third-party observation system, which permits the public to submit prior art references that may have an impact on the novelty or obviousness of published PCT applications, allows third parties to be directly involved in the PCT international search and examination process.

CHAPTER 2

PCT Procedures

The benefits an applicant receives from the Patent Cooperation Treaty are numerous, making the PCT a cost-effective option for anyone with an interest in international patent protection. In this chapter, we will discuss best practices for preparing to file a PCT application. The first step is to determine if the case is eligible for the PCT.

1. Requirements to File under the PCT

The treaty provides that at least one of the applicants filing a PCT application must be a national or a resident of a PCT member country.[1] If no applicant meets that requirement, the application cannot be accepted.

The laws of each member country determine who can be named as an applicant. In nearly all countries, applicants may be either natural persons or legal entities. Historically, the United States was an outlier; only inventors (i.e., natural persons) could be patent applicants, and

1. Article 9(1).

many PCT rules and procedures had to be drafted to comply with the U.S. requirement. However, on September 16, 2012, provisions of the America Invents Act permitting legal entity assignees to be applicants came into force. As a result, both natural persons and legal entities qualify to be named as patent applicants in all PCT member countries.

Because the actual persons or entities to be named as applicants may vary from one PCT member country to the next, it may be necessary to name different applicants for different countries. This is easily accomplished and will be discussed in detail later in this chapter.

For an application to be filed under the PCT, it is sufficient that at least *one* of the applicants named in the application is a national *or* a resident of a PCT member country.

---

2. Making an Ineligible Application Eligible: Applicants-of-Convenience

The requirement that at least one applicant be a national or a resident of a PCT member country has proven problematic when none of the applicants meet the requirement. To overcome this problem, you can name a person or entity from a PCT member country as an additional PCT applicant. The ordinary practice for doing this involves choosing a person from any PCT member country as an applicant for a country of low (or no) commercial interest for patent protection. Naming this applicant-of-convenience in the PCT application qualifies the application for filing under the PCT.

Suppose, for example, that an entity in Argentina (currently not a PCT member country) desires to file a PCT application, but all of the applicants are Argentine nationals and residents. If a national or resident of a PCT member country, such as an agent in the United States, is listed as one of the applicants, but only in respect of a PCT member country of low commercial interest to the Argentinian entity (in other words, a country in which the Argentinian entity has little interest in seeking patent protection), the application would qualify for filing under the PCT, because the application would then have an applicant who is a national or resident of a PCT member country.

The inclusion of an applicant-of-convenience has been successfully used by many practitioners and will not be questioned during the international phase. By adding the applicant-of-convenience to the application, the requirements of PCT Article 9(1) are met. For an application filed using this tactic, an assignment of at least a small percentage of the application to the applicant-of-convenience in the selected country of low commercial interest should, as a best practice, be executed and retained. Should the use of an applicant-of-convenience to allow filing under the PCT ever be challenged, the assignment can show that the applicant-of-convenience had the legal right to be named as the applicant for the specific country at the time the PCT application was filed.

3. Where to File an International Application

PCT applicants file their applications with a receiving office (RO), which is, generally speaking, a division or section of a national or regional patent office that is set up to receive PCT applications (hence the name). Most PCT member countries and regional patent offices have established their own ROs located within their own patent offices,[2] and each RO is competent (that is, has the authority) to receive and process PCT applications filed by nationals and residents of that country or region. For any national or regional office to be a competent receiving office for a given application, therefore, at least one applicant must be able to file with that office by reason of nationality or residence. Where there are joint applicants from two or more countries—for example the United States and Japan—the applicants may file their application either at the RO operated by the USPTO (referred to as the RO/US) or at the RO operated by the Japan Patent Office (referred to as the RO/JP), since both are competent. In addition to the nationality or residency requirement, the application must be in a language accepted by the receiving office. To file in the RO/US, the application

2. A few PCT member countries, for example, the United Arab Emirates, Barbados, and Sri Lanka, do not operate a PCT receiving office. Nationals and residents of those countries can only file PCT applications in the receiving office operated by the International Bureau of the World Intellectual Property Organization in Geneva, Switzerland.

must be in English, so if the joint applicants in the above example drafted their application in Japanese, they would either need to file the application in the RO/JP or translate their application into English.[3]

The International Bureau (IB) of the World Intellectual Property Organization (WIPO) also acts as a receiving office, known as the RO/IB. The RO/IB accepts applications from nationals and residents of all PCT member countries and accepts PCT applications in any recognized language in the world. It serves as an important alternative to a national or regional RO.

3.1 Choosing the Receiving Office

U.S. applicants have the choice of two ROs: the RO/US or the RO/IB. European applicants generally have the choice of three ROs: their national RO, the RO operated by the European Patent Office (known as the RO/EP), and the RO/IB. Given that an applicant may select any competent RO available, how do you decide which RO to use? A few best practices may aid in the selection. In some cases, the RO decision may be language-dependent. For example, if your application is not in English (or a language accepted by the local RO), using the RO/IB or a competent receiving office accepting the language of the application is best. In other cases, national laws may be of consideration. If you do not have a U.S. foreign filing license, or if the national security laws require filing your application in a specific country, then using the RO/US or that specific country's receiving office is best.[4]

Figure 2.1 lists additional attributes that may be key to selecting the most appropriate RO. As you can see, there are advantages and restrictions associated with each choice.

---

3. In contrast, the RO/JP accepts applications in both English and Japanese, so if the applicants prepared the application in English, they would still have the choice of filing with either the RO/US or the RO/JP. The PCT Applicant's Guide homepage, a database maintained by WIPO at http://www.wipo.int/pct/en/appguide/index.jsp, lists the language or languages in which applicants may file their applications and request forms for each RO. Annex C (Receiving Offices) on the Guide's homepage provides links to every PCT member country.

4. Compliance with national security requirements is the filer's responsibility. Filing a PCT application in the RO/US, or in the RO of any PCT member country having a national security requirement, is sufficient to meet the requirement.

RO Attribute	RO/US	RO/IB
Language(s) accepted	English	Any recognized language
Agents	Patent agents/attorneys registered to practice before the USPTO	Entities entitled to practice before the competent national/ regional RO
National security	International applications are automatically reviewed by the USPTO where the invention was made in the U.S.	Compliance with local law is applicant's responsibility
Certified priority documents available through the RO	U.S. national applications and PCT applications filed with the RO/US	PCT applications filed with the RO/IB and documents available via the WIPO Digital Access Service
Electronic filing options	Via EFS Web	Via PCT SAFE
Physical filing options[1]	Hand carry, U.S. Mail, Express Mail	Hand carry, fax,[2] courier services, postal services
Competent searching authorities	U.S., EP, KR, AU, and RU	All ISAs available through all competent national/regional ROs
Restoration of priority criterion	Unintentional	Due Care and Unintentional
Fee for priority restoration	US$1,410	None
Transmittal fee	US$240	CHF 100
Currency accepted at filing	USD	CHF, USD, EUR
Methods of payment accepted	Check, U.S. deposit account, credit card, wire transfer	Check, wire transfer, WIPO deposit account, credit card

[1] The filing date for most physical methods of filing will be the date the complete international application is received at the RO. "Express Mail Post Office to Addressee" service of the United States Postal Service (USPS) is the exception in the RO/US. Under 37 C.F.R. § 1.10, the filing date will be the date that the complete international application is deposited with the USPS. (The RO/US levies an additional fee of US$400 (US$200 for a small entity) on applications not filed electronically.)

[2] The filing date will be the date the complete application arrives at the RO/IB in Geneva, Switzerland. Mechanical failure when sending a fax is entirely at the applicant's peril.

Figure 2.1
Factors to Be Considered When Selecting a Receiving Office

The authors believe that for applications filed by U.S. applicants, the RO/US is generally the better choice, especially if the PCT application is claiming priority to one or more earlier U.S. applications (provisional or nonprovisional). Using the RO/US provides for national security clearance (foreign filing license), allows you to fill the need to supply certified U.S. priority documents at no cost by checking a box on the request form, permits easy electronic filing via EFS-Web, and allows payment via a U.S. deposit account or credit card.

The RO/IB, however, may be the better choice if you need to request restoration of priority (you can request restoration using either criterion of unintentionality or despite the exercise of due care required by the circumstances, and the RO/IB charges no fee, unlike the RO/US; for more on restoration, see Chapter 5). The RO/IB is also the better choice if your application is not in English.

You can carry out similar analyses if you have the option of filing in other competent ROs. All ROs do a good job of receiving and processing international applications. Your choice of RO should be based on the options that the different offices provide and on case logistics.

In addition to including an applicant-of-convenience to permit a normally ineligible application to be filed under the PCT, including an applicant-of-convenience can also allow an international application to be filed in an otherwise noncompetent RO.

4. Requirements for an International Filing Date

When preparing to file a PCT application, it is important to keep in mind the minimum requirements for an RO to accept your application and accord it an international filing date.

If any one of the requirements is missing, your application cannot be accorded an international filing date, and you will need to correct the defects.[5] It is thus extremely important that you pay careful attention to the formal requirements of PCT filing.

Minimum Requirements for Acceptance of Application and Accordance of International Filing Date

- At least one applicant must be a national or resident of a PCT member country.
- The application must be in a language prescribed by the RO.
- The application must contain at least
  - an indication that the application is intended as a PCT application,
  - a request that has the effect of designating all member countries that are party to the PCT on the day of filing,
  - the name of at least one applicant,
  - something that appears to be a description, and
  - something that appears to be a claim.

---

5. Completing the Request Form and Options Available at Filing

The PCT provides numerous helpful options, many of which are selected at the time of filing the PCT application. To get an understanding of the various PCT options and features as well as to learn how and when to use them, this section will outline the PCT request form[6] and provide comments on each section. The paper-based PCT/RO/101 request form, which is available in an editable PDF format at http://www.wipo

---

5. See Chapter 5 for a way to secure an initial filing date in the absence of a description and/or claim, as well as for the safeguard built into the PCT if the application is filed with a noncompetent RO based on nationality and residence of the applicants or if the application is not in a prescribed language.

6. The request is the PCT cover/data sheet that accompanies the patent specification. The term "request" comes from the first sentence of the form, which says: "The undersigned requests that the present international application be processed according to the Patent Cooperation Treaty."

.int/export/sites/www/pct/en/forms/request/ed_request.pdf,[7] will form the basis for this discussion. An electronic version of the request form, available through the use of the PCT SAFE (Secure Applications Filed Electronically) software, has the same features and options as the paper-based request form.

The PCT request form is available free of charge and is updated periodically. It is important to use the most recent version of the form. When new options and features are added to the PCT, any necessary language for using the new options and features is built into the most recent version of the request.

5.1 Getting Started

To begin, if you are new to the PCT, you should become familiar with the PCT Applicant's Guide, which is available electronically, free of charge, at www.wipo.int/pct/en/appguide/index.jsp. The Applicant's Guide is well indexed and provides a detailed explanation of the PCT process. It also contains annexes giving specific information about each member country, both in general and as an RO. Additionally, each office that acts as an international searching, international preliminary examining, and supplementary international searching authority has a separate annex for each function. Finally, there is an annex on entering the national phase in each member country.

5.2 The Request

The screenshots of the request form in this portion of the chapter come from the sample request form available on the WIPO website at http://www.wipo.int/export/sites/www/pct/en/forms/request/filled_request.pdf.

7. The collection of PCT forms can be accessed on the WIPO website at www.wipo.int/pct/en/forms/index.html or on the USPTO website at http://www.uspto.gov/patents/init_events/pct/Chapter1.jsp.

PCT

REQUEST

The undersigned requests that the present international application be processed according to the Patent Cooperation Treaty.

For receiving Office use only

International Application No.

International Filing Date

Name of receiving Office and "PCT International Application"

Applicant's or agent's file reference *(if desired) (12 characters maximum)* CHOCO 95549

Box No. I TITLE OF INVENTION

PROCESS FOR FOLDING WRAPPING PAPER FOR CHOCOLATES

Figure 2.2
Box No. I, PCT Request

By stating that the "application is to be processed according to the [PCT]," the standard-form language of the request ensures that you have satisfied one of the requirements for obtaining an international filing date (i.e., that you intend your application to be a PCT application). It also provides for a file reference number of up to 12 characters so the filing can be easily identified within your own docketing system.

The title of the invention is indicated in Box No. I. The title shown in Box No. I must be *identical* to the title appearing on the first page of the specification. If it is not, you will receive an "Invitation to Correct Defects" requiring you to conform the listed titles. For clarity, it is recommended that you show the title in all upper case letters.

5.3 The Applicant(s) and Inventor(s)

Box No. II provides a place for listing the applicant (additional applicants should be listed in Box No. III). If there are multiple applicants, the applicant identified in Box No. II may prove important. As we will discuss in Section 5.4 of this chapter, if (1) you have not appointed an agent or common representative, (2) a previously appointed agent renounces his or her appointment, or (3) the International Bureau (IB) cannot communicate with the entity named in Box No. IV ("Agent or Common Representative; or Address for Service"), the first applicant named in the request that can file with the RO will be "deemed" the common representative; all notices will then be sent to that deemed common representative. Consequently, the applicant named in Box No. II should preferably be an entity who is a national or resident of the country where the PCT application will be filed and who is best suited to fill this backup correspondent role. In most cases, a legal entity who is the primary owner of the invention will fulfill this role. If the entity listed in Box No. II is a natural person and is also an inventor, the appropriate box should be checked.

Box No. II APPLICANT ☐ This person is also inventor

Name and address: *(Family name followed by given name; for a legal entity, full official designation. The address must include postal code and name of country. The country of the address indicated in this Box is the applicant's State (that is, country) of residence if no State of residence is indicated below.)*

CANDY WRAP UNLIMITED, INC.
300 Colorado Street
Baltimore, Maryland, 21201-4307
United States of America

Telephone No. (+1-301) 876-5432

Facsimile No. (+1-301) 876-5555

Applicant's registration No. with the Office

E-mail authorization: Marking one of the check-boxes below authorizes the receiving Office, the International Searching Authority, the International Bureau and the International Preliminary Examining Authority to use the e-mail address indicated in this Box to send, notifications issued in respect of this international application to that e-mail address if those offices are willing to do so.
☒ as advance copies followed by paper notifications; or ☐ exclusively in electronic form (no paper notifications will be sent).
E-mail address: candy@anumma.com

State *(that is, country)* of nationality: US

State *(that is, country)* of residence: US

This person is applicant for the purposes of: ☒ all designated States ☐ the States indicated in the Supplemental Box

Box No. III FURTHER APPLICANT(S) AND/OR (FURTHER) INVENTOR(S)

☒ Further applicants and/or (further) inventors are indicated on a continuation sheet.

Figure 2.3
Boxes No. II and No. III, PCT Request

For clarity, names of legal entities and the surnames of natural persons should be in all upper case letters.

If the PCT application is being filed in a country that assigns registration numbers to applicants (e.g., Japan), the number should be listed in the space provided. The United States does not assign numbers to applicants; this is not a "customer number." Therefore, U.S. applicants should leave the space blank.

The PCT is moving toward a paperless system. As part of this effort, applicants can choose to (1) receive advanced copies of PCT notices by e-mail followed by an official paper notice or (2) receive PCT notices by e-mail only. To select either option, check the appropriate box and provide the e-mail address. At the time of this writing, only the IB is sending notices or advanced copies by e-mail. If the paperless system is an attractive option, you should first try receiving advanced copies by e-mail followed by the official paper notice. Once the system proves to be reliable, you can request the full paperless option in subsequent filings.[8]

You should list the state (i.e., country) of nationality and state (i.e., country) of residence for all the applicants. However, when you file with the RO/US, it is not a defect if you provide this information only for one applicant so long as that applicant is a national or resident of the United States.[9] You should use the *full* official country name—*United States of America*—or the two-letter ISO country code—i.e., *US*—instead of variations such as USA or United States. The RO will make an ex officio correction if you get the country name wrong, however.

When you file your application, you automatically designate all current PCT member countries, and your designation encompasses all the types of protection available in each member country (e.g., utility model protection).[10] In other words, you will have the right to enter the national phase in any designated PCT member country and to seek whatever type of protection for inventions that country provides. There are currently 146 PCT member countries; some countries are also members of one of the four regional patent offices associated with the PCT (European Patent Office (EP), Eurasian Patent Office (EA), African Regional Intellectual Property Office (ARIPO), and African Intellectual Property Office (OAPI)). You do not have to decide whether to seek a regional patent or a national patent, or both, until you enter the national phase.

8. If the application is being handled by an agent or common representative, or if an address for correspondence is listed in Box No. IV, electronic advanced copies/notices will be sent to the e-mail address indicated in Box IV rather than the e-mail address listed in Box No. II.

9. As a general rule, each applicant's nationality or residence should be provided on the form, even if it is not a PCT member country.

10. From 1978, when the PCT came into force, until January 1, 2004, applicants had to designate the PCT Contracting States that they wished to reserve for national phase entry at the time they filed their PCT applications, and if they were interested in seeking alternative forms of protection, such as a utility model, they had to so indicate along with the designation. Additionally, applicants had to pay a designation fee associated with the first few designations (the number varied from time to time).

You have the right to name different applicants for each one of the designated countries, but this is rarely done. Currently, all PCT member countries allow a legal entity to be the applicant on a patent application. In most cases, the applicant for all PCT member countries will be a single entity. Although typical, this situation is far from universal. How you list applicants for PCT member countries should match the legal ownership of the application in each country *at the time of filing*. For example, a U.S. corporation might be named as the applicant for the United States, Canada, and Mexico, a Brazilian subsidiary as the applicant for the PCT member countries in Central and South America, a Japanese subsidiary as applicant for the PCT member countries in Asia and India, and a European subsidiary as the applicant for the PCT member countries in Europe and Africa. In another situation, two or more legal entities (or natural persons) may jointly own the application in one or more countries. In some situations, one entity may own the application in some regions while another entity is the owner in others. The PCT system easily accommodates all permutations and combinations of applicants and countries.

In the typical situation mentioned above, a single legal entity is the applicant for all countries; a convenient check box is available in Box II of the request for this indication. For all other situations, mark the check box for "the States indicated in the Supplemental Box." In the Supplemental Box (see below), the countries for which the named entity is applicant can be indicated.

If there is more than one applicant, the appropriate check box at the bottom of Box No. II should be marked. Additional applicant(s) are listed in Box No. III on the "continuation sheet" of the request form.

Box No. III FURTHER APPLICANT(S) AND/OR (FURTHER) INVENTOR(S) *If none of the following sub-boxes is used, this sheet should not be included in the request.*	
Name and address: *(Family name followed by given name; for a legal entity, full official designation. The address must include postal code and name of country. The country of the address indicated in this Box is the applicant's State (that is, country) of residence if no State of residence is indicated below.)* JONES, Mary 1600 South Eads Street Arlington, Virginia 22202-2913 United States of America	This person is: ☐ applicant only ☐ applicant and inventor ☒ inventor only *(If this check-box is marked, do not fill in below.)* Applicant's registration No. with the Office
State *(that is, country)* of nationality:	State *(that is, country)* of residence:
This person is applicant for the purposes of: ☐ all designated States	☐ the States indicated in the Supplemental Box

Figure 2.4
Box No. III continuation sheet, PCT Request

Box No. III allows listing of the second and subsequent applicants as well as the inventors (use as many sheets as necessary to complete the listing). The procedure for completing Box No. III is essentially the same as for Box No. II with the following exceptions:

- Phone numbers and e-mail addresses are not required. (The "backup" correspondence role is most always filled by the entity listed in Box No. II.)
- There are check boxes for indicating whether the named entity is "applicant only," "applicant and inventor," or "inventor only." (The entity listed in Box II *must* be an "applicant" and *may* also be an inventor.)

If the listed entity is a legal entity or a natural person who is not an inventor, "applicant only" should be indicated.

If the listed person is an inventor and is to be an applicant for at least one PCT member country, then the second box, "applicant and inventor," should be marked, and the countries for which he or she is an applicant should be indicated by marking the check box for "all designated states" or "the States indicated in the Supplemental Box."

If the listed person is an inventor but is not an applicant for any member country, then "inventor only" is the proper indication.

Some countries, like Japan and the United States, require that the inventor(s) be listed in the application at the time of filing. Listing the inventors (as "inventor only" or as "inventor/applicant" as appropriate) in Boxes II and/or III fulfills this obligation. If the inventors are not listed in Boxes II and/or III, the obligation to list them in the application at the time of filing may also be fulfilled by using the first of the five declarations that may be filed in conjunction with the international application. The five declarations will be discussed in detail in Section 6 of this chapter.[11]

---

11. If you do not list the inventors in the request, you can still add them later by filing a change under Rule 92*bis*, or you can furnish them to the national office at the time of national phase entry. The PCT Applicant's Guide provides details for each country that requires the listing of inventors.

5.4 Agents, Common Representatives, and Address for Correspondence

Most PCT applications will be filed by an *agent* representing the applicant(s) for the PCT procedure.

> To be an agent for a PCT application, the agent must be entitled to practice before the receiving office where the case will be filed.

Only a person registered with the USPTO can be an agent for an application filed in the RO/US. Any agent qualified to practice before the receiving office where an application was filed can automatically represent the case before the other PCT international authorities and the International Bureau. To be an agent for an application filed with the RO/IB, the agent must be able to practice before one of the competent receiving offices where the application could have been filed based on the nationality and residence of all applicants listed in the request. Therefore, if you are a qualified U.S. agent, you are also qualified to file and prosecute applications with the RO/IB, provided the applicant (or one of the applicants) is a U.S. national or resident. Once appointed, the PCT permits agents to appoint sub- or associate agents. Where applications contain more than one applicant, the agent appointed by all of the applicants and having the authority to act on behalf of all of them is referred to as the *common agent.*

In general, applicants can represent themselves before their patent office; no professional representation is required. This is also true under the PCT. Because PCT applications often name several applicants, any one of the applicants can handle the application before the RO and other international authorities. As a result, the PCT has a special category called *common representative.* A common representative is one of the applicants who is appointed by all the other applicants as their representative. As with a common agent, any act by the appointed common representative is considered an act by all of the applicants. In cases where there are multiple applicants, naming the primary corporate applicant as the common representative allows the corporation's patent department to handle the prosecution during the international phase. (The address for the common representative indicated in Box No. IV does not have to be same as the address indicated in Box No. II or III.)

An agent or common representative can be appointed in a variety of ways, but the most common is through a power of attorney related to a specific PCT application or a general power of attorney covering all PCT applications.

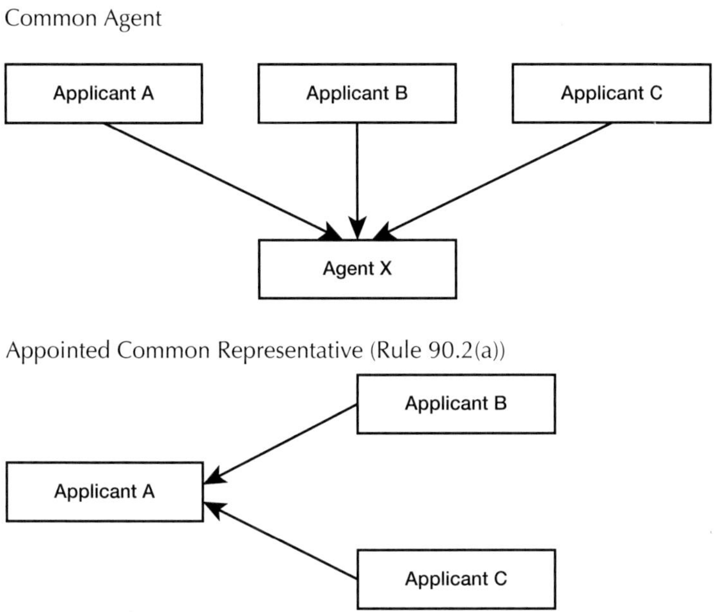

Agent X is the common agent that has been appointed by all applicants.
Applicants B and C (e.g., the applicant/inventors) appoint Applicant A (e.g., the corporate applicant) as their common representative.
Applicant A must be a national or resident of a PCT-Contracting State in order to be appointed as the common representative.

Figure 2.5
Common Agents and Common Representatives

The common representative concept is very useful, particularly in corporate practice. If Applicant A is the primary legal entity/owner and Applicants B and C are subsidiary companies or other applicants, having the subsidiary companies or other applicants appoint the primary legal entity as the common representative gives the primary legal entity control over the entire PCT process.

Doing this, however, puts the primary legal entity in the position of having to prosecute the application through the international phase, a task the legal entity may not want to or be able to perform. This issue can be circumvented by the legal entity subsequently appointing an agent.

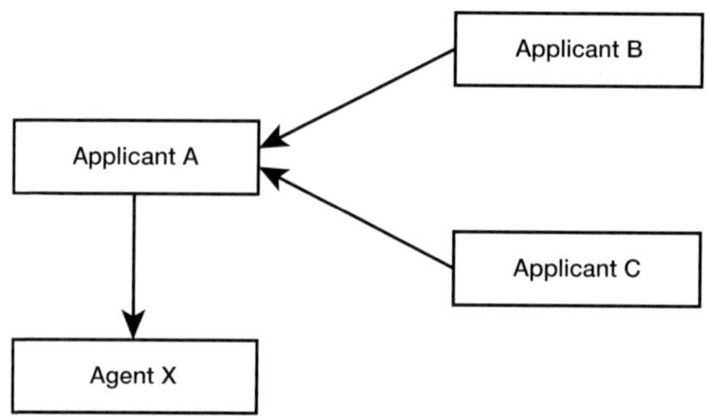

Applicant A, who has been appointed by the other applicants as their common representative, appoints Agent X.
Agent X can sign all documents for all applicants, including any withdrawal (Rule 90.3(c)), on behalf of the appointed common representative.

Figure 2.6
Agent of the Common Representative

Because authority from all the other applicants has been given to the common representative, the agent appointed by the common representative has complete authority to take any action required during the international phase.

As mentioned earlier, in the event a PCT authority (be it the RO, IB, or the International Searching Authority) cannot contact the appointed agent, for example because the agent has renounced his or her appointment, the authority will communicate with the first applicant named in the application who can file with the RO. This applicant will be "deemed" the common representative. A deemed common representative can take most actions, such as filing a demand, making amendments, or adding or correcting priority claims. Because the deemed common representative has not been appointed by all of the applicants, however, the deemed common representative cannot affect the withdrawal of an application, a designation, or a priority claim. All of those actions require the signatures of all of the applicants. A deemed common representative can appoint an agent to represent the case before the international authorities, but the agent's authority to act will be limited in the same manner as the deemed common representative.

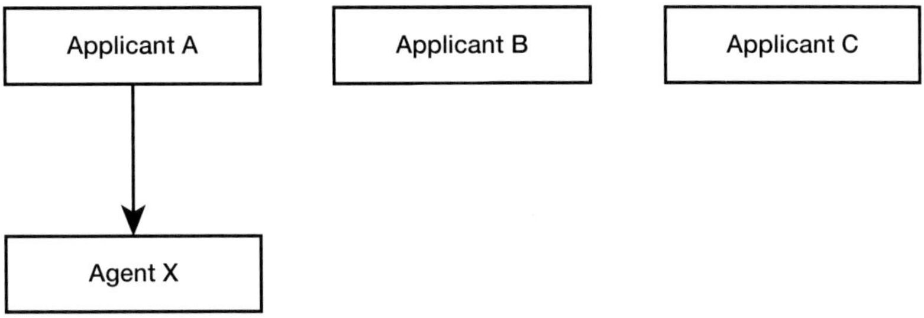

Figure 2.7
Deemed Common Representative

The indication relating to an appointed common agent or common representative is made in Box No. IV on the request form.

Box No. IV AGENT OR COMMON REPRESENTATIVE; OR ADDRESS FOR CORRESPONDENCE

The person identified below is hereby/has been appointed to act on behalf of the applicant(s) before the competent International Authorities as: ☒ agent ☐ common representative

Name and address: *(Family name followed by given name; for a legal entity, full official designation. The address must include postal code and name of country.)*	Telephone No.
DAVIS, Catherine 2500 Virgina Avenue, N.W. Washington, D.C. 20037-1902 United States of America	Telephone No. 1-202-557-3054 Facsimile No. 1-202-557-3060 Agent's registration No. with the Office 44,111

E-mail authorization: Marking one of the check-boxes below authorizes the receiving Office, the International Searching Authority, the International Bureau and the International Preliminary Examining Authority to use the e-mail address indicated in this Box to send, notifications issued in respect of this international application to that e-mail address if those offices are willing to do so.

☒ as advance copies followed by paper notifications; or ☐ exclusively in electronic form (no paper notifications will be sent).

E-mail address: davispatents@anumma.com

☐ **Address for correspondence:** Mark this check-box where no agent or common representative is/has been appointed and the space above is used instead to indicate a special address to which correspondence should be sent.

Figure 2.8
Box No. IV, PCT Request

If a common representative will be handling the application directly, the appropriate name and correspondence address should be listed in Box No. IV.

There may be instances when an applicant wants an agent to handle the case, but the agent is not competent to file the international application with the RO. One example would be a Canadian company that owns an invention in which all of the inventors are Canadian nationals and residents. If the corporation wants the application to be handled by their U.S. agent (who may be well versed in the technology or who is prosecuting the parent U.S. application), what can be done? Since there are no U.S. nationals or residents listed as applicants, the case cannot be filed in the RO/US, and a U.S. agent cannot be named as the agent because, in fact, the case should be filed in the Canadian receiving office (RO/CA) or the RO/IB by a Canadian agent. If the applicant nevertheless wants the U.S. agent to handle the case, the U.S. agent should be listed as the "Address for Correspondence," and neither the Agent nor Common Representative box should be checked. This will result in all of the correspondence being sent to the U.S. agent. However, the U.S. agent will have no authority in the case and will not be able to sign any documents.[12] When a signature is required, one of the applicants will have to sign. In this example, the application should be filed in the RO/IB and not the RO/CA. The RO/CA requires a Canadian agent to be appointed for all PCT applications if the applicant is not also the inventor.[13]

5.5 Designations and Types of Protection

Until 2004, applicants had to specifically designate which PCT member countries were of interest and the type of protection desired *at the time of filing their PCT application*. The treaty still requires a PCT application to designate at least one member country at filing, but the procedure for doing so has changed. The PCT request form now contains in Box No. V a statement designating all PCT member countries on the date of filing and for all types of protection available through the PCT.[14]

---

12. A U.S. agent could handle this case directly before the RO/US or RO/IB as agent if a U.S. national or resident was listed as an applicant for at least one PCT member country. (See previous discussion regarding applicant-of-convenience.)

13. This example points out the importance of checking the PCT Applicant's Guide when unusual situations arise. Information such as the requirement that a Canadian agent being necessary to file in the RO/CA if the applicant is any entity other than the inventor is found in the annexes to the PCT Applicant's Guide. *See* http://www.wipo.int/pct/en/appguide/index.jsp.

14. Types of protection available through the PCT include patents, patents of addition, utility models, innovation patents, an so forth. Industrial design and trademark protection cannot be secured under the PCT.

Box No. V DESIGNATIONS

The filing of this request **constitutes under Rule 4.9(a) the designation** of all Contracting States bound by the PCT on the international filing date, for the grant of every kind of protection available and, where applicable, for the grant of both regional and national patents.

However,

☐ DE Germany **is not designated** for any kind of national protection

☐ JP Japan **is not designated** for any kind of national protection

☐ KR Republic of Korea **is not designated** for any kind of national protection

(The check-boxes above may only be used to exclude (irrevocably) the designations concerned if, at the time of filing or subsequently under Rule 26bis.1, the international application contains in Box No. VI a priority claim to an earlier national application filed in the particular State concerned, in order to avoid the ceasing of the effect, under the national law, of this earlier national application.)

Figure 2.9
Box No. V, PCT Request

As can be seen, Box No. V also permits applicants to irrevocably exclude the designation of Germany (DE), Japan (JP), or Korea (KR). You should *not* mark any of the check boxes that permit the exclusion of those designations unless you are filing a PCT application that claims priority to a German, Japanese, or Korean national application. This very special situation owes its rationale to German, Japanese, and Korean national law.

The national laws of Germany, Japan, and Korea provide that an earlier-filed application will automatically become abandoned upon filing a subsequent DE, JP, or KR application on the same subject matter and claiming priority to the earlier application. In other words, the earlier-filed application is automatically abandoned in favor of the later-filed application. Since a PCT application designating DE, JP, or KR is equivalent to "a subsequent national filing," the filing of the application will trigger the abandonment of the earlier-filed priority application. Abandonment may not be the result an applicant wants, however.[15] The purpose of the check boxes in Box No. V, which make it easy for applicants with pending German, Japanese, and Korean priority applications on the same subject matter not to designate these countries, is to avoid this result.

What saves applicants who mistakenly mark a checkbox is that exclusion of the designation of any of the three countries *must* be

15. If the elimination of the designation of JP or KR is not made in the request, the earlier-filed JP or KR priority filing will be abandoned 15 months from the filing of the priority application. The automatic abandonment of an earlier-filed DE application will only occur if the international application is filed in the RO/DE in the German language.

accompanied by a priority claim to an earlier-filed application in that country. If the priority is not claimed in the PCT application, the applicant will be notified by the RO and invited to add a priority claim to the excluded country. If the applicant does not add the required priority claim, the RO will ignore the checked box requesting exclusion of the designation.

U.S. applicants will almost *never* want to exclude the designation of Germany, Japan, or Korea in Box No. V. Before marking any of the checkboxes, you should ensure that (1) the PCT application is claiming priority to a German, Japanese, or Korean application; (2) the priority claim to the earlier filing in any one of those countries has been made in Box VI; and (3) marking the checkbox and thereby preventing the automatic abandonment of the priority application is the best strategy.

5.6 Claiming Priority in a PCT Application

All PCT member countries are also party to the Paris Convention for the Protection of Industrial Property. Therefore, a PCT application can claim priority to one or more earlier-filed applications under the Paris Convention. Additionally, priority can be claimed to applications filed in non-Paris Convention member countries provided the country is a member of the World Trade Organization (WTO).

Box No. VI PRIORITY CLAIM AND DOCUMENT

The priority of the following earlier application(s) is hereby claimed:

Filing date of earlier application *(day/month/year)*	Number of earlier application	Where earlier application is:		
		national application: country or Member of WTO	regional application: regional Office	international application: receiving Office
item (1) 26 October 2011 (26.10.2011)	61/274,654	US		
item (2) 13 December 2011 (13.12.2011)	11187654.4		EP	
item (3)				

☐ Further priority claims are indicated in the Supplemental Box.

Figure 2.10
Box No. VI, PCT Request

Box No. VI of the request form provides space for up to three priority claims. You can make additional claims in the Supplemental Box.

The request form has space for the filing date, application number, and country where the earlier application was filed. If the earlier application is a regional application, there is a box to indicate the appropriate regional office (for example, EP), and similarly, if the earlier application is an international application, a box to indicate the RO. Note that under the PCT, all dates listed should be written out in "day-month-year" format (for example, 10 August 2012) and also in numeric format, dd.mm.yyyy (10.08.2012). Since the PCT operates in many different languages, including the numeric format, with the day preceding the month, is essential since it will be understood by all. If there are more than three priority claims, you should check the appropriate box and include the additional claims in the Supplemental Box of the request.

5.7 The PCT and U.S. Continuation Practice

A U.S. application may, under 35 U.S.C. § 120, claim the benefit of the filing date of an earlier-filed U.S. nonprovisional application,[16] provided the conditions of 35 U.S.C. § 120 are met. A PCT application designating the United States is equivalent to a U.S. domestic filing for all purposes. Therefore, a PCT application designating the United States can be a continuation or continuation-in-part of an earlier-filed nonprovisional U.S. application, and, likewise, an international application designating the United States can serve as the basis for a later-filed continuation or continuation-in-part. Though the earlier U.S. nonprovisional application must be pending on the international filing date, there is no requirement under 35 U.S.C. § 120 that the subsequent U.S. application be filed within 12 months of the earlier-filed nonprovisional application. If you want the U.S. designation in a PCT application to claim the benefit of the filing date of an earlier-filed U.S. nonprovisional application, you should identify in the Supplemental Box the "parent" U.S. application number, its filing date, and its relationship to the PCT/US designation. If the filing date of the earlier application is within 12 months of the

16. U.S. applications may, of course, also claim priority to earlier-filed provisional applications under 35 U.S.C. § 119(e).

international filing date, it can also serve as a Paris Convention priority claim for designations other than the United States. Therefore, you should also list the earlier U.S. application in Box No. VI. If there is only one U.S. parent application, you can make the domestic benefit claim at the time of national stage entry, or you can add it within four months of U.S. national stage entry under 35 U.S.C. § 371. However including the information in the Supplemental Box is recommended.[17] If the U.S. designation is part of a chain of multiple domestic benefit claims, the listing is critical because the USPTO may deny the PCT/US designation as a bridge to multiple earlier U.S. applications if the cross-reference is not in the PCT published application.

5.8 The Supplemental Box

The "Supplemental Box" has been mentioned several times in this chapter. This multi-use box is used when an applicant is named only for certain countries; for indicating priority claims when there are more than three; for naming more agents than will fit into the space in Box No. IV; and for indicating the realtionship between the U.S. designation and earlier nonprovisional U.S. applications. You should include it as part of the PCT application only when it is needed.

17. By listing the latest U.S. parent application in the Supplemental Box, the applicant keeps all options for obtaining patent protection in the United States either by entering the U.S. national stage under 35 U.S.C. § 371 or by filing a continuing application under 35 U.S.C. §§ 120 and 365(c) that claims domestic benefit of the PCT application under the so-called "bypass route." In a bypass route application, the listing in the Supplemental Box may be required to gain the benefit of all earlier-filed U.S. applications.

Supplemental Box *If the Supplemental Box is not used, this sheet should not be included in the request.*	
1. *If, in any of the Boxes, except Boxes Nos. VIII(i) to (v) for which a special continuation box is provided,* ***the space is insufficient*** *to furnish all the information: in such case, write "Continuation of Box No...." (indicate the number of the Box) and furnish the information in the same manner as required according to the captions of the Box in which the space was insufficient, in particular:*	
(i) ***if more than one person is to be indicated as applicant and/or inventor*** *and no "continuation sheet" is available: in such case, write "Continuation of Box No. III" and indicate for each additional person the same type of information as required in Box No. III. The country of the address indicated in this Box is the applicant's State (that is, country) of residence if no State of residence is indicated below;*	
(ii) *if, in Box No. II or in any of the sub-boxes of Box No. III, the indication* ***"the States indicated in the Supplemental Box"*** *is checked: in such case, write "Continuation of Box No. II" or "Continuation of Box No. III" or "Continuation of Boxes No. II and No. III" (as the case may be), indicate the name of the applicant(s) involved and, next to (each) such name, the State(s) (and/or, where applicable, ARIPO, Eurasian, European or OAPI patent) for the purposes of which the named person is applicant;*	
(iii) *if, in Box No. II or in any of the sub-boxes of Box No. III,* ***the inventor or the inventor/applicant is not inventor for the purposes of all designated States****: in such case, write "Continuation of Box No. II" or "Continuation of Box No. III" or "Continuation of Boxes No. II and No. III" (as the case may be), indicate the name of the inventor(s) and, next to (each) such name, the State(s) (and/or, where applicable, ARIPO, Eurasian, European or OAPI patent) for the purposes of which the named person is inventor;*	
(iv) *if, in addition to the agent(s) indicated in Box No. IV, there are* ***further agents****: in such case, write "Continuation of Box No. IV" and indicate for each further agent the same type of information as required in Box No. IV;*	
(v) *if, in Box No. VI, there are* ***more than three earlier applications whose priority is claimed****: in such case, write "Continuation of Box No. VI" and indicate for each additional earlier application the same type of information as required in Box No. VI.*	
2. *If the applicant intends to make an indication of the wish that the international application be treated, in certain designated States, as an application for a patent of addition, certificate of addition, inventor's certificate of addition or utility certificate of addition: in such case, write the name or two-letter code of each designated State concerned and the indication "****patent of addition,****" "****certificate of addition,****" "****inventor's certificate of addition****" or "****utility certificate of addition,****" the number of the parent application or parent patent or other parent grant and the date of grant of the parent patent or other parent grant or the date of filing of the parent application (Rules 4.11(a)(i) and 49bis.1(a) or (b)).*	
3. *If the applicant intends to make an indication of the wish that the international application be treated, in the United States of America, as a continuation or continuation-in-part of an earlier application: in such case, write "United States of America" or "US" and the indication "****continuation****" or "****continuation-in-part****" and the number and the filing date of the parent application (Rules 4.11(a)(ii) and 49bis.1(d)).*	US, continuation, 12/987,654 filed 16 March 2011 (16.03.2011)

Figure 2.11
Supplemental Box, PCT Request

5.9 Priority Documents

In principle, you have an obligation to submit a certified copy of each priority application to the receiving office or the IB.[18] If you have filed your priority application(s) with the USPTO and you file your PCT application with the RO/US, however, all you have to do in Box No. VI is to mark the first checkbox following the phrase "Furnishing the priority document(s)" (see Figure 2.12), which requests the receiving office to prepare and transmit to the IB certified copies of all priority applications. The IB will supply copies to all national and regional offices. If the priority application was filed in a different office, depending upon the office in which the priority application was filed, you may be able to ask the IB to obtain a certified copy of the application from the WIPO Digital Access Service (DAS) by marking the other checkbox in Box No. VI. You will find a detailed discussion of these options in Chapter 3.

If you are not able to take advantage of either option, however, you should send a certified copy of your priority application(s) directly to the IB after the IB has received the record copy of your application from the receiving office (you will know that the IB has received the record copy when you receive Form IB/301). The IB will make the priority documents available on its Internet site upon publication. You should file the priority documents by 16 months of the priority date, but they will be considered to have been timely filed if the certified copies are received by the IB no later than the date of publication of the international application. If you are unable to file the certified copies within this time limit, you will still have the opportunity to supply them to each national office within a reasonable time limit after national phase entry.

Figure 2.12 is an example of an application that was filed in the RO/US. The application lists priority claims to three applications: a U.S.

---

18. There are several filings under the PCT where applicants have the choice of filing needed documents with either the receiving office or the IB. Provided an applicant has received Form PCT/301 from the IB indicating that the IB has received the record copy of the application, it is always best to file the needed document with the IB. In these instances, it is the IB that must take action based on the filing, and filing with the RO merely delays the arrival of the document at the IB and risks loss of the document.

provisional application; a United Kingdom application; and a U.S. non-provisional application.

Filing date of earlier application *(day/month/year)*	Number of earlier application	Where earlier application is:		
		national application: country or Member of WTO	regional application: regional Office	international application: receiving Office
item (1) 17 March 2010 (17.03.2010)	61/274,654	US		
item (2) 8 December 2010 (08.12.2010)	1018767.4	GB		
item (3) 16 March 2011 (16.03.2011)	12/987,654	US		

☐ Further priority claims are indicated in the Supplemental Box.

Furnishing the priority document(s):

☒ The **receiving Office** is requested to prepare and transmit to the International Bureau a certified copy of the earlier application(s) *(only if the earlier application(s) was filed with the receiving Office which, for the purposes of this international applicati on, is the receiving Office)* identified above as:

☐ all items ☒ item (1) ☐ item (2) ☒ item (3) ☐ other, see Supplemental Box

☒ The **International Bureau** is requested to obtain from a digital library a certified copy of the earlier application(s) identified above, using, where applicable, the access code(s) indicated below *(if the earlier application(s) is available to it from a digital library)*:

☐ item (1) access code ______ ☒ item (2) access code #####______ ☐ item (3) access code ______ ☐ other, see Supplemental Box

Figure 2.12
Box No. VI (Priority Claim), PCT Request

In the scenario exemplified in the form above, because priority applications 1 and 3 were filed in the USPTO, the applicant can ask the RO/US to prepare the certified copies and forward them to the IB. While the RO/US provides this service at no charge to the applicant, other ROs may levy a charge. Because the second priority application was filed in the UK Patent Office and not in the USPTO, the applicant cannot ask the RO/US to obtain the necessary certified copy. Instead, the applicant has two options to supply the needed UK priority document: (1) order a certified copy from the UK Patent Office and send it to the IB, or (2) because the UK office is party to the WIPO Digital Access Service for Priority Documents (DAS), the applicant can take the necessary steps to have the UK Patent Office make the document available to the IB through the DAS.

Once a certified copy of a priority application has been made available to the IB, no national or regional office should ask the applicant to supply one when the PCT application enters the national or regional phase.[19]

It is important to note that under the PCT, no national office can cancel a priority claim if you failed to supply the priority document during the international phase; each national office must give you an opportunity to directly supply a certified copy during the national phase. If you did not arrange for the document to be supplied to the RO or IB, you should send a copy to the national office(s) when entering the national phase. Although each national office must give you a window of opportunity to submit a certified copy, the national office is not required to notify you that the document is not in the file in sufficient time to comply with the window of opportunity.

The IB will send you a copy of form PCT/IB/304 upon receipt of each priority document. Before entering the national phase, you should check the PCT file wrapper to ensure that a form is present for each priority application. This is your proof that the required documents were received by the IB. If the PCT/IB/304 form is missing for any or all of the priority documents, you will need to ascertain why the IB did not receive the documents and to correct the matter, or take steps to obtain certified copies for submission to the national/regional offices within the acceptable time limits under local practice.

5.10 Searching Matters

Box No. VII calls for listing your choice of international searching authority (ISA). Choosing the ISA is discussed in detail in Chapter 3.

Box No. VII also provides the opportunity to bring other prior art searches to the attention of the searching examiner. In some instances, this may result in a reduction in the international search fee (Annex D to the PCT Applicant's Guide details available cost reductions and the conditions to qualify for those cost reductions).

19. PCT Rule 17.

To list one or more previously conducted searches for consideration by the search examiner, you must complete the appropriate section of the request form and, where the search results are not otherwise available to the ISA, supply a copy of the previous search results and the cited prior art.

Continuation of Box No. VII USE OF RESULTS OF EARLIER SEARCH, REFERENCE TO THAT SEARCH

☒ The ISA indicated in Box No. VII is requested to take into account the results of the earlier search(es) indicated below (*see also Notes to Box VII; use of results of more than one earlier search*).

Filing date *(day/month/year)*	Application Number	Country *(or regional Office)*
13 December 2011 (13.12.2011)	11187654.4	EP

☐ **Statement (Rule 4.12(ii))**: this international application is the same, or substantially the same, as the application in respect of which the earlier search was carried out except, where applicable, that it is filed in a different language.

☒ **Availability of documents**: the following documents are available to the ISA in a form and manner acceptable to it and therefore do not need to be submitted by the applicant to the ISA (Rule 12*bis*.1(f)):

☒ a copy of the results of the earlier search,*
☒ a copy of the earlier application,
☐ a translation of the earlier application into a language which is accepted by the ISA,
☐ a translation of the results of the earlier search into a language which is accepted by the ISA,
☒ a copy of any document cited in the results of the earlier search. *(If known, please indicate below the document(s) available to the ISA):*

☐ **Transmit copy of results of earlier search and other documents** (*where the earlier search was* ***not*** *carried out by the ISA indicated above but by the same Office as that which is acting as the receiving Office*): the **receiving Office** is requested to prepare and transmit to the ISA (Rule 12*bis*.1(c)):

☐ a copy of the results of the earlier search,*
☐ a copy of the earlier application,
☐ a copy of any document cited in the results of the earlier search.

* Where the results of the earlier search are neither available from a digital library nor transmitted by the receiving Office, the applicant is required to submit them to the receiving Office (Rule 12*bis*.1(a)) (*See item 11. in the check-list and also Notes to Box No. VII*).

Figure 2.13
Box No. VII, PCT Request

6. Helpful Declarations that Are Available under the PCT

Anyone involved in international patent practice has experienced the extra effort required to comply with local formal requirements. At the request of PCT users, and with the approval of the PCT member countries, the IB modified the request form to include optional declarations that permit applicants to comply with certain national requirements during the international phase. If you choose to file one or more of the available declarations, no national office can require you to supply the actual documentation communicated in the declaration unless the office reasonably doubts the truth of the declaration.

There are five declarations that applicants can file with an international application. Applicants have complete freedom to use any one or more of the declarations to save the effort required to prepare, legalize (if needed), and file the actual documents with each national office when they enter the national phase. Applicants who choose not to utilize any of the five declarations need to comply with the relevant national requirements as part of the national phase entry process.

The available declarations include

1. the identity of the inventors;
2. the applicant's entitlement to apply for and be granted a patent;
3. the applicant's entitlement to claim priority of an earlier application;
4. the declaration of inventorship (U.S. only); and
5. the declaration relating to nonprejudicial exposures and exceptions to lack of novelty.

Each declaration requires specific wording, and if you choose to use a declaration, you must use the wording found in the instructions to the request form to ensure that the declaration will be accepted by all national and regional offices.

The full text of declarations timely filed during the international phase[20] are published together with their respective PCT application on PATENTSCOPE, the PCT database. If you plan on taking advantage of the opportunity to file declarations, you must so indicate in Box No. VIII of the request form, as follows:

Box No. VIII DECLARATIONS

The following **declarations** are contained in Boxes Nos. VIII (i) to (v) *(mark the applicable check-boxes below and indicate in the right column the number of each type of declaration)*:			Number of declarations
☐	Box No. VIII (i)	Declaration as to the identity of the inventor :	
☒	Box No. VIII (ii)	Declaration as to the applicant's entitlement, as at the international filing date, to apply for and be granted a patent :	1
☒	Box No. VIII (iii)	Declaration as to the applicant's entitlement, as at the international filing date, to claim the priority of the earlier application :	1
☐	Box No. VIII (iv)	Declaration of inventorship (only for the purposes of the designation of the United States of America) :	
☐	Box No. VIII (v)	Declaration as to non-prejudicial disclosures or exceptions to lack of novelty :	

Figure 2.14
Box No. VIII, PCT Request

20. In order for the declarations to be published together with their respective PCT application, they must be received by the IB prior to completion of the technical requirements for publication.

6.1 Box No. VIII(i)

The declaration as to the identity of the inventor is useful for applicants who do not mention the names of the inventors in Box Nos. II and III of the request form, but who want to fulfill their obligations to include the names of the inventors in the application, as required by the United States, Japan, and other countries.[21] While the declaration as to the identity of the inventor serves a helpful purpose, the better practice is to name the inventors in Boxes II and III. If there is a change in inventorship during the international phase, the declaration cannot be amended after the IB completes technical preparations for publication of the application (15 days prior to scheduled publication), nor can the declaration be withdrawn. If the inventors are named in Boxes II and III and there is a change in inventorship, the names of the inventors can easily be changed under PCT Rule 92*bis* at any time up to 30 months from the priority date. All you need to do is to file a request for the change with the IB.

6.2 Box Nos. VIII(ii) and VIII(iii)

For countries that require it, verifying the right to apply for and be granted a patent and/or the right to claim priority to an earlier-filed application can be accomplished by using the second and third of the five available declarations. For most international applications, a corporation, university, or other legal entity will be the applicant for all PCT member countries. When the applicants are not the inventors, some countries require evidence showing that the right to apply for and be granted a patent was assigned or otherwise transferred to the applicant by the inventors. Further, if the applicant listed in any priority filing differs from the applicant listed in the international application, some countries require evidence showing the applicant in their country

---

21. To determine if a country requires the names of the inventors, check the National Chapter Summary in the PCT Applicant's Guide for that particular country.

obtained the right to claim priority from the applicant shown on the priority document.[22]

In some cases, a country may require submission of evidence that the applicant in their country has the right to apply for and be granted a patent and/or has the right to claim priority to an earlier application. In such cases, the country requiring submission will often require the submitted evidence (a copy of an assignment document or other proof) be legalized through their consulate or under the Hague Convention via apostile. The legalization process takes time and costs money to complete. Such effort is unnecessary if the second and/or third declarations are filed in conjunction with the international application.

If either or both of these declarations are submitted, no country can ask the applicant for the actual (legalized) documents unless they reasonably doubt the veracity of the declarations. In order to utilize either of these two delarations, the documents effecting the transfer of rights *must* be effective before the international (PCT) filing date. As is the case with declarations (i) and (v), the declaration is made by the applicant or by the person signing the request form on behalf of the applicant. Declaration (iv) must be signed by the inventors.

It is important that any person signing an international application containing any one of declarations (i), (ii), (iii), or (v) verify the declaration is accurate as of the international filing date to prevent making a false declaration. There is no mechanism under the PCT for withdrawing a declaration.

Figures 2.15 and 2.16 are samples of declarations (ii) and (iii) illustrating one version of the standardized wording.

22. Article 4(A)(1) of the Paris Convention states: "*Any person who has duly filed an application for a patent*, or for the registration of a utility model, or of an industrial design, or of a trademark, in one of the countries of the Union, *or his successor in title*, shall enjoy, for the purpose of filing in the other countries, a right of priority during the periods hereinafter fixed." (emphasis added).

Box No. VIII (ii) DECLARATION: ENTITLEMENT TO APPLY FOR AND BE GRANTED A PATENT

The declaration must conform to the standardized wording provided for in Section 212; see Notes to Boxes Nos. VIII, VIII (i) to (v) (in general) and the specific Notes to Box No. VIII (ii). If this Box is not used, this sheet should not be included in the request.

Declaration as to the applicant's entitlement, as at the international filing date, to apply for and be granted a patent (Rules 4.17(ii) and 51*bis*.1(a)(ii)), in a case where the declaration under Rule 4.17(iv) is not appropriate:

in relation to this international application,

CANDY WRAP UNLIMITED, INC., is entitled to apply for and be granted a patent by virtue of the following:

an assignment from JONES, Mary, to CANDY WRAP UNLIMITED, INC.,

dated 16 March 2010 (16.03.2010).

Figure 2.15
Box No. VIII(ii), PCT Request

Box No. VIII (iii) DECLARATION: ENTITLEMENT TO CLAIM PRIORITY

The declaration must conform to the standardized wording provided for in Section 213; see Notes to Boxes Nos. VIII, VIII (i) to (v) (in general) and the specific Notes to Box No. VIII (iii). If this Box is not used, this sheet should not be included in the request.

Declaration as to the applicant's entitlement, as at the international filing date, to claim the priority of the earlier application specified below, where the applicant is not the applicant who filed the earlier application or where the applicant's name has changed since the filing of the earlier application (Rules 4.17(iii) and 51*bis*.1(a)(iii)):

in relation to this international application,

CANDY WRAP UNLIMITED, INC., is entitled to claim priority to earlier application number US 61/999,999, by virtue of the following:

an assignment from:

JONES, Mary, to CANDY WRAP UNLIMITED, INC., dated 16 March 2010 (16.03.2010)

and

in relation to this international application,

CANDY WRAP UNLIMITED, INC., is entitled to claim priority to earlier application number US 12/987,654, by virtue of the following:

an assignment from:

JONES, Mary to CANDY WRAP UNLIMITED, INC., dated 15 March 2011 (15.03.2011)

Figure 2.16
Box No. VIII(iii), PCT Request

The PCT SAFE software includes the standardized wording. For other forms of the request, the wording can be found in the notes to the request form and in the PCT Administrative Instructions Sections 211–215. All national and regional offices have agreed to accept these declarations in lieu of filing legalized copies of the actual documents. There may be instances, however, where the national or regional office requirements regarding the filing of assignments differ from the provisions in other parts of local law. If your local agent recommends filing the actual evidence *and* has a sound legal basis from outside the patent law, it is best to have the requested documentation filed.

Declarations (ii) and (iii)—right to apply for/be granted a patent and right to claim priority to an earlier filed application, respectively—are very useful and can save time and effort when entering the national phase. They should be used whenever the appropriate transfer of rights has occurred as of the international filing date.

6.3 Box No. VIII(iv)

The inventor's declaration required in every U.S. patent application can be prepared and filed with the PCT application. The United States accepts the PCT Rule 4.17(iv) declaration of inventorship when it is properly filled out and executed. The declaration of inventorship sheet of the request form can be filed with the PCT application, or it can be added to the request form within 16 months from the priority date, provided that, as with the other declarations, any declaration received prior to the completion of technical preparation for publication is considered to have been received on the last day of the 16-month time limit.[23]

The ability to have the inventors execute an acceptable U.S. declaration early in the PCT process can be particularly useful for applicants from outside the United States. This procedure can help applicants avoid having to locate the inventors at the time of U.S. national stage entry in order to have them execute a U.S. declaration form. For applicants from the United States who plan to enter the U.S. national stage from their international application, it is equally acceptable to have the inventors sign the standard U.S. declaration at the time of filing, hold it in their files, and submit it at the time of U.S. entry at 30 months or within the applicable time limits under U.S. law.

23. *See* PCT Rule 26*ter*.

If the declaration of inventorship sheet of the request form is filed after the international filing date, the international application number must be inserted onto the sheet.

Under the provisions of the Leahy-Smith America Invents Act (AIA), there are two methods of filing the U.S. Inventor's Declaration; only one of the methods, however, can be used when filing the inventor's declaration under PCT Rule 4.17(iv). In the first method, U.S. law accepts an inventor's declaration listing signed by all of the inventors. Different copies of the declaration can be submitted, with each copy signed by one or more inventors, but each copy must list all of the inventors. This practice is the same as is applicable under the pre-AIA rules and is the method acceptable for filing with the international application under PCT Rule 4.17(iv).

Under the AIA, the USPTO will also accept a series of individual declarations, each naming and signed by a single inventor, provided the series of individual declarations is accompanied by an Application Data Sheet (ADS) naming all the inventors. Because there are no provisions under the PCT for filing an ADS with a series of individual declarations, this method is not acceptable for filing with an international application under PCT Rule 4.17(iv).

If an applicant chooses not to file the inventor's declaration with the international application under PCT Rule 4.17(iv), but decides to file the declaration at the time of national stage entry or within other time limits established under U.S. law, either method of declaration practice is acceptable. An applicant is only limited to one method when filing the inventor's declaration with the international application under PCT Rule 4.17(iv).

6.4 Box VIII(v)

The final available declaration concerns the statement of "non-prejudicial disclosures and exceptions to lack of novelty." Some countries have "grace periods" as part of their laws concerning the novelty of inventions. For example, Japan has a six-month grace period for public exposures by the inventor, successor in title, or third parties obtaining knowledge from the inventor; Canada has a similar 12-month grace period. These grace periods provide the applicant with an interval following a qualifying public exposure to file a patent application without having the qualifying public exposure count against the novelty of the invention. (In countries without such provisions, any public exposure prior to filing a patent application would destroy the novelty of the invention.)

Some countries having grace periods, such as Japan, Mexico, and Brazil, require that an applicant seeking to use the grace period to protect the novelty of the invention following a qualifying public exposure reveal the details of the public exposure to the patent office at the time of filing. Normally, the applicant would file a declaration stating the timing and nature of the exposure at the time of filing or, in the case of an international application, at the time of national phase entry. PCT declaration (v) gives applicants an opportunity to supply this information at the time of filing the international application, thereby avoiding the need to file individual declarations upon national phase entry.

This declaration is available for use whenever the case circumstances require it. There is, however, no requirement to file this declaration under the PCT. The appropriate declaration can always be filed in each country requiring it upon national phase entry. Before deciding to utilize this declaration, an applicant should carefully consider all of the consequences associated with its filing:

- The details of the public exposure will be published with the international application and will be available to the patent offices in all PCT contracting states as well as to all third parties.
- The definition of what constitutes a public exposure may vary by country, particularly if the exposure is made for experimental trials. There is always a risk that such a declaration may bring one or more countries to conclude that the exposure is admitted prior art even if there is doubt under local law that the exposure was novelty destroying.

Choosing to forgo this PCT declaration in favor of filing the particulars only in those countries requiring it and in their local language may prove to be the better decision when there is a qualifying exposure prior to filing. Be sure to carefully check the current status of each local law on this issue and alert the local agent to all the facts prior to making a national phase entry. Grace period qualifications vary by country. Some run from the actual exposure to the local filing date; some limit grace period applicability to only a few types of exposures. Some countries allow their grace period to run from the local filing date *or* priority filing date (if priority is claimed).

7. Sequence Listings

7.1 Sequence Listings

An increasing number of applications are directed toward inventions in the field of biotechnology that involve specific nucleotide and/or amino acid sequences. In order to properly search the disclosed sequences in the biotech database, sequence listings must be provided. When an international application discloses one or more nucleotide and/or amino acid sequences, the description must contain a sequence listing that complies with Annex C of the PCT Administrative Instructions and the WIPO standard for presentation of these sequences (currently WIPO Standard ST.25, which is the standard for the presentation of nucleotide and amino acid sequence listings in patent applications). When filing a PCT application containing a sequence listing, the form in which the sequence listing is presented directly relates to the overall cost of filing.

At present, the PCT requires that sequence listings be presented in a text format (.txt) compliant with Annex C/WIPO Standard ST.25 for at least the purposes of conducting a search of the claimed invention.[24] If a sequence listing is presented in the application in any way other than an Annex C/ST.25 compliant form, a compliant version must be supplied to allow the search to be carried out. If no ST.25 compliant sequence

24. At the time of this writing, the Trilateral Offices (USPTO, EPO, and JPO) are working toward a revised standard utilizing XML rather than TXT format. Practitioners in the biotechnology arena will need to double-check the WIPO standards prior to preparing a sequence listing to insure compliance with the applicable standard at the time of filing.

listing is supplied by the applicant, the International Searching Authority will search the invention only to the extent possible without the aid of the sequence listing. This can result in the ISA issuing a Declaration of Non-Establishment of International Search Report[25] where all of the claims are directed to specific sequences. An Annex C/ST.25 compliant sequence listing can be prepared using PATENTIN software, available free of charge from the European Patent Office website at http://www.epo.org/patents/Grant-procedure/Filing-an-application/European-applications/Filing-options/PatentIn-filing-software.html, or from the USPTO website at http://www.uspto.gov/web/offices/pac/patin/patentin.htm.

When a PCT application is filed electronically, you only need to file one copy of an Annex C/ST.25 compliant sequence listing. That one copy serves as both the sequence listing part of the description and the copy needed by the ISA for search purposes. On rare occasions, a sequence listing is so large that it cannot be filed electronically because it exceeds the maximum file size acceptable to EFS-Web (the e-filing system used by the RO/US). In that situation, applicants should separately file the compliant sequence listing on physical data carriers on the same day as the electronically filed application. When filling out Box No. IX of the request form (CHECK LIST for EFS-Web filings), mark the appropriate box in item (g). Confusion can result if Box No. IX of the request is not properly filled out. If the compliant sequence listing is submitted *as the sequence listing part of the description*, item (g) of Box No. IX should be marked. If the compliant listing is submitted for purposes of search, together with a PDF or paper copy of the sequence listing as the sequence listing part of the description, item (f) should indicate the number of sheets of the sequence listing, and item 9 in the right-hand column of Box No. IX should be marked to indicate that the Annex C/ST.25 copy is "furnished only for the purposes of international search." In this situation, the applicant must make a statement confirming that "the information recorded in electronic form submitted under Rule 13*ter* is identical to the sequence listing as contained in the international application" and item 10 in the right-hand column. If

25. Form PCT/ISA/203.

a single compliant sequence listing is submitted but it is not properly identifed as being "part of the description," issues may arise during the national phase if the unidentified compliant copy is not transmitted to the national offices by WIPO.

The international filing fees are calculated on the number of sheets that make up the PCT application. There is a fixed fee for the first 30 sheets and a "per sheet" fee for each sheet in excess of 30 (see discussion of fees to follow). When an Annex C/ST.25 compliant sequence listing is filed as part of an electronically filed international application, there is no fee for the compliant sequence listing part of the description. To avoid confusion and additional charges for those sheets, you should not include a copy of the sequence listing in image format (for example, PDF or TIFF) as part of the electronically filed international application. If the sequence listing is filed on paper or in noncompliant image format as part of an electronically filed international application, the number of sheets of the sequence listing are counted in the total number of sheets making up the PCT application. You will have to supply a compliant copy to the ISA.

If an Annex C/ST.25 compliant sequence listing is not filed with the application but is provided later to the ISA for purposes of search only (i.e., the sequence listing filed with the application is in PDF format or is on paper), some international searching authorities will levy a late filing fee. Annex D of the PCT Applicant's Guide indicates those ISAs that levy a fee for later furinishing of the Annex C/ST.25 sequence listing (for example, the ISA/EP and ISA/KR levy this fee).

Sequence listings should be provided electronically and properly indicated to be part of the description in an Annex C/ ST.25 compliant format. Filing a single copy of a sequence listing in Annex C/ST.25 compliant format properly indicated to be the sequence listing part of the description is sufficient for all purposes during the international phase, including disclosure and search.

7.2 Boxes IX and X; Completing the Request

Box IX of the request provides for a listing of the items being filed with the PCT application. There are two versions of Box IX, one suited for filings made on paper and one for filings made in the RO/US by EFSWeb. The two are similar in content, but the EFSWeb version allows for submission of sequence listings in electronic format as part of the description (which are not included in the page count), while the version for paper filings does not (see discussion above).

Box No. IX CHECK LIST for EFS-Web filings - this sheet is only to be used when filing an international application with RO/US via **EFS-Web**

This international application **contains** the following:	Number of sheets	This international application is **accompanied by** the following item(s) *(mark the applicable check-boxes below and indicate in right column the number of each item)*:	Number of items
(a) request form PCT/RO/101 (including any declarations and supplemental sheets) . . . . :	8	1. ☒ fee calculation sheet . . . . :	1
(b) description (excluding any sequence listing part of the description, see (f), below) . . . . . :	24	2. ☐ original separate power of attorney . . . . :	
(c) claims . . . . :	3	3. ☐ original general power of attorney . . . . :	
(d) abstract . . . . :	1	4. ☐ copy of general power of attorney; reference number: . . . . :	
(e) drawings (if any) . . . . :	4	5. ☐ priority document(s) identified in Box No. VI as item(s) . . . . :	
(f) sequence listing part of the description in the form of an **image file** (e.g. PDF) . . . . :		6. ☐ Translation of international application into *(language)*: . . . . :	
		7. ☐ separate indications concerning deposited microorganism or other biological material . . . . :	
Total number of sheets (including the sequence listing part of the description if **filed as an image file**) . . . . :	40	8. ☐ *(only where item (f) is marked in the left column)* copy of the sequence listing in electronic form (Annex C/ST.25 text file) not forming part of the international application but **furnished only for the purposes of international search** under Rule 13*ter*. . . . . :	
(g) sequence listing part of the description ☐ filed in the form of an **Annex C/ST.25 text file** ☐ WILL BE filed separately on physical data carrier(s), on the same day and in the form of an **Annex C/ST.25 text file** Indicate type and number of physical data carrier(s)		9. ☐ *(only where item (f) is marked in the left column)* a statement confirming that "the information recorded in electronic form submitted under Rule 13*ter* is identical to the sequence listing as contained in the international application" as filed via EFS-Web: . . . . :	
		10. ☐ copy of results of earlier search(es) (Rule 12*bis*.1(a)) . . :	
		11. ☐ other *(specify)*: . . . . :	
Figure of the drawings which should accompany the abstract:	3	**Language of filing** of the international application:	English

Figure 2.17
Box No. IX, PCT Request

In addition to using Box IX to indicate the contents of the PCT application at the time of filing, the applicant also uses this box to indicate the language of filing as well as the drawing (if any) the applicant thinks should be published with the abstract. The applicant's choice of drawing will be reviewed by the International Searching Authority, who will accept the applicant's choice or will indicate in the search report that another figure better represents the invention.

Box X provides a place for the applicant, agent, or common representative to sign the request form. If signed by a registered U.S. agent or attorney, the registration number before the USPTO should be indicated after the typed name if not listed in Box IV. If the request is being filed electronically and an "s-signature" is being used to sign the submission, then the registration number should appear after the name or included between the slant marks of the s-signature (i.e., /Catherine Davis, Reg. No. 44,111/). If the application is signed by all of the applicants in Box X, this will be taken as an appointment of the agent or common representative listed in Box IV. If signed by an agent or a common representative, then, when needed, separate powers of attorney appointing the agent or common representative signed by the applicants will be required. (Many international authorities have waived the requirement to submit a power of attorney in most instances. There are, however, circumstances where submission of powers of attorney will be required even though the Authority has waived the requirement in most instances—withdrawal of the application, a priority claim, or a designation.)

Box No. X **SIGNATURE OF APPLICANT, AGENT OR COMMON REPRESENTATIVE** *Next to each signature, indicate the name of the person signing and the capacity in which the person signs (if such capacity is not obvious from reading the request).*
Catherine Davis Catherine Davis

Figure 2.18
Box No. X, PCT Request

8. Biological Deposits

Some biotechnology applications require the deposit of biological material to enable the practice of the claimed invention. In countries that are members of the Budapest Treaty, making a deposit in one of the treaty-recognized depositories (such as the American Type Culture Collection or ATCC) is sufficient for all Budapest Treaty member countries. The rules concerning when the deposit must be made vary across countries. Some countries (like Japan) require the deposit be made prior to filing the international application and the identifying information be part of the international application. The required information on each deposited biological material can be furnished on the PCT/RO/134 form and included within the description. Other countries are not so strict, allowing later deposits and reporting of the identifying information. When filing a PCT application, applicants should ensure that they meet the most stringent of the deposit requirements to maintain the flexibility to enter the national phase in all PCT member countries. Non-Budapest Treaty states may require a separate deposit be made in an approved local depository *before the international filing date.*

Annex L of the PCT Applicant's Guide provides the requirements in each country in which the national law contains provisions concerning the deposits of microorganisms and other biological material. For information on the local practice in countries not covered in Annex L, you should check with local patent offices or agents to determine their requirements.

> For invention disclosures requiring the deposit of biological material, it is important for applicants to check the requirements related to the deposit and reporting of indentifying information in Annex L of the PCT Applicant's Guide or the local patent office or with a local agent. Any deposits and reporting of information should meet the local requirements of the most stringent country of interest to the applicant to help ensure successful national phase entry and prosecution.

9. Fees under the PCT

There are a variety of fees associated with the filing and processing of a PCT application. With the wide variety of currencies around the world and the fluctuating exchange rates, being aware of the fee structure and how the fees are set will help the applicant ensure that proper payments are made in a timely manner.

Depending on circumstances, you may be required to make payments to any one or all of the international authorities including the RO, ISA, IB, SISA, and IPEA. Fees must be paid in a currency accepted by that international authority. Other than for the initial filing and international search fees, which are paid to the receiving office, applicants will be working with and paying the other international authorities or the IB directly. A summary of the various fees is found in the Figure 2.19.

Authority Collecting the Fee	Fees Required for Every Application	Fees that May Be Required Depending on Circumstances
Receiving Office (RO)	- transmittal fee (fee set and collected by the RO) - international filing fee (fee set by the IB; collected by the RO) - international search fee (set by the ISA; collected by the RO)	- fee for each sheet over 30 (set by the IB; collected by the RO) - fee for priority document - late payment fee - late furnishing fee (for translation) - fee for copies of documents - fee for requesting restoration of priority
International Searching Authority (ISA)	None	- additional search fees (where there is a lack of unity of invention) - protest fee - fee for copies of documents - fee for late sequence listing filing

International Bureau	None	- special fee for publication of request for rectification of obvious mistakes
		- special fee for publication of information concerning priority claim considered void
		- fee for early publication (before issuance of ISR)
		- fee for copies of documents
		- fees related to supplementary search:
		  - supplementary search fee (set by SISA; collected by the IB)
		  - supplementary search handling fee
		- late payment fee

(continued)

Figure 2.19
Summary of Fees Under the PCT
(Unless otherwise noted, fees are set and collected by the listed authority)

Authority Collecting the Fee	Fees Required for Every Application	Fees that May Be Required Depending on Circumstances
Supplementary International Searching Authority (SISA)	None	- review fee (for finding of lack of unity) - fees for copies of documents (where applicable)
International Preliminary Examining Authority (IPEA)	None	- fees related to filing a Demand: - preliminary examination fee (set by the IPEA) - handling fee (set by IB; collected by IPEA) - late payment fee - additional examination fee (where there is a lack of unity of invention) - protest fee (where applicable for challenging finding of lack of unity) - fee for copies of documents - fee for late sequence listing filing

Figure 2.19 *(continued)*

At the time of filing, you will need to pay a transmittal fee, an international filing fee, and an international search fee. If the application, including the request form, is more than 30 sheets, you will also have to pay an excess sheet fee for each sheet over 30. These fees are paid to the receiving office in the currency accepted by that office. The RO/US only accepts U.S. dollars. Payment may be made in any form acceptable to the USPTO in its domestic practice including by credit card, U.S. deposit account, check, or wire/bank transfer.

For filing of applications, the RO/IB accepts fees in Swiss francs, Euros, and U.S. dollars. Fees may be paid to the RO/IB by credit card, WIPO deposit account, wire/bank transfer, or check.[26] When paying fees to any of the international authorities, the payment must be made

26. The IB, in its capacities other than as a receiving office, only accepts payment in Swiss francs. Credit card payments can be made using the e-payment service offered by WIPO.

in the accepted currency. For example, if paying the fees for filing a Demand for International Preliminary Examination with the International Preliminary Examining Authority in the Republic of Korea (IPEA/KR), the fees must be paid in Korean Won. When paying any additional search fees to the ISA/EP, the payment must be made in Euros.[27] The PCT Applicant's Guide lists the acceptable currencies for each of the international authorities. Fees required for other than filing the international application will be discussed later in the sections relating to the specific items requiring payment of fees.

Under the PCT, an applicant always has one month after filing to pay the fees related to filing the PCT application (or request a supplementary search or file a Demand for international preliminary examination) without penalty.

You have one month to pay the fees to the RO. The RO will send the applicant a Notification Concerning Payment of Fees (PCT/RO/102 form) for every application, either informing the applicant that the fees have been paid in full or that fees are due. If the fees are not paid within the one-month time period, the RO will issue a PCT/RO/133 form inviting the applicant to pay the missing fees together with a late payment fee. If the missing fees are paid later than the one-month time limit but before the RO issues the PCT/RO/133 form, the fees are considered to have been timely filed, and no late payment is due. Otherwise, the late payment fee together with the outstanding fees must be paid. If these fees are not paid within the time limit set forth in the invitation, the RO will declare the international application withdrawn for failure to pay the fees by issuing a PCT/RO/117 form. If the missing fees together with the late payment fee are received by the RO later than the set time limit but before the RO issues the PCT/RO/117 form, the fees will be considered to have been timely paid.

Under the PCT, the late fee is equal to 50 percent of the missing amount. If a partial payment was timely made, the late penalty will be

27. The EPO no longer accepts checks for payment of fees. Applicants must pay by wire/bank transfer, credit card, or EPO deposit account.

calculated only on the unpaid amount. There is, however, a minimum and a maximum late fee. For fees paid to the RO at the time of filing, the minimum late fee is equal to the transmittal fee, and the maximum late fee is equal to 50 percent of the international filing fee. (Note that if an applicant underpays the fees by a small amount, the penalty will be assessed at the minimum. At the time of this writing, in the RO/US, this amounts to US$240.)

The search copy will not be forwarded to the ISA until the search fee has been paid. This can delay receipt of the international search report and written opinion of the ISA.

Fee	RO/US (or selected ISA)	RO/IB
Transmittal Fee	240.00[1]	US$107.00 (CHF 100)
International Filing Fee[2]	1419.00	US$1,419.00 (CHF 1330)
Fee for each page over 30	16.00	16.00 (US$ equiv. of CHF 15)
International Searching Authorities		
—ISA/US	2,080.00	2,080.00
—ISA/EP	US$2419.00 USD (EUR 1875)	US$2,419.00 (EUR 1875)
—ISA/KR	US$1,167.00 (KRW 1,300,000)	US$1,167.00 (KRW 1,300,000)
—ISA/AU	US$2,282.00 (AUD 2,200)	US$2,282.00 (AUD 2,200)
—ISA/RU	US$217 (RUB 6750)	US$217 (RUB 6750)

[1] There is an additional transmittal fee charge of US$400 (US$200 for a small entity) for applications not filed electronically in the RO/US.

[2] The international filing fee is reduced by the local equivalent of CHF 100, 200, or 300 for various forms of electronic filing. See the PCT Applicant's Guide for details of qualifying conditions for these fee reductions.

(continued)

Figure 2.20

Typical Costs of Filing an International Application by U.S. Applicants

(Costs listed are in US$ as of 1 January 2013 for an English language application)

Fee	RO/US (or selected ISA)	RO/IB
Minimum late payment fee	240.00	107.00 (equiv. of transmittal fee)
Maximum late payment fee	709.50	709.50 (equiv. of 50% of filing fee)
Fee for late filing of sequence listing in ST.25 compliant form for search		
—ISA/EP	EUR 220 (paid to ISA)	N/A
—ISA/KR	KRW 112,500 (paid to ISA)	N/A
—ISA/US & ISA/AU	0.00	N/A
—ISA/RU	RUB 2,050 (paid to ISA)	
Fee for RO obtaining certified copy of U.S. priority document	0.00	N/A
Requesting restoration of priority	1,410.00	0.00

Figure 2.20 *(continued)*

Because the fees are set in local currency (CHF, EUR, KRW, AUD, and RUB for the above example), the U.S. dollar equivalents change frequently with currency fluctuations. Be sure to verify the actual costs at the time of filing with the information in the PCT Applicant's Guide or the fee tables in the most recent PCT Newsletter to insure payment of the proper fees, avoiding overpayment or the possibility of having to pay a late fee.

The amounts of all other fees can be found in the PCT Applicant's Guide.

The PCT does not charge fees for many actions taken by applicants. For example, there is no fee for

- requesting an extension of time to correct formal defects.
- the number of claims in the application.
- a late response to most communications (e.g., an invitation to correct defects).

- requesting correction of an obvious mistake.
- requesting changes in indications concerning the applicant, inventor, agent, and so forth under Rule 92*bis*.
- requesting restoration of priority rights in many ROs (see PCT Applicant's Guide).
- requesting incorporation of priority document matter into the international application (by reference).

If a PCT application is filed and the fees are paid, it may be possible to request a refund of some of the fees if the application is withdrawn. To obtain a refund of the international filing and international search fees, the international application must be withdrawn by filing a request for withdrawal *signed by all of the applicants listed in the case (or their appointed (common) agent or common representative)* with the receiving office. If the withdrawal is made before the RO has sent the record copy of the application to the International Bureau, the international filing fees will be refunded. If the withdrawal is made before the RO has sent the search copy of the International Searching Authority, the search fee will be refunded. Be sure to expressly request a refund with the notice of withdrawal. The transmittal fee will not be refunded in most cases. If the applicant believes a refund is due and no refund is made, the applicant should take up the matter with the RO.[28]

28. Applicants must move quickly if they desire a refund of fees paid to the RO/US. At the time of this writing, the RO/US was forwarding record and search copies within one to two weeks of receipt.

CHAPTER 3

International Search and Preliminary Examination

1. Overview of the System

The international search is one of the highlights of the PCT system. Article 15 of the PCT mandates that every international application will undergo an international search carried out by one of the International Searching Authorities (ISA). Based on the international search, the ISA produces an International Search Report (ISR) listing the relevant prior art. Although not mentioned anywhere in the Treaty, Rule 43*bis* of the regulations provides that, in addition to the ISR, the ISA will establish a written opinion (WO) for each international application on whether the application appears to be novel, non-obvious, and industrially applicable. The ISR is published with the application 18 months after the filing date of the priority application, and the WO remains in the confidence of the applicant, the ISA, and WIPO until entry into the regional or national phase.[1]

The ISR consists mainly of a listing of references to published patent applications, patents, and technical journals that may affect the patentability of the claimed invention. The WO is a preliminary, nonbinding opinion on whether the invention is patentable in light of the search results. Unless an applicant requests international preliminary examination pursuant to Chapter II of the PCT, the WO forms the basis of an International Preliminary Report on Patentability,[2] which WIPO communicates to designated offices upon entry into the regional or national phase.

Receiving a favorable ISR and WO can greatly facilitate the prosecution of international applications in the national phase. In the past, many PCT applicants tended to dismiss the international search procedure as a necessary but unimportant formality. Recent developments in the PCT, however, especially the Patent Prosecution Highway (PPH),[3] have given the international search new importance and made it imperative that applicants pay attention to and make appropriate decisions during the international search process.

The primary objectives of the international search process are to help applicants evaluate their chances of obtaining patents in PCT member countries and to provide applicants with opportunities during the international phase to remedy flawed applications. A favorable ISR and WO tends to indicate a strong patent application with a good chance of speedy grant in the national phase. An applicant then may have the right to apply for expedited processing based on PPH bilateral agreements between the USPTO and the other ISAs. But if an applicant receives an unfavorable response from an ISA, all is not lost. The applicant can

1. In May 2012, the United Kingdom proposed that the written opinion be published along with the search report and no longer remain confidential until the entry into regional or national. While the proposal was greeted favorably, it had not yet been adopted at the time of drafting this chapter.

2. IPRP (Chapter I); form PCT/IB/373.

3. Chapter 10 provides a detailed analysis of the PPH procedure.

use the PCT to amend the claims under Article 19 procedure and may seek international preliminary examination under Chapter II of the treaty. This permits amendment to claims, description, and drawings and allows responses to the ISR and WO. Alternately, the applicant may use the results to formulate effective arguments in the national stage.

This chapter will provide an understanding of the international search process and highlight the options and choices available to applicants.

2. Scope of the International Search

The objective of the international search is to discover "relevant prior art," which is defined in Rule 33.1(a) of the PCT Regulations as:

> [E]verything which has been made available to the public anywhere in the world by means of written disclosure (including drawing and other illustrations) and which is capable of being of assistance in determining that the claimed invention is or is not new and that it does or does not involve an inventive step (i.e., that it is or is not obvious), provided that the making available to the public occurred prior to the international filing date.

Given the enormity of the world's prior art, it is not surprising that the PCT definition is limited to written disclosures and excludes oral ones. Since many countries, including most of Europe, Japan, Argentina, Brazil, Canada, India, Republic of Korea, and Russia, provide that oral disclosures, even those made outside the country, also constitute prior art, it is inevitable that the international search may leave some relevant disclosures uncovered. Moreover, although the PCT defines prior art as extending to "anywhere in the world," practical realities, including the particular language abilities of the examiners, dictate that international authorities restrict their searches geographically or linguistically. Accordingly, while Article 15(4) of the PCT directs ISAs to "endeavor to discover as much of the relevant prior art as its facilities permit," Rule 34 of the PCT Regulations permits authorities to focus their searches on the PCT minimum documentation, which includes patent documents and technical literature from major industrialized countries.

3. Understanding the ISR and WO

Theoretically, any time after the 16th month from the date of priority (or nine months from the PCT application filing date if there is no prior application), a copy of the ISR and WO will be transmitted to the applicant, although the timing of the communication will vary depending on the backlog of the ISA. As mentioned above, the heart of the ISR consists of a listing of prior art references (that is, references primarily to published patents, patent applications, and technical journal articles) that might have a bearing on the invention's novelty or inventive step (non-obviousness). For each reference cited, the report contains an indication by the examiner of the relevance of the cited prior art to the particular claim or claims of the invention that is the subject of the international application. For example, an A reference indicates that the cited document defines the general state of the prior art but is not of particular relevance to the patentability of the claimed invention. An X reference, on the other hand, indicates that in the opinion of the examiner, the cited document, taken on its own, destroys the novelty or inventive step of one or more of the invention's claims. Similarly, a Y reference indicates that in the opinion of the examiner, the cited document, in combination with one or more other documents, destroys the inventive step of one or more of the invention's claims, because the combination makes the invention obvious to a person skilled in the art. A quick glance at the list of cited prior art documents, the references that are assigned to them, and the claims to which they apply provides a good initial view of the strength of the international application and the extent to which the claims or description of the invention will need to be amended to make the invention patentable.

In addition, the report may contain observations concerning the requirement of unity of invention as well as whether certain claims were found to be unsearchable (because they concern subject matter that the ISA does not search or because they were unclear or improperly drawn) or whether the requirements were met concerning the filing of sequence listings if the invention concerns nucleotide or amino acid sequences.[4]

4. See Chapter 2 for more on the filing of sequence listings.

The PCT requirement of unity of invention differs somewhat from the U.S. restriction requirement. If, in the opinion of the patent examiner, an application relates to more than one inventive concept, the examiner will declare a lack of unity of invention and will search only the first claimed invention unless the applicant pays additional search fees. Each ISA determines the amount of its additional search fees, which are payable directly to the ISA in its local currency.

The WO, which issues together with the ISR, is the examiner's non-binding view on whether the invention appears to be patentable in light of the results of the international search. Box No. 5 of the WO contains the examiner's opinion, supported by citations and explanations, on which of the invention's claims meet the requirement of being novel, possessing inventive step, and being industrially applicable, and which do not. The WO also indicates the validity of the priority application, which may have important implications for the determination of the international filing date and, if the examiner is unable to establish the WO, on the reasons therefor. A favorable WO that does not raise issues of serious patent-destroying prior art evidences a strong patent application with a good chance of speedy grant in the national phase. A WO with at least one claim that the examiner concludes has novelty, inventive step, and industrial applicability also may qualify for PPH treatment in various national phase offices, which will likely guarantee that the application receives speedy processing in those offices and, most likely, a favorable outcome.

If, on the other hand, the ISR and WO are unfavorable, PCT Article 19 permits applicants to amend their claims in order to distinguish their inventions from the prior art cited in the ISR. And PCT Article 34 permits applicants to seek international preliminary examination, which authorizes amendments not only of claims but also of the description and drawings, and gives applicants a means to respond to the ISR and WO. If applicants do not wish to engage the formal procedures of Articles 19 and 34 but still wish to respond to the ISR and WO, they may file informal comments with the International Bureau, which will in turn communicate those comments to the designated offices during the regional or national phase.[5] And in cases where the ISR and WO

5. See pp. 87 *et seq.* for more information on Articles 19 and 34 and informal comments.

reveal that the invention is simply not patentable, regardless of any amendments the applicant may file, applicants may choose to abandon the application and thereby save the time, effort, and money that entering the regional or national phase would require, or they may opt to ensure the invention's continued confidentiality by withdrawing the application prior to publication.

The format of an ISR, which is an eight-page document, can be viewed at http://www.wipo.int/export/sites/www/pct/en/forms/isa/isa 210.pdf. The WO, which is a ten-page document, is available at http:// www.wipo.int/export/sites/www/pct/en/forms/isa/isa237pdf. And finally, when WIPO communicates the WO to designated offices as the International Preliminary Report on Patentability (IPRP) (see Chapter 1), WIPO simply attaches a cover sheet to the WO. That cover sheet can be viewed at http://www.wipo.int/export/sites/www/pct/en/forms/ib/ib 373.pdf.

4. Selecting an ISA

The first step in the international search process is choosing the ISA that will carry out the search. The choice must be made at the time of filing the PCT application, and applicants indicate their selection by filling in the two-letter country code of their chosen ISA in Box VII of the PCT request form. A patent examiner in the selected ISA will carry out the international search in accordance with uniform, detailed International Search and Preliminary Examination Guidelines. The Guidelines, which resemble a national practice manual, were agreed upon after lengthy discussion by all of the ISAs.[6] The international search is a unilateral process with no additional input from the applicant and no opportunity to intervene.

6. The Guidelines are available at http://www.wipo.int/export/sites/www/pct/en/texts /pdf/ispe.pdf, with a brief addendum relating to third-party observations, added July 2012 and available at http://www.wipo.int/export/sites/www/pct/en/texts/pdf/ispe_2add.pdf.

Although there are a total of 15 operating ISAs,[7] U.S. applicants have a choice of five:

- the USPTO (US),
- the European Patent Office (EP),
- the Korean Intellectual Property Office (KIPO),
- IP Australia (AU), and
- Rospatent (the Russian Patent Office—RU).[8]

To take advantage of the right to select one of the above five ISAs, at least one of the applicants—assuming there are joint applicants—must either be a resident or a national of the United States, and the applicants must file their application with the RO/US or the RO/IB. In other words, in the case of joint applicants from different countries, the applicants may choose any ISA provided that (1) it is an ISA that at least one of the applicants is entitled to choose and (2) the applicants file their application with an RO that is competent to deal with the ISA that has been selected. So, for example, if a U.S. national and a Japanese national jointly file a PCT application, the applicants may select any ISA available to U.S. nationals (the five ISAs listed above) or Japanese nationals (the Japan Patent Office). Assuming the applicants would like Japan to serve as the ISA, they must file their application with either the Japan receiving office or the RO/IB. As mentioned in Chapter 2, it is important to keep in mind that the RO/IB is the universal catch-all receiving office; applicants from any country are free to use it, and it is entitled to deal with any ISA.

4.1 Factors in Selecting an ISA

There are several factors that applicants should consider in selecting an ISA, including cost, quality, timeliness, competencies, availability of PPH, and linguistic search-scope.

7. The patent offices of the following countries or regions serve as ISAs: Austria, Australia, Brazil, Canada, China, the European Patent Office, Spain, Finland, Israel, Japan, Korea, Russia, Sweden, the United States, and the Nordic Patent Institute. In addition, Egypt has been designated an ISA but has not yet begun operations.

8. The USPTO, in agreement and cooperation with the recipient ISA, has the authority to determine which ISAs are available to U.S. applicants.

Cost

Every ISA charges an international search fee, which is paid directly to the receiving office, together with the international filing fee and the transmittal fee. The amount of the international search fee varies considerably from one ISA to another, but one common characteristic is that no ISA will begin an international search until the fees have been paid. If receiving a prompt ISR and WO is important, applicants should therefore not delay in paying filing, transmittal, and search fees.

Figure 3.1 shows the comparative fees for international search as of the time of drafting this chapter. An up-to-date schedule of fees can be found in the most recent issue of the PCT Newsletter, available at http://www.wipo.int/pct/en/newslett/index.html.

Figure 3.1 shows international search fees as of January 1, 2013.

US	$2,080
EP	$2,419
KR	$1,167
AU	$2,282
RU	$217

Figure 3.1
International Search Fees

If minimizing costs at the time of filing is the principal factor in selecting an ISA, Rospatent and KIPO are compelling choices. However, if the overall cost of prosecution in a particular patent office is a significant factor, the choice is unfortunately more complex than simply accounting for the amount of the search fee. The reason for the complexity is that the cost of additional fees that may become due farther down the prosecution time line will most likely be affected by the ISA an applicant chooses.

For example, choosing the United States as an ISA will result in a lower search fee if the applicant enters the U.S. national stage. Moreover, if the results of the international search or preliminary examination are positive for novelty, non-obviousness, and industrial applicability with respect to the claims in the national stage application, the U.S. national stage search and examination fee will be waived entirely. And the European regional phase search fee will be reduced by about 20 percent.

If Europe is expected to be an important market for an invention and European regional phase prosecution will therefore be a priority, choosing the EPO as an ISA may make financial sense despite the high cost. This is because the European international search fee will be partially offset by the European search fee (the fee that is paid when entering the European regional phase—€1,165 at the time of drafting this chapter), the cost of which will be reduced to zero.[9] And if an applicant does not anticipate having a particularly strong market preference but thinks there is a risk that the international search may find a lack of unity of invention (that is, that the application claims more than one inventive concept), applicants may wish to turn to KIPO, because the basic fee is relatively inexpensive and the fee for searching the additional inventions as determined by the ISR is the lowest available (about $198.00 for each additional invention, payable in Korean Won directly to KIPO).[10]

Therefore, although the choice of ISA is fairly straightforward if minimizing international filing fees is the overriding objective, the choice becomes more complex once reducing prosecution costs in important markets is factored into the equation. Unfortunately, selecting an ISA is also not as simple as looking at the cost alone.

Quality and Timeliness

There may be almost as many views about the comparative quality of the work performed by the ISAs as there are users of the system. Most of the views are anecdotal. All ISAs are required to follow the International Search and Preliminary Examination Guidelines, but the reality is that ISAs tend to view the international guidelines through the lens of their own national practices; therefore, search tactics and procedures may vary somewhat from one ISA to another. It is reassuring, however, that

9. The cost of the European search fee will be reduced by €190 if the USPTO is the international searching authority.

10. An analysis of the concept of unity of invention and how to deal with it can be found in Chapter 7.

whenever tests are carried out to compare the search results of the various ISAs, the differences prove to be insignificant.

Anecdotally, the general view has been—and continues at the time of drafting this chapter—that the quality of the EPO was consistently high, USPTO was mixed, KIPO varied by technology area (excellent for electronics), IP Australia was too limited (see discussion of competency, below), and for Rospatent, it was too early to tell. The USPTO is the only ISA of the five to outsource the international search to private searching entities. Although this arrangement has not resulted in a decrease in the quality of U.S. international search, it does mean that the U.S. national stage examiner will not be the same as the examiner who carried out the international search. As a result, U.S. examiners tend to place less reliance on the results of the international search than applicants might expect.

As for timeliness, ISAs are supposed to issue ISRs and WOs by the end of the 16th month from the priority date. The purpose of this deadline is to ensure that (1) ISRs will be published along with their corresponding international application at the 18-month publication date, and (2) applicants will have the opportunity to withdraw their applications before publication if the ISR and WO demonstrate that the inventions are not patentable. Recently, all of the ISAs available to U.S. applicants have come reasonably close to meeting the 16-month deadline, or at least to communicating the ISRs and WOs before the 18-month publication of the application, and timeliness is generally better than it has been in the past ten years. At the time of drafting this publication, IP Australia had the best timeliness record, followed in order by Rospatent, the USPTO, the EPO, and KIPO.

The ability of an ISA to carry out international searches on a timely basis is related in large part to the number of searches the authority has to carry out. The USPTO is a case in point. Several years ago, the USPTO's record for international search was abysmal, but because the USPTO saw its workload as an ISA decrease by almost 50 percent since 2007 (largely due to the addition of KIPO as an available alternative), it no longer suffers from infamous delays in issuing ISRs and WOs. Currently in last place, KIPO has been laboring under the burden of its own success. Its popularity as an ISA for U.S. applicants far exceeded its expectations; as a result, its record of delivering timely ISRs and WOs has dropped greatly, although it has been able to meet its international search obligations in almost all cases by the 22nd month. Now that Rospatent has replaced KIPO as the least expensive ISA, it will be interesting to see whether increased use of Rospatent will take some of the pressure off KIPO, allowing KIPO to improve its timeliness record, while adding pressure to Rospatent.

International Searching Authority	Total Number of ISRs Issued in 2011	Percentage of ISRs Issued Within 17 Months
AU	3,139	89.4
EP	71,432	61.3
KR	27,034	16.9
RU	1,008	71.2
US	16,285	69.0

Figure 3.2
ISA Filing Statistics
Source: 2012 PCT Yearly Review, WIPO

Worksharing

In order to minimize the disparities in search and examination quality among the ISAs as well as maximize the potential for collaboration, efforts have been made to enhance cooperation and worksharing during the international phase. One project, first proposed in June 2009, was the PCT Collaborative Search and Examination Pilot, which tested the feasibility of and potential for collaborative work among examiners at the USPTO, EPO, and KIPO. A primary examiner from one office prepared an ISR and WO and submitted it to two peer examiners, who commented on or complemented the ISR and WO with additional prior art. The primary examiner then issued the ISR and WO including the comments and prior art cited by the peer examiners. At the time of writing, the Pilot had experienced success with peer examiners adding prior art that would otherwise not have been included in the ISR and WO.

Several other pilots were also being tested through the Trilateral Offices (the EPO, Japan Patent Office, and USPTO) and IP5 (the Trilateral Offices plus KIPO and the Chinese State Intellectual Property Office (SIPO)). It was still uncertain whether any of the pilots, if they became permanent, would result in higher search fees and, if so, whether those fees would be cost effective from an applicant's perspective. It is nevertheless reassuring to know that the ISRs are cognizant of the need to minimize disparities while maximizing the quality of international search and that they are making efforts to achieve those goals.

4.2 ISA Competencies

ISAs may refuse to search international applications where the subject matter is any of the following:[11]

- scientific and mathematical theories;
- plant or animal varieties or essentially biological processes for the production of plants and animals, other than microbiological processes and the products of such processes;
- schemes, rules for or methods of doing business, performing purely mental acts, or playing games;
- methods for treatment of the human or animal body by surgery or therapy, as well as diagnostic methods;
- mere presentations of information; and
- computer programs to the extent that the ISA is not equipped to search prior art concerning such programs.

Though patent offices worldwide uniformly refuse to grant patents for mere theories or presentations of information, there is division among offices concerning the extent to which man-made organisms, business methods, methods of medical or surgical treatment, or software-related inventions are patentable. If an invention concerns one of the more controversial subject matter areas, applicants need to ensure that the ISA they select will carry out an international search and will not declare that the invention is one for which they will not establish an

11. *See* Article 17(2)(a) of the PCT and Rule 39 of the PCT Regulations.

ISR. In the unhappy event that the ISA issues a declaration of nonestablishment of the ISR in lieu of the search report itself,[12] the applicant may need to proceed to the national and regional phase without the benefit of an international search. In such cases, the ISA will still issue a WO, but the WO will not include any statements as to the novelty, inventive step, or industrial applicability of the claimed invention.

For example, the EPO, which excludes business methods from patentability, has expressly agreed that it will not search PCT applications filed by nationals or residents of the United States that contain one or more claims relating to business methods. The EPO defines the particular types of business method claims that it will not search in accordance with Class G06Q (and various subclasses) of the International Patent Classification (IPC), which categorizes business method-related inventions as follows:

> G06Q: Data processing systems of methods, specially adapted for administrative, commercial, financial, managerial, supervisory or forecasting purposes; systems of methods specially adapted for administrative, commercial, financial, managerial, supervisory or forecasting purposes, not otherwise provided for.

Therefore, if a PCT application contains any claim that may fall within the contours of the excluded class, the EPO should not be selected as the ISA. However, the United States and Korea both permit the patenting of business methods that meet the statutory requirements of patentability, and those offices would therefore make far better choices as an ISA.

Similarly, for inventions directed to methods of treatment of the human or animal body by surgery or therapy, the United States or Russia are logical choices as ISAs; both offices search national applications relating to methods of treatment and therefore will search international applications as well.

12. The ISA communicates its declaration in form PCT/ISA/203. In the event that only a few of the claims are directed to unpatentable subject matter but the invention as a whole is patentable, the ISA may choose to search all but the unpatentable claims.

Lack of Clarity

Examiners may also issue declarations of nonestablishment of the ISR where the description or drawings fail to meet the requirement for clarity or support of the claims to the extent that no meaningful search can be carried out.[13] Even if the claims were not lacking in clarity, the EPO, in particular, has on occasion issued a declaration of nonestablishment of the ISR because the application contained too many independent claims relating to the product that was the subject matter of the application or to the process for making or using the product.[14] The declarations of nonestablishment of an ISR reflected the European practice of permitting one independent claim for each category of claim.

One lesson that may be learned from this situation is that becoming familiar with the peculiarities of the different ISRs and learning how to anticipate them can help maximize the benefits of international search. When selecting the EPO as the ISA, for example, a good model to follow in order to limit the number of claims comes from the WIPO Administrative Instructions[15] and the International Search and Preliminary Examination Guidelines.[16] The texts mirror each other in expressly permitting the inclusion of any one of the following combinations of claims of different categories in the same PCT application.

- In addition to an independent claim for a given product, include an independent claim for a process specially adapted for the manufacture of the said product, and an independent claim for a use of the said product; or
- In addition to an independent claim for a given process, include an independent claim for an apparatus or means specifically designed for carrying out the said process; or
- In addition to an independent claim for a given product, include an independent claim for a process specially adapted for the manufacture of the said product and an independent claim for an apparatus or means specifically designed for carrying out the said process.

---

13. PCT Article 17(2)(a)(ii).
14. *Id.*
15. Annex B, para. (e).
16. Part III, chap. 9, para. 10.12.

Claiming as those examples suggest will help ensure that your application is found to neither lack unity of invention nor fail to comply with the prescribed requirements to such an extent that no meaningful search could be carried out.

Special Limitations with Respect to Australia

When the United States and Australia agreed in 2008 that IP Australia would serve as an ISA for applications filed by nationals and residents of the United States, Australia limited the scope of applications it would search. Australia declared that it not only lacked competence to search inventions directed to business methods but it also lacked competence to search inventions directed to mechanical engineering or analogous fields of technology.

The subject matter for which Australia is *not* a competent ISA, in accordance with the International Patent Classification, is as follows. It is an extensive list:

A01-AGRICULTURE; FORESTRY; ANIMAL HUSBANDRY; HUNTING; TRAPPING; FISHING, all classes except:

> A01H, A01N, A01P (i.e., new plants or processes of obtaining them thereof, Preservation of human, animals bodies or plants, biocidal, pest repellent, pest attractant or plant growth regulatory activity of chemical compounds or preparations)

A21-BAKING; EQUIPMENT FOR MAKING OR PROCESSING DOUGHS; DOUGHS FOR BAKING all classes except:

> A21D (i.e. Treatment of flour or dough for baking)

A22-BUTCHERING; MEAT TREATMENT; PROCESSING POULTRY OR FISH

A23N-MACHINES OR APPARATUS FOR TREATING HARVESTED FRUIT, VEGETABLES OR FLOWER BULBS IN BULK

A23P-SHAPING OR WORKING OF FOODSTUFFS

A24-TOBACCO; CIGARS; CIGARETTES

A41-47 PERSONAL AND DOMESTIC ARTICLES (e.g., headgear (A42), footwear(A43), haberdashery (A44))

A61-MEDICAL OR VETERINARY SCIENCE, all classes except:

A61K, A61L, A61P and A61Q (i.e., preparations for medical, dental or toilet purposes, methods, apparatus for sterilising materials or objects, chemical aspects of bandages, dressings, absorbent pads, or surgical articles, therapeutic activity of chemical compounds, use of cosmetics or similar toilet preparations)

A62-LIFE-SAVING all classes except:

A62D (i.e., chemical means for extinguishing fires, processes for making harmful chemical substances harmless, or less harmful, by effecting a chemical change, composition of materials for coverings or clothing for protecting against harmful chemical agents; composition of materials for transparent parts of gas-masks, respirators, breathing bags or helmets; composition of chemical materials for use in breathing apparatus)

A63-SPORTS; GAMES; AMUSEMENTS

B06-GENERATING OR TRANSMITTING MECHANICAL VIBRATIONS IN GENERAL

B21, B23-B27 all except:

B23K (i.e., soldering or unsoldering; welding; cladding or plating by soldering or welding; cutting by applying heat locally, e.g., flame cutting; working by laser beam)

B31-MAKING PAPER ARTICLE WORKING PAPER

B60-B68 all except:

B60L, B60M and B60Q (i.e., electric equipment or propulsion of electrically propelled vehicles; magnetic suspension or levitation for vehicles; electrodynamic brake systems for vehicles, in general, power supply lines, or devices along rails, for electrically propelled vehicles, arrangement of signalling or lighting devices, the mounting or supporting thereof or circuits therefor, for vehicles in general)

D01-D07 Textiles all except:

D06L, D06M, D06N, D06P, D06Q (i.e., bleaching, treatment of fabrics, dyeing or printing textiles, decorating textiles)

E01-E06 FIXED CONSTRUCTION

E21-EARTH OR ROCK DRILLING; MINING

F01-F04 MACHINES

F15-F17 ENGINEERING ELEMENTS, ACTUATORS, STORAGE OR DISTRIBUTION OF GASES OR LIQUIDS

F41-F42 WEAPONS, AMMUNITION

G04-HOROLOGY

GO6-COMPUTING; Calculating; Counting

G10-MUSICAL INSTRUMENTS

G11-INFORMATION STORAGE

If an applicant selects Australia as the ISA to search an application concerning an invention that falls within one of the above IPC classes, the Australian office will send the application back to the RO/US, and the RO/US will have to notify the applicant that Australia cannot carry out the search and that the applicant will have to choose another ISA. Of course, this takes time, may cost additional money in international search fees, and will almost certainly result in the late issuance of the ISR and WO. It is important, therefore, that an applicant select an ISA other than Australia when the PCT application claims a mechanical or other unsupported invention.

4.3 Effect of ISA Selection on PPH Use

Patent offices can, and often do, rely on the ISRs and IPRPs (Chapters I and II) to help in examination during the national phase. While smaller offices have always tended to rely heavily on the results of the international search, the need to deal with excessive backlogs in the large offices has led toward a push for patent office worksharing. The PCT-Patent Prosecution Highway (PPH) actualizes this push for patent office worksharing by directly reducing the amount of redundant work between any two offices for which the specific PPH applies. From a legal perspective, the current network of PCT-PPH arrangements applicable to U.S. applicants consists of a series of bilateral agreements between the USPTO and other national patent offices. Under the terms of these agreements, applicants who receive a WO from an applicable office indicating that at least one claim is patentable can request expedited ("fast track") examination from the other applicable office. Ultimately, this results in a faster and more efficient patent grant with a reduction in redundancy between the two offices. Figure 3.3 shows the PCT-PPH agreements available for each office as of June 2012.

ISA (WO with at least one patentable claim)	PCT-PPH Agreements
USPTO	Austria, Australia, China, European Patent Office, Spain, Finland, Japan, Korea, Russia, Sweden, Nordic Patent Institute
EPO	JP, US
KIPO	CN, JP, US
Australia IP	US
Rospatent	ES, FI, US

Figure 3.3
PCT-PPH Agreements

As Figure 3.3 shows, an applicant with a favorable WO as to novelty, inventive step, and industrial applicability will gain an advantage in obtaining faster protection in more countries through PCT-PPH if the search was performed by the USPTO. It should be noted that the advent of PPH 2.0, discussed in Chapter 9, further enables fast-track examination of related applications and that U.S. applicants should not let the lack of a PCT-PPH agreement alone discourage use of any particular ISA.

4.4 Linguistic Ability

Examiners in the different ISAs possess varying linguistic search skills. For example, examiners in the EPO must be able to search prior art documents that exist in English, French, and German, and many EPO examiners can search in other European languages as well. Examiners in KIPO can search documents in English and Japanese as well as Korean, and many can also search documents in Chinese. And examiners in Rospatent can search in English as well as in Russian, and many also possess Eastern European and Eurasian language skills. When seeking to exploit their inventions in a particular area or region, or where much of the prior art comes from a particular area or region, applicants may be best off having the international search conducted by an examiner who is capable of searching in the language of that area or region. As a patent's strength and its ability to withstand challenge frequently depend on the degree to which the relevant prior art has been uncovered and examined, it is important that prior art not be overlooked simply because it is in a language with which the examiner is unfamiliar.

4.5 Provision of Cited References

In order to evaluate the results of the international search and determine how you wish to respond, you need to access the prior art references cited in the ISR. Sometimes the cited references are easily retrievable on the web, but other times, for example, when the references come from foreign technical journals or foreign applications published by offices without easily accessible databases, the references may be hard to locate. Therefore, having the ISA provide copies of the cited references is a benefit that you cannot easily overlook. The five ISAs that U.S. applicants may use are the following:

1. the EPO provides paper copies of all cited references;
2. Rospatent provides paper copies of all cited references;
3. KIPO provides copies of cited references on a web page that applicants may download;
4. the USPTO provides copies of cited non-U.S. patent documents and non-patent literature; and
5. IP Australia provides copies of all cited references upon payment of A$50.00 for each document.

4.6 Some Strengths of Each of the ISAs

In the authors' opinion, the following are some of the major advantages of each ISA.

USPTO

Although considerably more expensive than KIPO or AU, choosing the USPTO as the ISA can provide a number of advantages to applicants. One of the most common reasons applicants choose the USPTO is because of the broader search coverage in comparison to other ISAs. Specifically, the USPTO is the only ISA that will conduct searches for subject matter directed toward business methods and methods of treatment of the human or animal body by surgery or therapy. This broader search coverage for PCT applications is, however, no different than any other prior art search the USPTO conducts. The USPTO searches and examines the same subject matter in an international application as it does in a national application.

Another commonly cited advantage of choosing the USPTO as the ISA is the potential cost savings upon entering the national phase, as well as the ease of payment of additional international search fees, if applicable. Upon entering the national phase, each designated office conducts its own prior art search. Not surprisingly, the designated office also charges the applicant a fee for this search. If the USPTO conducts the prior art search in the international phase, because a subsequent search in the national phase by the same authority tends to be redundant, the USPTO charges a lower fee upon entering the national phase. In fact, the U.S. national phase search and examination fee will be waived altogether if the WO is positive for novelty, inventive step, and industrial applicability with respect to all presented claims.

Furthermore, because the USPTO is such a well-established and respected searching authority, regardless of the outcome of the WO or IPRP (Chapter II), the EPO will also reduce its fees for a subsequent search by about 20 percent. Finally, because all subsequent fees (besides the basic international search fee) that are generated by an ISA must be paid directly to the ISA in the local currency, payments to the USPTO of these fees is much easier for U.S.-based applicants.

The most recent advantage to the USPTO as the ISA is the number of PCT-PPH agreements available. At the time of writing, the USPTO has PCT-PPH agreements with Austria, Australia, the EPO, Finland, Japan, Republic of Korea, Spain, Sweden, and a pilot program with Denmark. This is by far the most agreements by an office available as an ISA to U.S. applicants, as is further discussed below.

EPO

Although the EPO is the most expensive ISA, applicants may enjoy certain benefits in choosing the EPO as the ISA, especially if the applicant has plans to eventually exploit the technology disclosed in the application in Europe. The main difference between an EPO search and a search conducted by the USPTO is the patent classification system. Specifically, the EPO search is based on an international patent classification system rather than the U.S. classification. Another commonly cited difference is that typically, EPO examiners will have additional language capabilities. That is, EPO examiners may be able to locate potentially anticipatory art that has not been translated into English (German and French are the two most common additional languages). Because the application can still easily be amended prior to entering the national phase, the international phase is the time to find every bit of prior art out there that may be anticipatory. In fact, the limited language capability is one of the most commonly cited disadvantages of using the USPTO as the ISA. An experienced practitioner may say that because a prior art search will be conducted at the USPTO eventually anyway (during the national phase), applicants are forgoing a more comprehensive prior art search by multiple authorities by choosing the USPTO as the ISA. For this reason, applicants who are seeking to find as much potentially anticipatory art as possible will file their application with one RO, select a different office as the ISA, and request a Supplemental International Search Reports (SISR) by yet another ISA.

Other advantages include the option of employing the EPO as an International Preliminary Examining Authority (IPEA) to produce an IPRP (Chapter II). If the WO is unfavorable and the application is amended, demanding an IPRP (Chapter II) by the EPO can result in an early opinion by the EPO on the chances of obtaining a regional European patent. An EPO-generated IPRP (Chapter II) will also result in a reduction of the EP regional phase examination fee and possibly an earlier grant of an EP patent if the IPRP (Chapter II) is favorable.

KIPO

Despite the addition of Rospatent, KIPO remains an inexpensive ISA, and for that reason it continues to be a very popular choice for fee-conscious applicants. Besides the low basic international search cost, KIPO also has the least expensive fee for searching additional inventions in case of lack of unity of invention (one of the most common reasons that ISAs charge additional fees). Currently, KIPO charges

KRW 225,000 (approximately $187) for the additional search. If there is a lack of unity of invention, a partial international search will be carried out on the first-mentioned invention. When completed, the results will be sent to the applicant, together with an invitation to pay additional search fees. If an applicant is seeking an IPRP (Chapter II), KIPO, again, is the least expensive option.

In addition to the low cost, KIPO has a number of other qualities that make choosing it a good strategy. Namely, like their more expensive counterparts in the EPO, KIPO examiners have additional language capabilities. For starters, all South Korean examiners are fluent in both English and Korean, but many examiners' language capabilities also extend into other Asian languages—the most common being Japanese. KIPO also has designated PCT specialists and English language advisors to help English-speaking applicants.

Australia

Australia is currently the fastest and most timely of all the ISAs that U.S. applicants may choose. In fact, you are almost certain to receive an ISR and WO within 18 months of the priority date. However, as discussed above, IP Australia is not competent to act as an ISA for international applications filed by U.S. applicants in the RO/US or RO/IB with one or more claims directed to mechanical engineering or analogous technologies, including business methods.

If an applicant chooses to seek international preliminary examination and selects Australia to produce an optional IPRP (Chapter II), the AU national phase examination fee will be reduced significantly. One noted disadvantage is that, like the USPTO, AU examiners may restrict their search to prior art written in the English language.

Russia

Rospatent is the newest and least expensive ISA available to U.S. applicants. It remains to be seen how popular Rospatent will become as an ISA. One author's anecdotal experience with Rospatent found the office to be competent, professional, and capable of high-quality work. Until Rospatent establishes more of a track record, suffice it to say that if the cost of the PCT application is an especially significant factor, or if you are not particularly interested in or dependent upon the content of the ISR and WO, Rospatent currently provides the best option. In addition, Rospatent is the only available ISA, outside the United States, that will perform searches on applications directed to methods of treatment of the human or animal body by surgery or therapy.

5. The Procedure Following Receipt of the ISR and WO

5.1 Amending Your International Application

Once you have received and analyzed the ISR and WO, you have several options. If the ISR and WO are favorable, or if you think it would be preferable to amend your application before each national office when entering the regional or national phase, you should do nothing—except to prepare for entering the regional or national phase (see Chapter 6). If, however, your ISR and WO are unfavorable to patentability and you would like to take action in the international phase, you have three options, described below.

Filing Informal Comments

One option, which very few applicants take, is to file informal comments with WIPO. The informal comments, which usually are in the form of a letter, are neither sent to the ISA nor published, but WIPO includes them in your application file and communicates them to all designated offices upon entry into the regional or national phase.

Amending Your Application

The other two options while still in the international phase are to amend your PCT application, pursuant either to Article 19 or Article 34 of the treaty.

Article 19

Article 19 amendments are limited to amending the claims and are generally used to correct minor defects noted by the ISA in the ISR or WO. Article 34 amendments are much more comprehensive in that they allow applicants to amend the application's description and/or drawings as well as the claims.

Article 34

Article 34 amendments are ideal if you would like to perfect or improve your application while still in the international phase—especially if you would like to be able to take advantage of the applicable PCT-PPH arrangements (see Chapter 9). You cannot file Article 34 amendments on their own, however. They must be filed in conjunction with a demand for international preliminary examination and for the establishment of a second written opinion, which is communicated to designated national offices in place of the earlier WO as an International Preliminary Report on Patentability (Chapter II). Neither amendment may add subject matter to the original application.

5.2 Article 19 Amendments

Article 19 amendments must be filed directly with WIPO within 2 months from the mailing date of the ISR and WO, or 16 months after the priority date, whichever is later. An Article 19 amendment allows you only to amend the claims in the application. This type of amendment is particularly useful and is most commonly used to overcome damaging prior art references in the ISR and WO. The procedure for filing Article 19 amendments is governed by PCT Rule 46, which requires you to present your amendments on replacement sheets that contain a complete set of claims in replacement of the claims you originally filed. A letter must accompany the replacement sheets that

- Identifies the amended claims and indicates the difference between the amended claims and the claims as originally filed, by stating for each claim that
    - the claim is unchanged,
    - the claim is cancelled,
    - the claim is new,
    - the claim replaces one or more claims as filed, or
    - the claim is the result of the division of a claim as filed; and

- Indicates the precise basis for the amendments in the application as filed
  - so that the examiner may assess whether the amendments contain subject matter that extends beyond the disclosure of the application as filed.

In a statement "[p]roviding guidance on how to file amendments under Articles 19 and 34,"[17] WIPO gave the following example of how the accompanying letter should read:

> "Claim 1 amended; claims 2 to 7 unchanged; claims 8 and 9 amended; claims 10 to 14 cancelled; claims 15 to 17 unchanged; new claim 18 added.
>
> (i) Basis for the amendment: Claim 1 has been amended at lines 4 and 11 to 14 and now indicates that the filter comprises a periodic backwashing means serially coupled to a first and second chamber. The basis for this amendment can be found in original claims 2 and 4 as filed.
>
> (ii) Basis for the amendment: Concerning amended claims 8 and 9, the indication of 'quick-fire piston' is in paragraph Nos. 2 and 19 in the description as filed.
>
> (iii) Basis for the amendment: Claim 18 is new, the indication is in drawing No. III of the original application."

If you fail to comply with the requirement to include an accompanying letter, you risk having the designated national offices refuse to allow the amendments in the regional or national phase.

In addition to the mandatory accompanying letter, you may add a brief statement (limited to 500 words) explaining how the amendments affect patentability. The amendment and statement will be published together with the application, so they must be in the same language as the application and must not contain any disparaging comments about the ISR. Article 19 amendments may not add new matter; in fact, Article 19 amendments generally serve to narrow or limit the scope of

---

17. *See* http://www.wipo.int/pct/en/faqs/amendments_19_and_34.html#1.03.

the claimed invention. Moreover, Article 19 amendments are not examined in the international phase of the PCT process.

5.3 Article 34 Amendments and International Preliminary Examination

Fewer than 10 percent of all PCT applicants choose to file Article 34 amendments and to request international preliminary examination. Nevertheless, the Article 34 process, which is encompassed in Chapter II of the PCT, is the only way to amend an application's description and/or drawings during the international phase. To initiate the process, you file your amendments together with a Chapter II Demand[18] with one of the five ISAs (although the ISAs are called International Preliminary Examining Authorities (IPEA) at this stage when they carry out international preliminary examination under Chapter II). Generally, the demand must be filed within 3 months of the mailing date of the ISR and WO, or within 22 months of the priority date, whichever is later. International preliminary examination requires the payment of an international preliminary examination fee that goes to the IPEA as well as a small handling fee (the equivalent of 200 CHF) that goes to WIPO. You must pay both fees directly to the IPEA in the IPEA's local currency. In selecting the IPEA to carry out the examination, you may choose the same office that acted as the ISA, or you may choose one of the other five offices.

A demand for an international preliminary examination ultimately results in a second examination and generation of a second nonbinding written opinion on the novelty, inventive step, and industrial applicability of the claimed invention. This opinion is known as an International Preliminary Report on Patentability (IPRP (Chapter II)), and is usually communicated to the applicant on the 28th month following the priority date.

18. Form PCT/IPEA/401.

Why File a Demand

Applicants typically file Article 34 amendments in response to serious obstacles to patentability raised in the WO. With the advent of PPH, some applicants also use the Article 34 process to receive a favorable IPRP (Chapter II) so that they may take advantage of the growing number of PCT-PPH arrangements. In general, international preliminary examination can be a cost-effective way to advance PCT prosecution since it can eliminate some of the redundancy in responding to individual office actions in the regional or national phase. For applications destined to enter the national phase in a large number of countries, the effort and cost savings resulting from the elimination of all, or even some, of the issues raised in the ISR or WO can result in both cost savings and shorter pendency at national offices.

Some applicants, regardless of whether the ISR and WO were favorable, plan from the very start to file a demand for international preliminary examination simply to obtain a second opinion as to patentability. For those applicants, the goal is simply to identify as much of the relevant prior art as possible in order to ease national/regional phase processing and, to a lesser extent, reduce the possibility that later-found prior art could invalidate their issued patent should they need to enforce it.

The Article 34 Process

In many ways, Article 34 amendments are similar to Office Action responses in U.S. patent prosecution, except that Article 34 amendments are not obligatory. The format for filing the amendments is the same as that for Article 19 amendments. You must include replacement sheets, which preferably indicate the reason for the amendment, and the accompanying letter must indicate the basis for the amendment, always with reference to the application's description, claims, or drawings, as originally filed. The consequences for noncompliance with the Article 34 requirements are even harsher than with the requirements of Article 19. If you do not include the accompanying letter or if the letter fails to indicate the basis for the Article 34 amendment, the IPEA may proceed with international preliminary examination and establish the international preliminary report on patentability as if the amendment had not been made.

Also like Article 19 amendments, Article 34 amendments may include a brief statement (limited to 500 words) explaining how the amendments affect patentability. As with Article 19 amendments, Article 34 amendments also may not add new matter to the claims, description, or drawings. Unlike Article 19 amendments, however, Article 34 amendments are examined in the international phase of the PCT process.

Selecting an IPEA

The RO determines which ISAs are competent to serve as IPEAs and carry out international preliminary examination.

RO and ISA	Competent IPEAs
RO/US and ISA/US	US, KR, or RU
RO/US and ISA/EP	EP (unless biotechnology, business methods, or telecommunications invention), US, KR, or RU
RO/US and ISA/KR	KR, US, or RU
RO/US and ISA/AU	AU, US, KR, or RU
RO/US and ISA/RU	US or RU
RO/IB and any competent ISA	US, KR, AU (only if AU/ISA), EP (only if EP/ISA), RU, or other competent ISAs based on nationality of applicants

Figure 3.4
Selecting an IPEA

Naturally, there are some pros and cons to selecting the same office to conduct a follow-on examination. One advantage of selecting the same office to conduct the international preliminary examination is continuity. Rather than the possibility of the second authority differing in opinion from the first authority on the original application's patentability, continuing with the same authority will likely ensure that the focus of the IPRP (Chapter II) will be on the Article 34 amendments. In other words, the international preliminary examination will be more like an office action with the USPTO common to domestic practice.

However, there is also a downside to employing the same authority: forgoing a second authority's opinion on patentability. Because the opinions are nonbinding, prior to entering the national phase, applicants may prefer arming themselves with a diversity of opinions on the application's patentability. Which strategy to choose really depends on where you intend to enter the national phase and how many obstacles you must overcome in the ISR and WO. If you plan on proceeding in a large number of countries, many of which rely heavily on the results of an IPRP (Chapter I or II), you may be best served by continuing with the same authority. Alternatively, if you plan on filing in a smaller number of countries, particularly countries that carefully scrutinize national phase applications, you may elect to have a second authority perform the subsequent examination.

There are also important financial considerations in selecting an IPEA. Each office charges a different international preliminary examination fee; this fee may vary depending on whether the same authority served as the ISA. As previously noted, all fees must be paid directly to the IPEA in the local currency. Figure 3.5 gives an indication of the different international preliminary examination fees as of December 2012. Current fees can be found in the latest issue of the PCT Newsletter.[19]

IPEA	Fee When IPEA Served as ISA	Fee When IPEA Not ISA
USPTO	$600	$750
EPO	€1,850 (~ $2,445)	€1,850 (~ $2,445)
KIPO	KRW 450,000 (~$ 421)	KRW 450,000 (~ $421)
AU	A$590 (~$ 612)	A$820 (~ $850)
RU	RUB 2,700 (~ $89)	RUB 4,050 (~ $133)

Figure 3.5
International Preliminary Examination Fees (effective January 1, 2013)

Russia is by far the least expensive IPEA, irrespective of whether Rospatent served as the ISA, followed by Korea. However, just as in selecting the ISA, there are other considerations that may affect the overall price. Namely, some offices offer a reduction in the fees associated with national phase prosecution if they are the chosen authority to produce the IPRP (Chapter II). For example, if an applicant selects

19. *See* http://www.wipo.int/export/sites/www/pct/en/fees.pdf.

the Australian office to produce the IPRP (Chapter II), the Australian national phase examination fee will be reduced by one-third (A$300 instead of A$450). The EPO boasts the same benefit. An EPO-generated IPRP (Chapter II) will result in a reduction of 50 percent in the European regional phase examination fee; furthermore, if the IPRP (Chapter II) is favorable, the European patent may grant earlier. European regional phase prosecution costs will also be reduced by 20 percent if the USPTO produces the IPRP (Chapter II).

Figure 3.6 indicates the number of Chapter II Demands applicants filed in the five IPEAs in 2011.

IPEA	**Number of Chapter II Demands**
US	16,285
EP	71,432
KR	27,034
AU	3,139
RU	1,008

Figure 3.6
Number of Chapter II Demands by IPEA

As a final note, applicants may file both Article 19 amendments and a Chapter II Demand for international preliminary examination. Although rare, applicants occasionally take advantage of both procedures, for example, when they determine that it would be beneficial to amend the description or drawings to provide better support for their already-filed Article 19 amended claims. In such cases, the IPEA will carry out the international examination and prepare the IPRP (Chapter II) on the basis of the amended claims.

Copies of the Chapter II-related forms are available on the WIPO website.[20]

20. To view a Chapter II Demand, see http://www.wipo.int/export/sites/www/pct/en/forms/demand/ed_demand.pdf. The Written Opinion of the IPEA (form PCT/IPEA/408) is available at http://www.wipo.int/export/sites/www/pct/en/forms/ipea/ipea408.pdf. And the International Preliminary Report on Patentability (Chapter II) (form PCT/IPEA/409), which mimics the Written Opinion, is found at http://www.wipo.int/export/sites/www/pct/en/forms/ipea/ipea409.pdf.

6. Supplementary International Search

In addition to, or instead of, an IPRP (Chapter II), you have the option of having one or more supplementary international searches completed. These search requests may be submitted to any one of the supplementary international searching authorities (SISA) with payment of corresponding fees. The current SISAs are the Austrian Patent Office, EPO, Finnish Patent Office, Nordic Patent Authority, Rospatent, and Swedish Patent Office. Applicants may request a supplemental search as early as 19 months from the date of priority.

The ultimate product of the request is a Supplemental International Search Report (SISR). These reports are communicated to both the applicant and WIPO by the 28th month of priority. The purpose of an SISR is to reduce the likelihood of seeing new prior art cited in the subsequent national phases. Supplemental searches are most beneficial when important prior art may exist in a language that the selected ISA does not readily search, when the SISA has particularly relevant subject matter expertise, or when the ISA that an applicant may use does not search the subject matter that forms the basis of the applicant's application. In fact, supplemental international search has been used most by applicants with methods of treatment applications who have no ISA to turn to and therefore seek supplemental international search from Rospatent (which searches methods of treatment). Very few applicants to date have taken advantage of supplemental international search. In 2011, applicants filed only 41 such requests, 31 of which were filed with Rospatent.

7. Third-Party Observations

The newest tool available to users of the PCT system is the ability of third parties (that is, neither the applicant nor WIPO, the RO, ISA, or IPEA) to file observations during the international phase on published PCT applications that they believe lack novelty or inventive step. The time line for filing observations begins with an application's international publication date and continues until 28 months from the priority date.

If you wish to file third-party observations, you must do so electronically using the ePCT service[21] (see Chapter 11 for more on ePCT services), and you must observe certain formalities. For example, you may file only one observation on any particular international application, and that observation must consist of one to ten prior art citations accompanied by an indication of how each citation is relevant to the claimed invention's novelty or inventive step. Although you must include your name on the third-party observation form, you may choose to keep your identity confidential from the applicant, the patent offices, and the public. When WIPO receives an observation, it reviews it to make sure it conforms with the requirements of form and content; if it accepts the observation, it will notify its contents to the applicant, make the observation available on the PATENTSCOPE® database, and communicate it to the ISA (if the ISA has not yet issued the ISR), to IPEA (if the applicant files a Chapter II Demand), and to designated offices. Applicants are free to respond to an observation up until 30 months after the priority date, but they are not required to do so. It is up to each designated office to decide what use, if any, to make of a third-party observation. As the filer of an observation, you have no additional right to intervene in the processing of the PCT application in the international phase, but depending upon the national law concerned, you may be entitled to intervene again during the regional or national phase by filing observations or instituting opposition proceedings.

21. *See ePCT Third Party Observations: A Guide to Using WIPO's PCT Third Party Observation Service* at http://www.wipo.int/pct/en/epct/pdf/epct_observations.pdf.

CHAPTER 4

Post-Filing Procedures: Publication, Withdrawals, and Recording Changes

Following the filing of the PCT application, a number of events, procedures, and options are available. Chapter 3 examined the selection of the international searching authority, the international search report (ISR), and the written opinion (WO) of the international searching authority, amendments to the international application, and Chapter II international preliminary examination. In addition to these options and events, there are numerous safeguard procedures available to help you when things go wrong. These safeguards will be discussed in detail in Chapter 5.

In this chapter we will examine three key post-filing events and procedures: publication of the application including provisional protection; procedures to withdraw the international application, a priority claim, or a designation and the effects of withdrawal; and, finally, recording changes in the listing of applicants, inventors, and agents under PCT Rule 92*bis*.

1. Publication

1.1 The PCT Publication Process

The PCT publication process is one of the principal responsibilities of the International Bureau (IB). Like most regional and national patent laws, PCT Article 21 requires that all international applications be published as soon as possible following the 18-month anniversary of the earliest priority filing date. In addition to publishing the application as filed, the IB also publishes an abbreviated version of the ISR and any amendments entered under Article 19. At the same time, the IB ensures that portions of the case file at the IB are laid open to public inspection via PATENTSCOPE, the WIPO patent database search tool. The laid-open file will contain the full text of any of the five declarations filed with the international application, relevant data regarding any microbiological deposits made in conjunction with the application, and other information relevant to the application. The WO of the international searching authority is *not* published or laid open at 18 months, but will be publically available in the case file 30 months after the priority filing date.

Since April 1, 2006, the IB has published all applications electronically; PCT applications are no longer published in paper form. Applicants may request a paper copy of the publication from the IB, but because the electronic version of the publication is readily available and easily downloaded from the WIPO website,[1] there is generally no

1. You can access the electronic version of the publication through several routes. See http://www.wipo.int/patentscope/search/en/structuredSearch.jsf,orhttp://patentscope.wipo.int/search/en/search.jsf, or click on the PATENTSCOPE Search tab at http://wipo.int/patentscope/en.

reason for applicants to order a copy. When the application is published, the IB informs the applicant using form PCT/IB/311, which includes the international publication number (WO number) and the date of publication.[2]

International applications are published in one of the following ten languages; Arabic, Chinese, English, French, German, Japanese, Korean, Portuguese, Russian, or Spanish. If the publication is in a language other than English, the title and abstract of the application will also be published in English. The full bibliographic data on the front page of the publication will be in the language of publication, however, and each data entry is associated with a numeric INID code, which identifies each of the data fields. A listing of the INID codes can be found by clicking on the "HELP" tab at the PATENTSCOPE webpage.

Following publication and partial laying open of the electronic file at WIPO, the IB makes a copy of the publication available to most national offices in DVD format. A few offices (AU, CH, CN, JP, KP, KR, and US) routinely receive official copies from the IB, but the remainder of the national offices only receive official copies upon request following an applicant's entry into the national phase. When the application is published, the IB will issue form PCT/IB/308 to the applicant. This form can be used as proof that the designated national or regional offices have received a copy of the application from the IB or have agreed that any national requirement for the applicant to supply a copy of the PCT application will be considered fulfilled even though the actual receipt is postponed until requested.

Publication of PCT applications occurs on Thursdays. If the 18-month anniversary of the priority filing date falls on a Thursday, the IB will not publish the application on that day, but will publish it a week later. The goal is to publish each PCT application on the first Thursday following the 18-month anniversary, but publishing volume

2. Upon publication, the IB will assign a publication number to the publication. This will be in the form of "WO/yyyy/nnnnnn A#," where "yyyy" is the year of publication and "nnnnnn" is an identifying number. "A#" indicates the kind of publication being made. A complete list of the "Kind Codes" (as well as the INID codes) can be found via the "HELP" menu on the PATENTSCOPE webpage at http://patentscope.wipo.int/search/en/structuredSearch.jsf.

and logistics may delay the actual date of publication for an additional week or two, and occasionally longer. There may be times when you need to know in advance the actual scheduled date of publication of your application. In such cases, the applicant or agent of record can request the date from the IB. The request can be made by fax, e-mail, or telephone to the PCT InfoLine at WIPO.[3] Since the actual scheduled date of publication is confidential, the date will be sent to the fax number or e-mail address listed for the agent or common representative on the request form. The response may take a day or two.

The IB requires a period of time before the actual date of publication to technically prepare PCT applications for publication. The technical preparations are completed 15 days before the actual date of publication. Any changes to the publication, including stopping or postponing publication or making changes to the bibliographic information for publication, must be received by the IB prior to the completion of technical preparations for publication.

For example, if the actual scheduled date for publication is Thursday, November 1, the technical preparations will be completed 15 calendar days earlier on Wednesday, October 17. Therefore, any document that reaches the IB before October 17 will be taken into account for publication; later submissions will not.

Contents of the Published PCT Application

- Always published:
  - front page with bibliographic data and abstract
  - description, claims, and drawings, if any
  - international search report
- Published when applicable:
  - amended claims (and any statement) under Article 19
  - any declaration referred to in Rule 4.17 (Rule 48.2(a)(x))
  - any relevant data concerning deposited biological material furnished under Rule 13*bis* (Rule 48.2(a)(viii))
  - information regarding requests for restoration of right of priority (Rule 48.2(a)(xi))

3. PCT InfoLine fax: 41-22-338-83-39; e-mail: pct.infoline@wipo.int; telephone: 41-22-338-83-38.

  - statement concerning authorized requests for rectification of obvious mistakes received after publication (Rule 48.2(i))
  - information about a priority claim considered not to have been made (Rule 26bis.2(d))
- upon applicant's request with payment of a small fee:
  - information about the applicant's wish to correct or add a priority claim after the expiration of the time limit under Rule 26*bis*.1(a)
  - refused request for rectification of an obvious mistake (Rule 91.3(d))

1.2 Early Publication

An individual case strategy may call for publication before the 18-month anniversary of the priority filing date. You can obtain early publication under the PCT by expressly requesting the IB to do so. Once the IB receives the request for early publication, it will publish the application as soon as is practical. If the ISR has been issued by the ISA, there is no charge for early publication. If the ISR has not been issued, the IB will charge a fee for early publication since it will have to republish the application with the ISR following its issuance by the ISA.[4]

1.3 Availability for Licensing

Anecdotal data has shown that enterprises seeking to license technology frequently look to published PCT applications as a licensing resource. In order to more systematically promote the licensing of inventions contained in PCT applications, in January 2012, the IB began offering applicants the opportunity to list their inventions as "available for license." The request to have this indication included with the publication of the application is made on form PCT/IB/382.[5] The PCT/IB/382 can be filed with the application or submitted separately to the IB at any time between receipt of form PCT/IB/301, indicating that the IB has received the record copy from the RO, until 30 months after the priority

4. The fee is listed in Annex B2/IB in the PCT Applicant's Guide and is currently the equivalent of 200 CHF.

5. Form PCT/IB/382 is available on the WIPO website at http://www.wipo.int/export/sites/www/pct/en/forms/ib/editable/ed_ib382.pdf, or go to the PCT Forms page at http://www.wipo.int/pct/en/forms/index.html and scroll down to form PCT/IB/382.

date. Parties wishing to review PCT applications that are available for licensing should include this parameter in their Boolean logic searches in PATENTSCOPE.

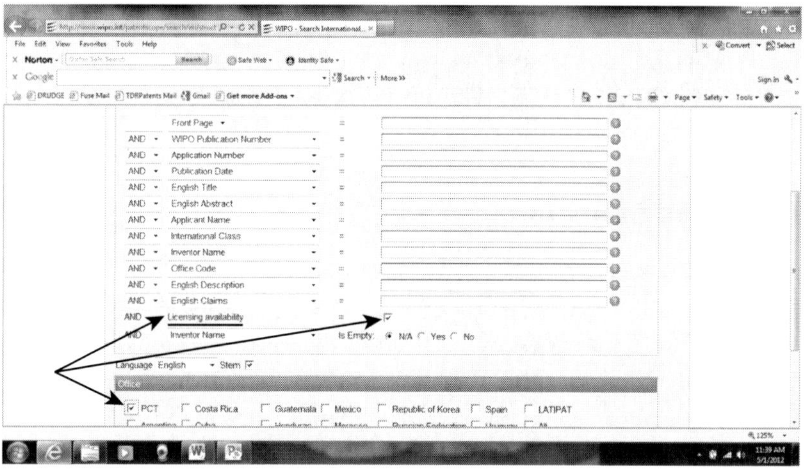

Figure 4.1
Finding PCT Applications Available for Licensing

2. Withdrawals and Stopping or Postponing Publication

As discussed in more detail in Section 2.1 below, you can withdraw a PCT application if the circumstances call for it. You do so by notifying either the RO or the IB; however, since the withdrawal process will be carried out by the IB, it is best to notify the IB directly. In addition to withdrawing the entire PCT application, you can also withdraw one or more country designations and/or one or more priority claims. If you have chosen to use the Chapter II international preliminary examination option, you may also withdraw the Demand or one or more elected states (i.e., countries). In that case, you must notify the international preliminary examining authority (that is, the office that you have selected to carry out the preliminary examination).

Withdrawals under Chapter II and withdrawals of designations under Chapter I are rare, but they are possible if case circumstances require. Withdrawing the entire international application or of one or more priority claims is more common. The only route to prevent publication of a PCT application is to withdraw the application before technical preparations for publication have been completed. However, you can delay publication, as well as other PCT deadlines calculated on the basis of the priority date, by withdrawing the earliest priority claim. Delaying publication may be a good tactic (provided there is no looming prior art) if you need additional time to decide the question of withdrawal. If you withdraw the earliest priority claim, *all PCT time limits that have not yet expired* will be recalculated based on the earliest priority claim remaining in the application. If all priority claims are withdrawn, the international filing date will serve as the new basis for all PCT deadlines. For example, withdrawing the earliest priority claim before the completion of technical preparations for publication will postpone the date of publication until 18 months after the earliest priority claim remaining in the application. Additionally, the following deadlines will also be postponed:

- filing a Demand for international preliminary examination (the later of 22 months from priority or 3 months from mailing of the ISR),
- requesting a supplementary international search (19 months from priority),
- requesting correction of obvious mistakes (26 months from priority),
- recording changes under Rule 92*bis* (30 months from priority),
- entering the national phase (30 months or more from priority), or
- any other deadline that has not yet passed on the date the priority claim is withdrawn.

Withdrawing a priority claim, however, will *not* permit an applicant to "recapture" a deadline that has already passed.

2.1 Stopping or Postponing Publication

There may be times when a withdrawal is necessary. For example, the ISR and WO may indicate that due to previously unknown prior art, there is no possibility of obtaining commercially meaningful patent protection. You must then decide either to let the disclosure publish (to help insure freedom to practice) or to stop publication to prevent the full contents of the disclosure from becoming public. Or, you may decide to stop publication when trade secret information that must not be allowed to publish has been inadvertently included in the disclosure. In any case, where publication must be stopped (or postponed), the IB *must* receive the notice of withdrawal before the completion of technical preparations for publication.[6]

Withdrawal of either the PCT application or a priority claim can be filed with the RO or the IB and takes effect on the date of receipt *by the IB*. Since filing with the RO will only delay receipt of the notice by the IB, in most cases you should file the notice directly with the IB.[7] Form PCT/IB/372 is recommended for filing the notice. Additionally, you can make the notice of withdrawal conditional: if the IB receives the notice too late to stop publication, the withdrawal will not take effect. Making the notice conditional will prevent the possibility that the application will publish but will be considered withdrawn.

Since withdrawal of the application, a priority claim, or a designation affects the scope of potential rights established at the time of filing, the IB requires that any notice of withdrawal be accompanied

---

6. When deciding whether to postpone or stop publication of the international application, be sure to consider filings made outside the PCT in countries that publish or lay open applications at 18 months. Though the applicant may be able to stop the publication of the international application, it may not be possible to stop the publication or laying-open of the priority filing or any filings made in non-PCT contracting states. If this is the case, withdrawing the international application or the earliest priority claim may not be the best strategy since the disclosure will be publicly available through other sources.

7. There is one exception: when the application has just been filed with the RO and the applicant seeks to withdraw the filing *and* recover any fees paid at the time of filing, the notice of withdrawal should be filed with the RO. If the notice of withdrawal is received by the RO before the record copy has been sent to the IB, the international filing fee will be refunded. The search fee will be refunded if the notice is received before the search copy is forwarded to the ISA. The transmittal fee will be kept by the RO and will not be refunded.

by the signatures of all entities named as applicants in the international application. For the IB to act on a notice of withdrawal, the notice must therefore be signed by all applicants or signed by a common representative or common agent *and* accompanied by powers of attorney (signed by all applicants) showing the appointment of the common representative or common agent.

While submitting a withdrawal notice may be necessary on some occasions, the consequences of withdrawal are significant. If the PCT application is withdrawn, it ceases to exist as an application in all PCT member countries; no national or regional phase entry is possible. If a priority claim is withdrawn, the application remains active, but the novelty and inventive step of the invention may be impacted by prior art occurring during the withdrawn priority period. Submitting a notice of withdrawal should be a last resort, and the consequences should be carefully considered.

Withdrawals

What	– international application, designations, demand, elections, priority claim
When	– before the expiration of 30 months from the priority date (before the technical requirements for publication have been completed where applicant desires to avoid publication)
How	– by a notice of withdrawal (use of form PCT/IB/372 recommended), signed by all applicants, their agent, or the appointed common representative, and filed with: • the RO, the IB, or the IPEA (Chapter II), if withdrawing international application or priority claim • the IB, if withdrawing demand or elections
Effect	– withdrawal effective upon receipt by appropriate authority (see above) – withdrawal has no effect in DOs/EOs where national processing or examination has already started – withdrawal of international application or designation • effect ceases in each designation concerned, with the same consequences as withdrawal of a national application in that state

(continued)

  - if notice of withdrawal is received by the IB before completion of technical preparations for international publication, there will be no international publication (withdrawal can be made conditional on receipt in time to prevent publication)
- withdrawal of demand or elections: withdrawal after expiration of Chapter I time limit for entry into the national phase is considered to be withdrawal of the international application in relation to the state(s) concerned
- withdrawal of priority claim: time limits that have not expired are re-computed on the basis of the revised priority date resulting from the withdrawal (to postpone publication, the notice of withdrawal must be received by the IB before completion of technical preparations for international publication; withdrawal can be made conditional on receipt in time to postpone publication)

2.2 Withdrawal of Application or Priority Claim after National Phase Entry

Filing a PCT application has the same effect as a national filing in each designated national or regional office. While no member country can require an applicant to enter the national phase before 30 months, applicants have complete freedom to enter the national phase prior to that deadline in any one or more national or regional offices and at any time during the international phase. This opens the possibility of entering the national phase early in one or more national or regional offices and then withdrawing the application or a priority claim in the PCT application *after* national phase entry in those offices. Entering the national phase in selected national offices and then withdrawing one or more priority claims may be advantageous in some instances. A withdrawal in the PCT application of a priority claim in the international phase has no effect in any national or regional office where national processing or examination has started (following early national phase entry).[8] This may present a strategic advantage. Depending on the national offices of interest, an applicant may enter the national phase in one or more coun-

8. *See* PCT Rule 90*bis*.6(a).

tries, ensure that national processing or examination has started, and then withdraw the priority claim in the PCT application. This strategy will extend the deadline for national phase entry in the remaining designated national offices as the deadline for entry will be recalculated based on the earliest priority date remaining in the application. An example of when this strategy might be useful is if some of the national offices of interest have an absolute novelty statute with no grace periods. In such cases, an applicant could enter those countries early, with the priority claim intact, followed by a withdrawal of the priority claim in the PCT application in the remaining countries. If the remaining countries of interest had grace periods or favorable novelty standards regarding any intervening prior art such that the priority claim was not necessary, national phase entry into these countries could occur by the extended time limit without negative consequences.

If this strategy appears to be beneficial for particular applications, you should work through your local agents to ensure that all needed steps for national phase entry have been taken and that the countries where early entry has occurred have started national processing or examination and will continue to honor the initial priority claims. You should also verify through your local agents that the states set for entry on the extended timing have applicable grace periods or favorable novelty statutes to ensure protection against intervening prior art. Keeping in mind that publication of priority claims is required under the Paris Convention, it may also be best to delay any of the early entries until after international publication so the priority claims are published as part of the international publication.

2.3 Provisional Protection

Many member countries offer provisional protection, which allows a patent holder to seek a reasonable royalty from a third party who has copied the invention between the date of publication and the date of grant. This provision helps protect patent applicants since their full, enabling disclosure becomes public on the date of publication, but the right to exclude others from using the invention does not vest until the date of grant. Each country that provides for this in their national law sets the conditions and limits on provisional protection.[9] In general, there are several steps to seeking provisional protection. Since the publication of the PCT application usually serves as the first publication of the enabling disclosure, one would hope that the publication would fulfill the publication requirement set forth in the national laws. In countries using the language in which the PCT application was published, the publication may well fulfill this requirement. Countries using a language other than the language of publication generally require an official publication in the local language to meet the publication requirement of the provisional protection laws. Regardless of language, some member countries predicate the start of provisional protection on receipt of a copy of the published application.

In the United States, provisional rights begin upon the application's English language publication under the PCT. If the application is not published in English, provisional rights start upon receipt by the USPTO of an English translation of the published PCT application.[10] In addition to the publication requirement, the ability to obtain a reasonable royalty depends on whether the claims as published are substantially identical to the claims granted by the USPTO[11] and also on a showing that the person conducting the offending acts[12] had actual notice of the publication.

3. Recording Changes: PCT Rule 92*bis*

It is not unusual for the bibliographic information related to any PCT application to change during the international phase. PCT Rule 92*bis* provides a simple and convenient method for an applicant to enter changes to the bibliographic data. A request for recording a change may

9. Each country's provisions on provisional protection are summarized in Annex B (General Information) of the PCT Applicants Guide, *available at* http://www.wipo.int/pct/en/appguide/index.jsp#E. Additional information concerning the countries that provide protection can be found in their respective national chapters attached to the Guide.

10. *See* 35 U.S.C. § 154(d).

11. *See* amendments under PCT Article 19 in Chapter 3.

12. *See* 35 U.S.C. § 154(d)(1)(A)(i & ii).

be submitted at any time from the date of filing through 30 months after the priority.[13] Applicants simply file a letter with either the IB or the RO describing the changes to be made. As with the case of requesting withdrawals of applications, best practices would call for communicating directly with the IB.

Rule 92*bis* changes can include:

- changing the name of the applicant;
- changing the address of the applicant, agent, or inventor;
- changing the nationality or residence of the applicant;
- adding or removing an applicant or inventor;
- making changes needed due to the death of an applicant or inventor; and
- changing the agent handling the application.

If the request for change is made by the agent or the common representative of record, the IB will record the change without further proof; however, national offices may require additional documentation regarding any change in the national phase. When the IB has recorded the change, it will inform the applicant as well as the designated national offices on form PCT/IB/306. These forms are available in the case file in PATENTSCOPE. Additionally, the bibliographic data on the first page in PATENTSCOPE will be updated with the changes.

If the applicant wants the change under 92*bis* to be taken into account for publication of the PCT application, the IB must receive the request before the completion of technical preparations for publication. If the request for recording a change arrives too late to be included in the publication, the IB will still enter it into the application data, but it will not be published.

If the request for recording a change is made by an entity who is not of record in the case, such as a new applicant or the agent for a new applicant, the IB will require proof that the new applicant has acquired the application (usually by requiring submission of the assignment or other document showing the transfer of ownership), and if the request

13. Requests for recording a change under Rule 92*bis* received by the IB after 30 months from priority will not be recorded.

is made by an agent for the new applicant, a power of attorney from the new applicant to the agent will be needed.

If the change is to be recorded in a number of PCT applications, such as following an address change in the agent of record in multiple applications, it is possible to submit the requested change for one of the cases and attach a list of the PCT application numbers of all of the other applications in which the change should be recorded. The IB will attend to the recording of the changes on all applications and issue a form PCT/IB/306 for each case.

Recording of changes under Rule 92*bis* is one of the most user-friendly features of the PCT. This is particularly true where there is a change in applicant for the majority of PCT member countries. While this change can be recorded during the national phase by following local procedures in each national office, it is generally much easier to submit a change under Rule 92*bis* to the IB before the expiration of 30 months from priority. In many countries, to change the applicant, you must pay agent and official fees and file assignments, either as local forms in dual languages or legalized true copies of the original assignment. In addition, transfer taxes and other fees may be levied. By entering the change during the international phase of the PCT under Rule 92*bis*, most of these formalities, and the work and cost associated with them, can be avoided. Some national offices may require filing of a proof of the transfer following national phase entry, but this is generally simpler and less labor intensive than recording the change under national practice in the national phase.

When case circumstances call for recording a change in the listed applicants, inventors, or agent/common representative or their addresses, recording the change under PCT Rule 92*bis* is almost always simpler and easier than entering the national phase and recording the change under national practice.

CHAPTER 5

Procedural Safeguards: Helpful Options When Things Go Wrong

The vast majority of PCT applications will travel through the PCT procedures without incident. Occasionally, however, something will occur at or after the time of filing that may jeopardize the application. To help protect applicants when things go wrong, there are numerous procedures available under the PCT to aid in getting applications back on track for the remainder of the PCT process. In Chapter 2, under Section 9, "Fees under the PCT," we discussed the procedures in place when required fees are not paid at the time of filing. Chapter 2 also promised an explanation of the safeguard in place to protect the applicant when the PCT application (or the Demand) is filed with a noncompetent office. Chapter 4 discussed stopping or postponing publication by withdrawing the PCT application or the earliest priority claim. In addition to a review of the procedures relating to payment of fees and stopping or postponing publication, and a discussion of what happens when papers are filed with a noncompetent authority, this chapter will discuss:

- Incorporation of priority-document matter by reference,
- Restoration of the right of priority following filing after the priority year,
- Adding or correcting priority claims,
- Correcting obvious mistakes in the PCT application,
- Reinstatement of rights by the national offices, and
- Review of international phase events by the national offices.

1. Fee and Refund Safeguards

Anytime a fee is due in association with the filing of a document during the international phase, applicants always have one month from the date of filing to pay the fee without penalty. This procedure holds for the initial filing of the application, requesting an optional supplementary international search, and filing a demand for international preliminary examination. Time limits are also applicable for payment of additional search or examination fees (following a finding of lack of unity of invention by the ISA/IPEA). In those cases, however, the invitations to pay additional fees will specify the time limit for paying.

If an applicant does not pay a fee within the one-month time limit, the RO, IB, or IPEA will send a notice regarding the unpaid fees. The notice will give the applicant a set period of time to pay the fee, but following the mailing of the notice, the payment must be accompanied by a late fee. The late fee is 50 percent of the delinquent payment. If the applicant has not paid the filing fees in whole or in part, then the late payment penalty is a minimum of the transmittal fee (currently $240 in the RO/US) to a maximum of 50 percent of the international filing fee (currently $709.50). In the case of late payment of the fees associated with a demand for international preliminary examination, the minimum late fee is equal to the Chapter II handling fee, and the maximum is double the handling fee. The handling fee varies by the currency accepted by the IPEA selected, but is the local equivalent of

CHF 200. If the fees required with a request for supplementary international search are not paid within the one-month time limit and the notice of delinquent fees has been mailed, the fee for late payment is 50 percent of the supplementary search handling fee (currently CHF 200).

The consequence of nonpayment of fees varies. If the international filing fee is not paid, the RO will declare the PCT application withdrawn. If the application is withdrawn, it will cease to exist for all member countries. The RO will not forward the search copy of the application to the ISA until the international search fee is paid. If the fees due with the Chapter II demand are not paid, the demand will be considered not to have been filed, and no international preliminary examination will take place.[1] If the fees for supplementary search are not paid, no supplementary search will be made.

Some applicants have relied on nonpayment of fees and the resultant declaration by the RO that the PCT application is withdrawn to prevent publication. There is no assurance that failure to pay the filing fees will prevent publication. You should never rely on lack of payment to stop publication. The RO will forward the PCT application to the IB regardless of whether the fees have been paid. This places the application in the queue for 18-month publication. With the short five and a half months between a filing at 12 months and the completion of technical preparations for publication, there is a significant chance the RO will not declare the application withdrawn in time to stop publication. If an applicant promptly responds to the invitation from the RO to pay fees and states that no fees will be paid, then the RO *may* act quickly enough to withdraw the application, thereby stopping publication, but there is no guarantee publication will be stopped.[2]

Applicants should never rely on non-payment of fees to stop publication. While lack of payment of fees will result in the application being declared withdrawn by the RO, there is no guarantee the declaration

1. For the three countries with reservations to current Chapter I timing of 30 months from priority (LU, TZ, and UG), failure to pay the fees due with the demand will result in the national phase deadline for these three national offices to be 20 months after priority, provided the demand was filed within 19 months of priority. See Chapter 2.

2. *See* PCT Rule 90*bis*.

will be made and transmitted to the IB in time to stop publication. To ensure publication is stopped, the applicant should expressly withdraw the application before the completion of technical preparations for publication (see Chapter 4).

If the ISA or the IPEA determines that there are multiple inventions claimed in the PCT application, they will invite the applicant to pay additional search or examination fees for each additional invention. If the applicant chooses to pay some or all of the additional fees, the inventions for which the fees have been paid will be searched or examined. The decision to pay any additional search or examination fees lies completely with the applicant and will not affect the status of the PCT application. The claims directed to any additional inventions for which fees have not been paid will remain in the application. The claims will continue through the PCT process unsearched or unexamined and will be available for national phase entry. In the national phase, however, the national offices may require additional fees or the applicant may be required to file divisional applications to continue prosecution of the unsearched or unexamined claims.[3]

2. Publication Safeguards

As discussed in Chapter 4, you can stop publication of the PCT application by withdrawing the PCT application, or you can postpone it by withdrawing the earliest priority claim. In order to stop or postpone publication, the IB must receive notice of withdrawal prior to the completion of technical preparations for publication. Additionally, the signatures of all entities listed as applicants in the PCT application must be supplied before the IB will act on the notice of withdrawal. The required signatures can be sent either directly or on powers of attorney appointing the signing common agent or common representative. A notice of withdrawal signed only by a deemed common representative will not be honored.

3. Unsearched claims will not be examined by the IPEA.

3. Safeguards Relating to Filings Made in Noncompetent Offices

In order for an RO to be competent to grant a filing date, the application must be in a language accepted by the RO, and at least one applicant must be able to file with the RO by reason of nationality or residence. For the RO/US to be able to grant a filing date, an application must be in English, and at least one of the applicants must be a national or resident of the United States. Given this requirement, it appears that an application filed in a noncompetent RO will not be given a filing date. If the application was filed with a noncompetent RO on the last day of the priority period, then it appears priority would be lost. Fortunately, this is *not* the case.

If a PCT application is filed with a noncompetent RO, the noncompetent office will stamp the date of receipt onto the application. Provided that at least one of the applicants is a national or resident of a PCT member country, the noncompetent RO will forward the application to the IB. In its capacity as a receiving office, the RO/IB accepts PCT applications in all languages and is competent to act as an RO for nationals and residents of all PCT member countries. The RO/IB will then become the RO for the application and will review the application and give it a filing date if the minimum requirements are met. It is important to note that the filing date assigned will be the date the application was received by the noncompetent RO.

Since the noncompetent RO had to process the initial filing and forward it to the RO/IB, it may require a fee equivalent to the transmittal fee be paid, currently $240.00 in the RO/US.[4] Upon receipt, the RO/IB will become the receiving office, and all fees due with the filing

---

4. In cases where the RO/US declares itself noncompetent, they will assess a fee equal to the transmittal fee. The RO/US will not forward the case to the RO/IB until this fee is paid. If, at the time of filing, the applicant is aware the RO/US is noncompetent and the application will be forwarded to the RO/IB, then only a fee equal to the transmittal fee should be paid to the RO/US. This avoids the need to seek a refund of any other fees that may have been paid with the filing.

(including the RO/IB's transmittal fee of CHF 100) will be owed to the RO/IB.[5] Any fees paid to the noncompetent RO, with the possible exception of the transmittal fee, will be refunded.

Upon receipt of the application from the noncompetent RO, the RO/IB will review the case to see if the agent representing the applicants is still competent to handle the application and also if the ISA selected is still competent. If either the agent or the selected ISA lacks competency (based on the nationality and residence of the applicant(s)), the RO/IB will contact the applicant for appointment of a new agent[6] or selection of a new ISA.

For example, if a U.S. agent filed a PCT application with the RO/US and all of the applicants were nationals and residents of Canada, then the RO/US would declare itself to be noncompetent, stamp the date of receipt onto the application, obtain any required national security clearance, collect $240.00, and forward the application to the RO/IB. The RO/IB will notify the applicant of the receipt and inform the applicant of the fees due. It will also inform the applicant that a U.S. agent is not competent to handle the application since the agent is not licensed before the RO/CA, which is the only national RO competent to receive the case. The applicant will have to appoint a Canadian agent or appoint the U.S. agent as address for correspondence. Presuming the U.S. agent selected one of the five ISAs competent for U.S. applicants, then the RO/IB will also require that an ISA competent for RO/CA filings be selected. In this case, only the ISA/CA is competent.

As a second example, if a PCT application having at least one U.S. national or resident among the applicants was filed by a U.S. agent in the RO/US but in a non-English language, for example, German, then the RO/US would declare itself noncompetent based on the language of

---

5. For applications transferred to the RO/IB, the one-month time period to pay fees without penalty begins on the date of receipt by the RO/IB and not the date of filing with the noncompetent office.

6. The applicant may choose to have the filing agent take on the role of address for correspondence. The filing agent will have no authority to sign any papers, and all papers will have to be signed by at least one of the applicants. This strategy allows the noncompetent agent to receive all correspondence and to continue working with the applicants in an unofficial capacity.

filing. The RO/US would stamp the date of receipt on the application, obtain any required national security clearance, collect $240.00, and forward the application to the RO/IB. The RO/IB will notify the applicant of receipt and inform the applicant of the fees due. In this case, however, the U.S. agent and the originally selected ISA are competent, because there is a U.S. national or resident among the listed applicants. The case will proceed in German; however, if the ISA selected does not search in German, then the applicant will have to supply a translation into a language accepted by the selected ISA. The ISA/EP is the only ISA available to U.S. applicants that will search in German.

A similar procedure is used if the applicant files a demand for international preliminary examination with a noncompetent IPEA or with an RO, ISA, or the IB. The noncompetent office will stamp the date of receipt of the demand and either forward it to the competent IPEA or, if there is more than one, to the IB. The IB will contact the applicant for instructions where to send the demand. The competent IPEA will consider the demand to have been filed on the date it was received by the noncompetent office. There is no fee associated with forwarding a demand.

4. Restoring Missing Parts or Elements by Incorporation by Reference

Since April 1, 2007, it has been possible to incorporate matter contained in the priority application(s) claimed in the request form into the PCT application *without loss of the filing date.* This procedure was first adopted by the Patent Law Treaty (PLT) and is one of two major procedures subsequently adopted by the PCT. It is important for U.S. practitioners to know that "incorporation by reference" under the PCT (and PLT) is different than incorporation by reference under U.S. domestic practice.

The incorporation by reference procedure recognizes two categories of missing matter:

1. Elements: all of the description or all of the claims.
2. Parts: part of the description or part of the claims or all or part of the drawings.

If an element is missing from a PCT application, the application will not qualify for an international filing date; both a description and at least one claim are required (see Chapter 2). If a part is missing, the application can be given a filing date. But if the missing part is critical to the enabling disclosure, the claimed invention may be unpatentable due to inadequate support.

Provided a missing part or element is entirely contained in the priority application(s), then using the incorporation by reference procedure will allow the applicant to bring the missing part or element from the priority document into the PCT application without loss of filing date.

To be eligible to use the incorporation by reference procedure, the request form filed as part of a PCT application *must* contain a statement conditionally incorporating the matter in the priority document(s) by reference. Figure 5.1 shows a statement in the form/RO/101.

> **Incorporation by reference:** where an element of the international application referred to in Article 11(1)(iii)(d) or (e) or a part of the description, claims or drawings referred to in Rule 20.5(a) is not otherwise contained in this international application but is completely contained in an earlier application whose priority is claimed on the date on which one or more elements referred to in Article 11(1)(iii) were first received by the receiving Office, that element or part is, subject to confirmation under Rule 20. 6, incorporated by reference in this international application for the purposes of Rule 20.6.

Figure 5.1
Incorporation by Reference Statement

> When filing a PCT application, the applicant should ensure that the most recent version of the request form or most recent version of PCT SAFE is used to prepare the request. This will ensure that any statements required to access PCT procedures (such as incorporation by reference) are included on the request form.

The confirmation of incorporation by reference must be filed with the RO in a timely manner. An applicant always has two months from the date of filing to confirm an incorporation by reference. If the RO or the IB invites the applicant to correct what appears to be a missing part or missing element, then the applicant has two months from the invitation's mailing date to submit any confirmation.[7]

7. The RO will always notify the applicant and invite correction if an element is missing since the application will not qualify for a filing date with a missing element. If a part is missing, then the RO or the IB may notify the applicant of the missing matter, but they are under no obligation to do so. It is the applicant's responsibility to double-check every filing to ensure there are no missing elements or parts before filing.

A confirmation submission should include

- a notice of confirmation,
- sheets containing the information to be incorporated by reference (suitable for inserting into the PCT application as filed),
- a copy of the priority application(s) containing the matter to be incorporated unless the priority documents have already been submitted or the RO has been asked to obtain a copy on the request form,
- a translation of the priority document(s) into the language of the application if they are in a different language, and
- an indication of where in the priority document(s) (and the translation if one is needed) the matter being added by incorporation by reference is contained.

If all of the information presented with the confirmation is found in the priority documents, then the incorporation by reference will be approved and the matter will be included in the PCT application and the subsequent publication. The filing date will remain unchanged. If, however, the RO concludes that all of the requirements for incorporation by reference are not fulfilled, for example, if a missing element or part is not entirely contained in the priority applications, then *the incorporated matter will be included and the PCT application will be assigned a later filing date* based on the date the missing element or part was received. This may not be the situation the applicant wants, particularly if the new filing date is outside the priority year. If a later filing date is not acceptable, then the applicant may request the missing part be disregarded and the original filing date restored.[8]

An applicant will receive a notice and invitation to correct if an element is missing from the application and may receive a notice and invitation if a part is missing. The applicant can respond to the invitation in one of two ways:

8. This is not an option in the event of a missing element. The application will not receive a filing date with an element missing. If the incorporation is denied, then the earliest date on which the application is qualified to receive a filing date is the date of receipt of the missing element.

1. The applicant can submit the missing element within the time limit and the application will be accorded a later filing date (PCT Article 11(2)), or
2. The applicant can confirm that the element or part is incorporated by reference. If all added matter is contained in the priority application(s), then the original international filing date is maintained.

Applicants should carefully consider the consequences of both options before responding to any invitation to correct missing elements or parts.

Even if the receiving office accepts a confirmation of incorporation by reference, the national offices may, to a limited extent, review the decision of the RO.

As with a number of procedures under the PCT, incorporation by reference is not compatible with the national laws of several member countries. Until those countries change their national laws, incorporation by reference, even if approved by the RO, will have no effect. In those countries, the applicant will have to decide to proceed with the case without the missing parts but with the original filing date, or to proceed with the added matter in place but with a later filing date.

The member countries having reservations to PCT rules relating to incorporation by reference (and any other PCT rule) can be found on the WIPO website.[9] At the time of this writing, the following countries have declared that the relevant rules regarding incorporation by reference are incompatible with their national laws.

- As an RO: Belgium, Cuba, the Czech Republic, Germany, Indonesia, Italy, Korea, and Mexico. These ROs will not accept confirmation of incorporation by reference requests related to applications filed with them.
- As a National Office: China, Cuba, the Czech Republic, Germany, Indonesia, Korea, Lithuania, Mexico, and Turkey. These national offices will not accept the confirmation of incorporation by reference approved by any RO. The outcome of the procedure will have no effect in these countries.

---

9. *See* http://www.wipo.int/pct/en/texts/reservations/res_incomp.html.

Reservations to PCT rules affect only the offices listed. Some of the countries (for example, the Czech Republic, Germany, Lithuania, and Turkey) are also members of a regional office (in this case, the EPO). Because none of the regional offices have filed a reservation to the applicable rules, applicants can achieve incorporation by reference in those countries through the regional route.

5. Restoring Priority for Filings Outside the Priority Year

The second PCT safeguard that originated in the PLT is the restoration of a priority claim for a PCT application filed outside the priority year. If a PCT application is filed outside the priority year *but within two months of the priority deadline*, the applicant may request restoration of the priority claim. The request for restoration may be submitted to the RO during the international phase or submitted to each national office upon entry into the national phase. Which authority to use is entirely up to the applicant and should depend on individual case strategy. If the applicant chooses to request restoration through the RO and is not successful, the applicant can revisit the issue in each country in the national phase.

The request for restoration of priority must be accompanied by a showing that the reason the application was not filed within the priority period was either in spite of due care required by the circumstances having been taken or unintentional. Each member country must apply one of these two criteria, or they may apply both.[10] The criteria applied by each PCT member country can be found at http://www.wipo.int/pct/en/texts/restoration.html.

For applicants utilizing the RO/US or the RO/IB, the applicable standards are

10. If national law of any state has a less stringent standard than the two mentioned, the national office may apply the local standard to requests for restoration made during the national phase.

- RO/US: applies the unintentional criterion only, and
- RO/IB: applies both criteria.

To request restoration of priority during the international phase, the PCT application must be filed within the two-month period following the expiration of the priority year, i.e., by month 14. Additionally, the request for restoration of priority must be filed with the RO within the same two-month period. If the application was filed within the two-month period but the request is not made of the RO within that period, the applicant will have to request restoration before each national office.

When filing a request for restoration of priority with the RO, the request must

- contain a statement giving the reasons for failure to file within the priority period,
- be accompanied by a declaration or other evidence to support said statement, and
- be accompanied by any fee set by the RO for processing the request.

The RO/US currently charges a fee of $1,410.00 for requesting restoration; the RO/IB does not charge a fee. U.S. applicants who miss the priority filing date would be well advised to file their applications and seek restoration with the RO/IB.

If the RO approves the request, the application will proceed with the priority claim in place. There is no assurance, however, that the restored claim will be considered valid in the national phase. All national offices may, to a limited extent, review the RO's decision.

If the RO denies the request for restoration of priority, the denied priority claim will not be declared void under the PCT; instead, it will remain in the application, *and it will serve as the basis for calculating all PCT timings*. Therefore, it is important to maintain the date of a priority claim in the firm's or company's patent docketing system, even though the priority claim relates to a denied request for restoration. Removal of the denied priority claim will result in all PCT deadlines being calculated up to one year too late. Maintaining the denied priority claim in the application is also important. The claim will be published and PCT timings maintained, which allows the applicant to revisit the issue of restoration before each designated national office. If the denied claim were removed from the case, the national offices may not allow the denied restoration request to be reconsidered during the national phase.[11]

If an applicant does not want to revisit the denied request for restoration in the national phase and would prefer PCT deadlines be based on the earliest valid priority claim remaining in the application, then the priority claim associated with the denied restoration request must be expressly withdrawn.[12]

The result of restoration of the priority claim varies with the restoration criterion (either "unintentional" or "in spite of due care") used by the individual member countries. If the priority claim is restored under the unintentional criterion, the restoration will be effective in all member countries accepting that criterion. If the priority claim is restored under the "in spite of due care" criterion, the restoration will be effective in all member countries, except those member countries that have filed a reservation of incompatibility with national law.

As discussed in the section relating to incorporation by reference, restoration of priority is not compatible with the national laws of several member countries. Until those states change their national laws, they are neither able to honor restoration approved by any RO, nor will they accept a request for restoration in the national phase.

As of this writing, countries that have national laws that will not allow their receiving office to consider a request for restoration include Algeria, Belgium, Brazil, Cuba, the Czech Republic, Germany, Greece, India, Indonesia, Italy, Japan, Korea, Norway, Philippines, and Spain. Applicants using these receiving offices will not be able to request restoration by the RO.

Applicants who are residents or nationals of any PCT member country (including countries that have filed reservations) may also use the RO/IB. The RO/IB accepts requests for restoration on the basis of both criteria—"unintentional" and "in spite of due care." Additionally,

11. Paris Convention Articles 4(D)(2) and 4(D)(5) require priority claims be published.

12. See Chapter 4.

the four regional offices associated with the PCT—the European Patent Office (EPO), the Eurasian Patent Office (EAPO), the African Regional Intellectual Property Organization (ARIPO), and the African Intellectual Property Organization (OAPI)—have not filed reservations to the PCT rules relating to restoration of priority. Applicants from countries that are also members of a regional organization can file and request restoration of priority via the regional RO.

The countries with laws that will not allow them to accept a decision by an RO to restore priority and will also not accept requests for restoration during the national phase include Algeria, Brazil, Canada, China, Colombia, Cuba, Czech Republic, Germany, India, Indonesia Japan, Korea, Lithuania,[13] Mexico, Norway, Philippines, Spain, and Turkey.[14]

6. Correcting or Adding Priority Claims after Filing

PCT Rule 26*bis* provides a method for applicants to correct erroneous priority claims and to add priority claims not included at the time of filing. Under Rule 26*bis*, an applicant is able to add or correct

- a missing priority claim,
- a missing priority date,
- a missing indication of the priority filing date, country of filing, or application number, and

---

13. Lithuania (LT) maintains its reservation to PCT Rule 49ter.1(g) and will not honor a decision to restore priority by a receiving office. LT has, however, withdrawn its reservation to PCT Rule 49ter.2(h) indicating the that requests for restoration will be accepted by the national office in the national phase.

14. Early drafts of this chapter included the United States among the countries that accepted neither an RO's decision to restore priority nor requests for restoration during the national phase. For U.S. applicants, the U.S. Senate had ratified the PLT in 2007, but Congress only recently adopted implementing legislation, which President Obama signed into law on December 18, 2012 (the Patent Law Treaties Implementation Act of 2012, Pub. L. No. 112-211 (Dec. 19, 2012)). The authors therefore hope that by the time this book goes to press, the United States will have withdrawn its reservation and will accept both restored priority claims and requests for restoration during the national phase.

- a priority filing date more than 12 months earlier than the international filing date.

If a defect in a priority claim is noticed by the RO or the IB, it *may* invite the applicant to submit a correction if

- the priority claim does not comply with the formalities of PCT Rule 4.10,
- the indications on the priority document do not match the corresponding information in the request, and
- if the international filing date is outside the priority period.

In most instances, if the applicant does not take corrective action in response to the invitation, the priority claim will be considered void for all PCT procedures. There are three important exceptions to this. The priority claim will not be considered void because

- the indication of the application number of the priority application is missing,
- an indication on the priority document is not the same as the indication in the priority claim, or
- the international filing date is outside the priority period but is within two months from the expiration of the priority period.

These exceptions are critical and help maintain the rights of the applicant. First of all, the Paris Convention only requires listing the country of filing and the priority filing date when filing the PCT application. The application number may be supplied at a later date, but the Paris Convention does require that all three pieces of information be published.[15]

There are a variety of reasons the information on the submitted priority document may not match the priority claim in the request. For example, there could be an error in the priority document or the priority claim, or a petition for correction of the filing date of the priority application may be pending. Keeping the priority claim in the

15. *See* Paris Convention Article 4(D)(1) and 4(D)(5).

application helps preserve an applicant's chance to seek correction in the national phase.

Finally, with availability of restoration of priority, any priority claim made outside the priority period but within two months of the priority deadline will remain in the application, will be published, and will serve as the basis for all timings under the PCT. This is true regardless of whether any request is made for restoration of priority or the outcome of any such request. Maintaining the priority ensures that the priority claim is published and helps preserve the applicant's ability to request restoration in the national phase.

A claim that is permitted by the national law of a member country is not affected in the national phase even if the claim would be void under the procedures of the PCT.

6.1 Additions or Corrections that Affect the Earliest Priority Claim

If a correction to the earliest priority claim or the addition of a priority claim with a filing date earlier than any other priority claim in the PCT application is needed, then the request must be submitted to the RO or the IB[16] within the later of

- four months from the international filing date, or
- the earlier of
  - 16 months from the originally filed earliest priority date, and
  - 16 months from the newly added priority date.[17]

All PCT deadlines that have not lapsed by the date the correction or addition is made will be recalculated on the basis of the corrected or added priority date. This rule allows the applicant the maximum time

16. Provided the applicant has received form PCT/IB/301, it is better to submit the change or addition to the IB. The applicant must also ensure that a certified copy of the priority application for any newly added priority claims is timely submitted to the RO or preferably the IB.

17. See PCT Rule 26*bis*.2(b) for certain instances when an additional month may be available for correcting the earliest priority claim. The additional month is not applicable to the addition of a claim.

consistent with the need to publish the application at 18 months from priority.

To aid in determining the last date to request a correction or addition, the PCT offers a Time Limit Calculator on the WIPO website (http://www.wipo.int/pct/en/calculator/pct-calculator.html), which allows applicants to quickly and easily determine any PCT deadline. For the time limit for adding or correcting the earliest priority claim, an applicant needs to fill in the international filing date, the earliest priority claim before the change, and the earliest claim after the change; the software will then calculate the deadline.

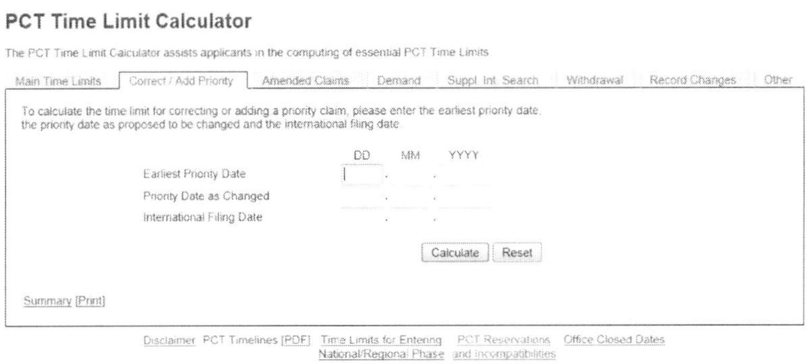

Figure 5.2
PCT Time Limit Calculator

6.2 Additions or Corrections that Do Not Affect the Earliest Priority Claim

The time limit for submitting changes or additions that do not affect the earliest priority date is somewhat simpler. For these changes and additions, the applicant will always have four months from filing to enter the change or addition. If 16 months from the earliest priority date falls after the four-month period, the applicant will have some additional time.[18]

18. *See supra* note 10.

6.3 Publication Related to Priority Claims

Paris Convention Article 4D requires publication of priority claims, including the country and date of filing and the application number. To help ensure that this requirement is met, if the priority claim is considered void, then the IB will publish information or a statement by the applicant concerning the priority claim. This procedure is the same for priority claims considered not void only because the application number is missing, the information on the priority document does not match the priority claim, or the PCT application was filed outside the priority period but within two months of the priority deadline. This publication may prove important to validating or restoring the priority right before the national offices. Many national offices will not consider a request for restoration or correction of a priority claim unless the relevant information has been published. In the example above, if there is a pending petition to correct the filing date of the priority application, an applicant would want to make this known to the public and the national offices including the filing date expected to be assigned upon granting of the petition. The IB makes this publication free of charge.

If an addition or a change to a priority claim is needed but the time limit for submitting the change has passed, the applicant may still take up the proposed change or addition in the national phase. To help guarantee consideration by the national offices is possible, it is important that the information relating to the change or addition is published. In this case, the applicant may ask the IB to publish the relevant information regarding the desired addition or change. This request can be submitted to the IB anytime up until 30 months from priority. There is a fee for the publication of this information (currently CHF 200).

7. Rectification of Obvious Mistakes

After filing a PCT application, an applicant may discover that there are one or more mistakes in the filing and that it would like to request correction. PCT Rule 91 provides for correction of obvious mistakes in the application as well as any other papers that may be submitted during the international phase. Since many corrections desired by applicants may be viewed as "new matter" under national laws, the standards for successful corrections of obvious mistakes are very high. Under the PCT, correction of a mistake may be authorized provided:

- It is *obvious* to the relevant authority that something other than what appears in the document concerned was intended, and
- Nothing else could have been intended other than the proposed rectification.

Before deciding to request correction of an obvious mistake, the applicant should compare the particulars of the mistake to the rectification standards. This comparison must be made in light of the information the authorizing authority may take into account when making its decision. If the mistake is in the description, claims, or drawings, the authorizing authority may only consider what is contained in the description, claims, or drawings as filed (or a correction thereof). If the mistake is in the request, the authority may also consider the contents of any papers submitted with the request and any papers in the authority's file for the particular application, including any priority document(s) that are available to the authorizing authority.

The interpretation of Rule 91 by the USPTO is set forth in MPEP Section 1836:

> Examples of obvious mistakes that are rectifiable include linguistic errors, spelling errors and grammatical errors so long as the meaning of the disclosure does not change upon entry of the rectification. Changes to chemical or mathematical formulas would not generally be rectifiable unless they would be common knowledge to anyone. A missing chemical formula or missing line of text would not be considered to be an obvious mistake subject to rectification.

The PCT Receiving Office Guidelines do not offer examples of rectifiable obvious mistakes.

If an applicant is going to request rectification of an obvious mistake, the request must be submitted to the authorizing authority no later than 26 months after priority. The appropriate authorizing authority is dependent on where the obvious mistake is located. If the mistake is in the:

- request or other paper submitted to the RO, the authorizing authority is the receiving office;
- description, claims, or drawings (Chapter I), the authorizing authority is the ISA;
- description, claims, or drawings (Chapter II) or in any amendment under Article 19 or 34, the authorizing authority is the IPEA;
- papers submitted to the IB, the authorizing authority is the IB.

As with incorporation by reference and restoration of priority, the national offices may, to a limited extent, review the decision authorizing the correction of an obvious mistake to ensure that if they were the authorizing authority, they would have reached the same conclusion.

8. Reinstatement of Rights by National Offices

If the deadline for national phase entry has passed and an applicant has not fulfilled the requirements for entry into the national phase in the countries of interest, PCT Rule 49.6 provides a method to seek reinstatement of rights before the national offices. The national offices accepting this procedure will require the applicant to state that the reason the initial entry deadline was missed was either "unintentional" or, at the choice of each national office, was missed "in spite of due care required by the circumstances."

The request for reinstatement must be made within two months of the date the cause for failure to timely enter the national passes or by 12 months from the original date for national phase entry, whichever expires first. Longer time limits may apply depending on applicable national law. The details for this procedure in each national office can be found in the national chapters in the PCT Applicant's Guide.

A few member countries have notified WIPO that Rule 49.6 is not compatible with their national laws. These include Canada, China, Germany, India, Korea, Latvia, Mexico, New Zealand, the Philippines, and Poland. None of the regional offices have filed a reservation to Rule 49.6. Reinstatement of rights is available via the regional route in any of these countries that are also members of regional offices. Some of the above-mentioned countries have filed reservations to Rule 49.6 because they have reinstatement procedures that are more favorable to applicants than those under the rule. For example, Canada permits up to 42 months to enter the national phase, provided an applicant pays a surcharge for late entry, and China allows a time limit of 32 months, also upon payment of a surcharge. Other countries, for example, Korea, simply do not allow reinstatement.

8.1 Review by the National Offices

In general, any action taken by the RO or the IB during the international phase that is not favorable to the applicant may be brought before the national office for review. If national law allows, the national office may ignore or reverse the decision or actions of the RO or IB. Of course, the issue must be brought before each individual country where review is desired.

CHAPTER 6

Entering the National Phase

The national phase follows the international phase and consists mainly of processing the PCT application in each national or regional patent office in which you have decided you want patent protection. The selected patent offices are known either as "designated offices" (DOs) or "elected offices" (EOs), while the nations or regions are appropriately called either "designated states" or "elected states." It should be noted that the distinction between the labels is entirely artificial and confusing. When, during the international phase, an applicant does not seek international preliminary examination under Chapter II of the PCT, and the applicant enters the national phase on the basis of an International Preliminary Report on Patentability I (IPRP I), patent offices are referred to as designated offices and the countries as designated states. Because the overwhelming percentage of applicants do not seek the benefits of Chapter II, national phase offices and countries most frequently bear the label "designated." Not surprisingly, offices and countries are called "elected" when an applicant has sought international preliminary examination and the applicant enters national phase on the basis of an International Preliminary Report on Patentability II (IPRP II). In either case, it is important to remember that the ultimate decision to grant or deny a patent in any designated or elected office remains solely within the jurisdiction of the designated or elected state.

If an Applicant Receives an:	*The Applicant Enters National Phase In:*
IPRP I	Designated Offices/Designated States
IPRP II	Elected Offices/Elected States

For simplicity's sake, we will refer to designated and elected offices as "national offices."

The process for entering the national phase is rather simple, but it involves several important requirements. Generally, it entails filing a form or an express request notifying the national or regional office that you desire a patent in that particular country or region. The exact process for making the request varies among countries, but universally, it must be completed prior to termination of the international phase. In addition, you must pay the required national or regional fee, which also varies from country to country, and, if necessary, provide a translation of the PCT application into the national office's official language. Other possible national phase requirements include the appointment of a local agent, the submission of powers of attorney, and the filing of permitted declarations. National offices normally may not begin to process or examine PCT applications prior to termination of the international phase, unless you enter the national phase early.

It is important to keep in mind that, with the exception of entering the national phase in the United States, the process of entering the national phase and prosecuting applications in PCT countries usually requires foreign patent counsel. It is therefore important to establish good working relations with reliable foreign patent counsel, because the fate of national phase PCT applications rests largely in their hands. It is also essential to remember that the burden of entering the national phase rests solely on you. Neither WIPO nor the receiving office (RO) nor the international searching authority (ISA) sends any notification about national phase entry deadlines or requirements. You are responsible for meeting the deadlines and requirements even if you have not yet received the ISR and WO from the ISA or the IPRP (Chapter II) from the international preliminary examining authority.

Once your application has entered the national phase, it will be processed and examined for the most part as if it were a directly filed national application. For example, if the national law requires that an applicant request examination, the same request must be made for a PCT national phase application. Unlike most directly filed applications, however, PCT applications will typically require some preliminary amendments in order to conform the application (especially the claims) to the national practice. Applicants generally have one month to file those preliminary amendments.

1. Deadlines for Entering the National/ Regional Phase

The normal time limit for entering the national phase is 30 months from the priority date. However, many national and regional offices, including the European Patent Office and the Indian Patent Office, have chosen to fix the time limit at 31 months from the priority date, while a few others—the Canadian Office in particular—excuse delays and provide yet additional time for national phase entry.

WIPO maintains an electronic time limit calculator, which automatically calculates the 30-month time limit on the basis of an application's priority date. The calculator is available on the WIPO website.[1]

The following charts identify PCT member countries that require national phase entry at 30 months, those that permit it at 31 months, and those that have other deadlines. A few PCT member countries that are also members of the European Patent Organization (EPO) or the African Regional Intellectual Property Organization (ARIPO) have "closed the national route," which means that an applicant may not enter the national phase in the closed route countries because their patent offices have chosen not to act as national offices; instead, in order to obtain a national patent, the applicant must enter the regional phase in the relevant regional office, obtain a regional patent, and then validate (or register) the patent in the national office. EPO and ARIPO countries that have closed the national route appear at the end of the charts.

1. *See* http://www.wipo.int/pct/en/calculator/pct-calculator.html.

Note that the newest members of the PCT as of the time of drafting this chapter—Brunei, Panama, Qatar, and Rwanda—had not yet made known whether they would be 30- or 31-month countries. Prudence therefore requires that they would be included in the 30-month group.

1.1 Deadlines for Entering the National/Regional Phase (as of May 2011)

Angola	Honduras	Portugal
Antigua and Barbuda	Israel	Romania*
Austria*	Japan	Saint Kitts and Nevis
Azerbaijan	Kenya	Saint Lucia
Bahrain	Lao People's Democratic Republic	Saint Vincent and the Grenadines
Barbados	Lesotho	Singapore
Belize	Liberia	Spain*
Brazil	Libyan Arab Jamahiriya	Sri Lanka
Chile	Madagascar	Sudan
Comoros	Malawi	Switzerland & Liechtenstein*
Cuba	Malaysia	Tajikistan
Dominica	Mexico	Thailand
Dominican Republic	Montenegro	Trinidad and Tobago
Egypt	Nicaragua	Tunisia
El Salvador	Nigeria	Turkmenistan
Gambia	North Korea	United Arab Emirates
Germany*	OAPI	United States of America
Ghana	Oman	Zambia
Grenada	Peru	Zimbabwe
Guatemala	Poland*	

*The 30-month deadline only applies for national phase entry. If the country is designated or elected for a European patent, the European Patent Office deadline of 31 months applies.

Figure 6.1
30-Month Countries/Regions

Albania	Eurasian Region (EAPO)	Papua New Guinea
Algeria	European Region (EPO)	Republic of Korea
ARIPO	Finland	Republic of Moldova
Armenia	Georgia	Russian Federation
Australia	Hungary	San Marino
Belarus	Iceland	Seychelles
Bosnia and Herzegovina	India	Sierra Leone
Botswana	Kazakhstan	Slovakia
Bulgaria	Kyrgyzstan	South Africa
Colombia	Lithuania	Sweden
Costa Rica	Mongolia	Syrian Arab Republic
Croatia	Morocco	The former Yugoslav Republic of Macedonia
Czech Republic	Mozambique	Ukraine
Denmark	Namibia	United Kingdom
Ecuador	New Zealand	Uzbekistan
Estonia	Norway	Vietnam

Figure 6.2
31-Month Countries/Regions

Canada	Normally 30 months, but the time limit can be extended to 42 months if applicant pays an additional fee
China	Normally 30 months, but the time limit can be extended to 32 months if applicant pays a surcharge upon entry
Indonesia	Normally 31 months, but the time limit can be extended if the applicant pays an additional fee for late entry into the national phase
Luxembourg**	20 months under Chapter I; 30 months under Chapter II
Philippines	Normally 30 months, but the time limit can be extended to 31 months if applicant pays an additional fee
Serbia	Normally 30 months, but the time limit can be extended by 30 days if the applicant pays an additional fee
Turkey	Normally 30 months, but the time limit can be extended to 33 months if applicant pays an additional fee. The time limit is 31 months if designated or elected for a European patent.
Tanzania***	21 months under Chapter I; 31 months under Chapter II
Uganda***	21 months under Chapter I; 31 months under Chapter II

**The 20-month deadline applies only for national phase entry. If the country is designated or elected for a European patent, the European Patent Office deadline of 31 months applies.
***The 21-month deadline applies only for national phase entry. If the country is designated or elected for an ARIPO patent, the African Regional Intellectual Property Office deadline of 31 months applies.

Figure 6.3
Other Countries

EPO Member Countries that Have Closed the National Route: Belgium, Cyprus, France, Greece, Italy, Latvia, Malta, Monaco, and Netherlands

ARIPO Member Country that Has Closed the National Route: Swaziland

Once an applicant has designated the national or regional offices, paid the required fees, and provided a translation, WIPO communicates all of the necessary documents in the application file to the selected national offices. This may include the published PCT application; any amendments to the claims; the priority application (if filed in the applicant's home country prior to entering the international phase); the International Preliminary Report on Patentability I or II (IPRP I or II), which consists of the ISR and WO of either the International Searching Authority or International Preliminary Examining Authority; and any possible supplementary search reports or third-party observations. Although the written opinion and IPRP are nonbinding, given the level of scrutiny and standardization in the international phase, if the results are favorable, the substantive examination in the national phase may be significantly eased in certain offices (for example, Singapore). With the advent of the PCT Patent Prosecution Highway (PCT-PPH), which will be explored in detail in Chapter 9, favorable results in the international phase can also result in expedited examination in the national phase.

1.2 The Four Patent Regions

In addition to the current 146 PCT member countries, four regional patent offices receive and process PCT applications. The four regional offices are the African Regional Intellectual Property Organization (ARIPO), the Eurasian Patent Office (EAPO), the European Patent Office (EPO), and the African Intellectual Property Organization (OAPI). Each office has its legal basis in a diplomatic treaty, each is supported by a secretariat, and each is made up of member countries. It is not necessary to be from a member country in order to prosecute an application in one of the offices, however, any applicant from any Paris Convention country can secure regional patent rights using of any of the offices. The member countries of the regional patent offices as well as the treaties that establish the offices and the name and location of the offices' secretariats are set forth in Figures 6.4 and 6.5.

ARIPO*:* Botswana, Gambia, Ghana, Kenya, Lesotho, Liberia, Malawi, Mozambique, Namibia, Rwanda, Sierra Leone, Somalia, Sudan, Swaziland, Tanzania, Uganda, Zambia, Zimbabwe
EAPO*:* Armenia, Azerbaijan, Belarus, Kazakhstan, Kyrgyzstan, Moldova, Russia, Tajikistan, Turkmenistan
EPO*:* Albania, Austria, Belgium, Bulgaria, Croatia, Cyprus, Czech Republic, Denmark, Estonia, Finland, France, Germany, Greece, Hungary, Iceland, Ireland, Italy, Latvia, Liechtenstein, Lithuania, Luxembourg, former Yugoslav Republic of Macedonia, Malta, Monaco, Netherlands, Norway, Poland, Portugal, Romania, San Marino, Serbia, Slovenia, Slovakia, Spain, Sweden, Switzerland, Turkey, United Kingdom, and the extension states of Bosnia and Herzegovina and Montenegro, which are not EPO member countries but recognize the grant of European patents
OAPI*:* Benin, Burkina Faso, Cameroon, Central African Republic, Chad, Congo, Equatorial Guinea, Gabon, Guinea, Guinea-Bissau, Ivory Coast, Mali, Mauritania, Niger, Senegal, Togo

Figure 6.4
Member Countries of the Regional Patent Offices

Office	Basic Legal Texts	Secretariat and Office Location
ARIPO	Lusaka Agreement and Harare Protocol	African Regional Intellectual Property Organization (Harare, Zimbabwe)
EAPO	Eurasian Patent Convention	Eurasian Patent Organization (Moscow)
EPO	European Patent Convention and EPC Implementing Regulations	European Patent Organisation (Munich, The Hague, Berlin, and Vienna)
OAPI	Bangui Agreement	African Intellectual Property Organization (Yaoundé, Cameroon)

Figure 6.5
Treaties that Establish Regional Patent Offices and Name and Location of Offices' Secretariats

1.3 Patent Grant

Patents granted by the EAPO and OAPI are automatically valid in all EAPO and OAPI member states, respectively.[2] This is not the case with respect to patents granted by the EPO and ARIPO, however. When the EPO and ARIPO grant patents, it is comparable to the grant of a bundle of national patents that become valid in each particular member country when the patent owner completes minimal registration or validation formalities. Typically, validation involves completing a simple request and paying the applicable fees. In the case of the EPO, validation may also entail providing a translation of the claims or the entire specification into the country's national language (see below for more on entering the regional phase in the EPO). In the case of an EAPO patent, though the application has to be translated into Russian in order to enter the regional phase, no additional translations are required, because the entire EAPO system operates in Russian. But, most important, in either case, no additional examination is required, and each member country must treat a regional patent as equivalent to a national patent and must grant the patent owner the same rights as would be conferred by a national grant.

2. Determining Where to Enter National Phase

2.1 Trends in Regional and National Phase Selection

Worldwide in 2010 (the latest year for which statistics were available), PCT national/regional phase entries accounted for over 54 percent of all nonresident applications received by patent offices worldwide. For U.S. applicants, the number is considerably higher: almost 70 percent of all foreign filings were made on the basis of PCT national phase entries. Out of a total of about 477,500 national phase entries in 2010, about 141,600 originated from U.S. applications. At the same time, most PCT

2. While the substantive patent law is the same across all EAPO and OAPI member countries, interpretations of the law may nevertheless differ from one country to the next, and a patent may be invalidated in one country and remain in force in the others.

applications only entered the national phase in a handful of countries or regions. In 2010, for every PCT application filed, applicants entered national/regional phase in an average of just 3.1 patent offices,[3] and 86 percent of all national phase entries were concentrated in just 10 patent offices.[4] Those figures are a strong indication that most applicants focus on a limited number of select markets in which they believe patent rights will be most beneficial. Figure 6.6 indicates the most popular countries for national phase entry for all PCT applicants.

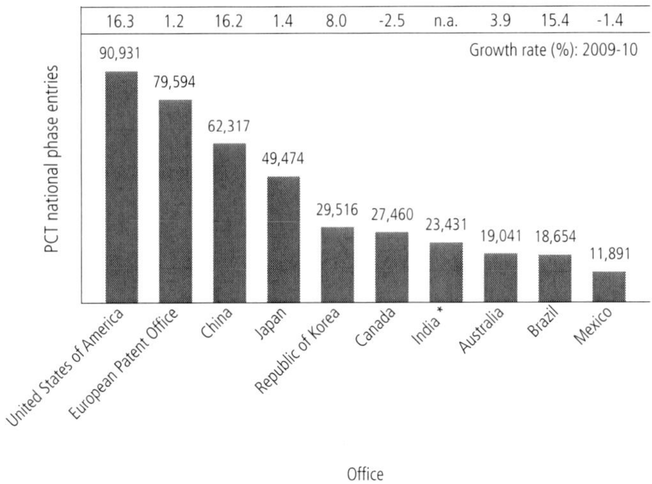

Figure 6.6
Most Popular Countries for National Phase Entry for All PCT Applicants
Source: WIPO, 2012 PCT Yearly Review

The same ten patent offices tend to be the most popular national phase entry destinations for PCT applications originating in the United States. For example, in 2010, the EPO received 23,708 PCT national phase entries from applications originating from the United States, and

---

3. This includes PCT applications that did not result in any national phase entry. The average of 3.1 was slightly higher for applications originating from high-income countries (3.2) and substantially lower for applications originating from middle-income countries (1.3). U.S. applicants tend to enter the national phase in slightly fewer countries than European applicants, but in slightly more countries than Japanese, Korean, Indian, or Chinese applicants. Source: WIPO, 2012 PCT Yearly Review.

4. Those offices, in descending order, were United States, EPO, China, Japan, Korea, Canada, India, Australia, Brazil, and Mexico.

China received 17,649. In contrast, the USPTO received only 14,070 national phase entries on the basis of PCT applications originating from the United States. This figure may indicate that a significant number of U.S. PCT applicants choose to proceed in the United States on the basis of either the "bypass route" (see more on the bypass route in Chapter 7) or a parallel-filed U.S. utility application. If the latter, it may also indicate that U.S. applicants are opting for prudence, caution, and flexibility over some of the cost-deferring benefits and efficiencies of the PCT system.

Chapter 9 provides guidance, strategies, and best practices on how to choose national phase countries, a process that should not be taken lightly. The primary purpose of this chapter is to describe the national phase entry procedure.

3. General Principles Regarding Entering the National Phase

While most of the mechanics of national phase entry will be performed by foreign associates whom you have appointed for each country or region (except in the case of national phase[5] entry in the United States), it is important to have an understanding of what national phase entry entails. A sense of familiarity and comfort with the process is especially important to ensure that the preparatory national phase entry work can be done in a timely manner and that no deadlines are missed. At its most basic, compliance with national phase entry requirements entails paying the national fees, furnishing a translation where required, and, if the PCT application has not yet been published, furnishing a copy. You may have to comply with other special requirements, but you must be permitted to do so after you have entered the national phase.

The PCT Applicant's Guide, available on the WIPO website at http://www.wipo.int/pct/en/appguide/index.jsp, provides information

5. While "national phase" is the generic term for converting a PCT application into a national or regional application, pursuant to § 371 of the U.S. Patent Act, 35 U.S.C. § 371, entering the national phase in the United States is actually referred to as entering the "national stage."

concerning the fees, requirements, and national phase entry practices of every national and regional office. The Guide, which you should get into the habit of consulting regularly, is an extremely valuable source of country-specific information. Although the basic requirements for national phase filings span all PCT member countries, each country adds its own particular spin, and national law and practice change regularly. The PCT Applicant's Guide is updated almost weekly and therefore provides the most up-to-date information generally available on national phase entry practice.

Commercial docketing systems are well programmed to inform you of the national phase entry deadline of 30 or 31 months from the priority period. What is important to remember, however, is that if the PCT application claims priority to two or more applications, the date must be calculated from the earliest filed application (you may still be able to enter the national phase on the basis of the later priority application, but your earlier priority claim will fail and your application may fail as well if there was intervening prior art).

Undoubtedly, the most difficult aspect of national phase entry is selecting the countries or regions where you want to pursue patent protection. Those responsible for making the country choices need to have sufficient time and information not only to carry out the task wisely and properly but also to communicate their choices with sufficient lead time to allow the preparatory work to occur. The most time-consuming aspect of that preparatory work is translating the application into the languages of the national phase countries that do not accept applications in English.

3.1 The Translation

The translation must encompass the application's description, claims, and any text matter in the drawings. Most countries also require a translation of the abstract, and some require a translation of the request form. If you have filed Article 19 or Article 34 amendments, you will need to furnish translations of the amended text (if you have requested international preliminary examination, you will need to submit a translation of the amendments annexed to the IPRP (II)), but some countries also require a translation of the original claims.[6] To meet the requirement of translating the text matter in drawings, it is not necessary to redo the drawings, but the translated text matter must appear on the drawings in place of the original text. PCT member countries may not require that a translation be certified by a governmental authority or official translator (unless the office later doubts the accuracy of the translation), but they may require the applicant or translator to verify with a signed statement that, to the best of her or his knowledge, the translation is complete and accurate.

Most local agents are willing to take on the responsibility of preparing the translation, but independent translation services that can prepare the translation for you also exist.

3.2 The Fees

You will have to pay national fees, which vary by country, in the local currency. If annual or renewal fees have become due before the start of the national phase (remember that a PCT application is considered the equivalent of a national application in every PCT member country, and in some countries, the fee clock begins to run the day you file your application), you will have to pay those as well. In most cases, the local agent will advance the fees, eliminating the need to make hurried currency transfers.

3.3 Foreign Associates

As mentioned above, you will be required to use a foreign patent attorney (also referred to as a foreign associate, foreign counsel, or foreign agent) to file and prosecute the national phase application in almost all national offices. Employing a foreign associate will require the execution of a power of attorney document, often in the foreign language. Though you may provide your own document, model power of attorney forms can be found on the WIPO site at http://www.wipo.int/pct/en/forms/pa/index.htm.

---

6. The specific requirements for each PCT country can be found in the PCT Applicant's Guide at http://www.wipo.int/pct/en/appguide/index.jsp#O0.

It may seem obvious, but it is worth stating that you need to work with foreign associates whom you respect, have confidence in, and can trust. Chapter 9 provides guidance and advice on selecting and working with foreign counsel. If you do not already have a working relationship with a foreign associate in a national phase country, it is important to begin the selection process well enough in advance to avoid a last-minute panic.

3.4 Entering the National Phase Early

It is not necessary to wait until the end of the international phase to enter the national phase. You are free to enter the national phase (and request examination in those countries where you must specifically make such a request) whenever you feel it would be most beneficial. Early national phase entry is not only quite common, but it can also be particularly advantageous when you want an early grant. The same national phase entry requirements apply regardless of when you choose to enter; however, it will probably be necessary for you to furnish a copy of the international application to the national office or regional office, or (and this is less preferable) you will need to ask the International Bureau to furnish the copy. Furnishing a copy of your application will certainly be necessary if the International Bureau has not yet published it and it is not available online.

When the International Bureau communicates copies of international applications to national or regional offices, they send the applicants a copy of form PCT/IB/308, entitled Second Supplementary Notice Informing the Applicant of the Communication of the International Application. If you have received a copy of the form, it is likely that the DO/EO has a copy of the application, but if in doubt, the form contains the name and telephone number of the WIPO officer handling your application, and you can contact that officer for verification.

3.5 Other Requirements

National offices may, and often do, impose additional requirements, but they may not do so as a condition of entry into the national phase, and they must give applicants the opportunity to fulfill the requirements after the start of national phase processing. Where a requirement is not at the time of national phase entry, most national offices will send an invitation to comply with the requirement by a particular deadline (or the national law will provide the deadline), and in most cases, that deadline will be two months from the date of the invitation. However, prudence and best practice dictate that if requirements can be fulfilled as part of, or even before, the national phase entry, they should be.

Rule 51*bis* of the PCT regulations spells out permissible additional requirements, which include the submission of documentation

- relating to the identity of the inventor;
- relating to the applicant's entitlement to apply for a patent;
- containing proof of the applicant's entitlement to claim priority of an earlier application where the applicant is not the applicant who filed the earlier application or where the applicant's name has changed since the date on which the earlier application was filed;
- containing an oath or declaration of inventorship; or
- concerning nonprejudicial disclosures or exceptions to lack of novelty.

Fortunately, there is a simple way to deal with those requirements, and it is contained in the PCT request form. Box No. VIII of the request form provides for the submission of optional declarations that respond to each of the requirements described in Rule 51*bis*. When a request form contains the declarations, a national office is not permitted to require any additional documentation or evidence unless it doubts the veracity of the declaration. The only exception is in the case of declarations relating to nonprejudicial disclosures or exceptions to lack of novelty, concerning which national offices may always ask for additional evidence. (See Chapter 2 for details concerning the submission of declarations.)

An additional subject of special requirements concerns priority documents. In general, since applicants have already made copies of their priority documents available to the International Bureau during the international phase, the International Bureau undertakes responsibility for furnishing priority documents to national offices during the national phase, and national offices may not require applicants to furnish additional certified original copies. Moreover, national offices are not supposed to require translations of priority documents into the office's national language unless the validity of the priority claim is in question or a portion of the priority document has been incorporated into the international application. Nevertheless, some national offices require all applicants to submit an uncertified photocopy of their priority application and filing receipt, and some may require a translation of the priority application, but in that case, they will need to provide a deadline for its submission.

Some national offices make available the use of a special form to enter the national phase. Although countries cannot condition successful entry on the use of such a form, it is wise to use it wherever applicable.

4. Missed Deadlines

As discussed in Chapter 5, mistakes happen, and applicants sometimes miss national phase entry deadlines. The PCT provides a partial solution in PCT Rule 49.6, which provides for the restoration of rights in the event that applicants fail to enter the national phase on time. Under Rule 49.6, applicants who miss the deadline may, within the following two months, request a DO to restore their rights and permit them to enter the national phase if their failure to enter on time was either unintentional or despite the exercise of all due care, depending on the standard that the national office has adopted.[7] As the terms indicate, it is easier to make out a case of unintentionality than a case of all due care, but in both cases, it is up to the national office to determine whether the standard has been met. A national office is free to charge a fee for the privilege of filing a request and may require the submission of supporting evidence.

7. The standard that each country has adopted is provided in the "national chapters" section of the PCT Applicant's Guide.

Rule 49.6 also provides that national offices may refuse to permit late national phase entry altogether if their national law does not permit it. As of July 2012, the following countries had given notice of their refusal to permit late national phase entry: Germany, India, Korea, Latvia, Mexico, New Zealand, Philippines, and Poland. On the other hand, some offices are more forgiving and permit restoration of rights as a matter of course or, upon payment of a fee, beyond the two-month deadline of Rule 49.6. Canada, for example, permits late entry for up to a year beyond the 30-month deadline, and China permits late entry for up to two months, with no questions asked.

5. Saving Money and Hassle

The most effective way to save money and hassle while entering the regional phase is to try to capture efficiencies during the international phase. For example, it is much less expensive and less complicated to record assignments, name changes, or other PCT Rule 92*bis* changes[8] with the International Bureau during the international phase, rather than having to file the changes with every national or regional phase office separately. You may also save money by avoiding excess claim fees that many regional or national offices charge (with the EPO probably having the most draconian excess fees). The best ways to avoid excess claim fees are by inserting multiple claim dependencies into the application, cancelling claims, and incorporating claim language into the description. Taking measures such as those may not only reduce filing costs but may also speed up examination.

The next two chapters provide some detail on national phase procedures in the United States and the two other most popular destinations for national phase entry of PCT applications filed by U.S. applicants: Europe and China.

---

8. Rule 92*bis* changes are changes that the International Bureau will make to the data in the request or demand forms pertaining to changes in the person, name, residence, nationality, or address of the applicant, or in the person or name and address of the agent, the common representative or the inventor.

CHAPTER 7

Entry into the U.S. National Phase

1. General Information

A PCT application has two parts or phases. The first is the international phase, and the second is the national phase. In the United States, the international phase is completed by 30 months, by which time the applicant must have entered into the national phase or the application will become abandoned. An applicant need not wait until the 30 months, but can enter into the United States national phase before the 30 months if the applicant wants U.S. national application processing to begin early. Additionally, to the extent that the applicant misses the 30-month deadline, there are ways to revive the application, which will be discussed later.

1.1 National Stage and Bypass

In the United States, there are two ways to enter into the national phase. One is by continuing the national route from the PCT application. This will be referred to as the "national stage."[1] National stage entry is the typical procedure that is used to enter the national phase in all of the other PCT member countries.

However, in the United States, there is a second method of entering the national phase that is unique to U.S. practice. This method is referred to as the "bypass" route. This chapter will discuss both of those methods in detail; it will explore the benefits and problems of each and analyze the detailed routines necessary to take advantage of each method.

National Stage

Entering the national phase using the national stage route is governed by § 371 of the U.S. Patent Act, 35 U.S.C. § 371. Under § 371, you essentially continue prosecution of the same PCT application but as a national application. A PCT application designating the United States is considered a pending U.S. application under § 365(c) of the Patent Act. Thus, while it is in the international phase, a PCT application is already considered a pending U.S. application. Proceeding under § 371 into the national stage is simply continuing the same application that preexisted.

Bypass

On the other hand, using the bypass route, you essentially are filing a separate and new continuation application of the pending PCT application. Because a PCT application during the international phase is a pending U.S. application, under § 120 of the Patent Act, you can file a continuation application at any time during the life of that pending U.S. application. The bypass is essentially the filing of a new application under 35 U.S.C. § 111(a), as a continuation application claiming the benefit of the PCT application under § 120. While the continuation or bypass application benefits from the earlier priority date, it is essentially a brand new application.

---

1. Pursuant to U.S. Patent Act, 35 U.S.C. § 371, entering the national phase in the United States is referred to as entering the "national stage."

These two routes are shown in the depiction in Figure 7.1.

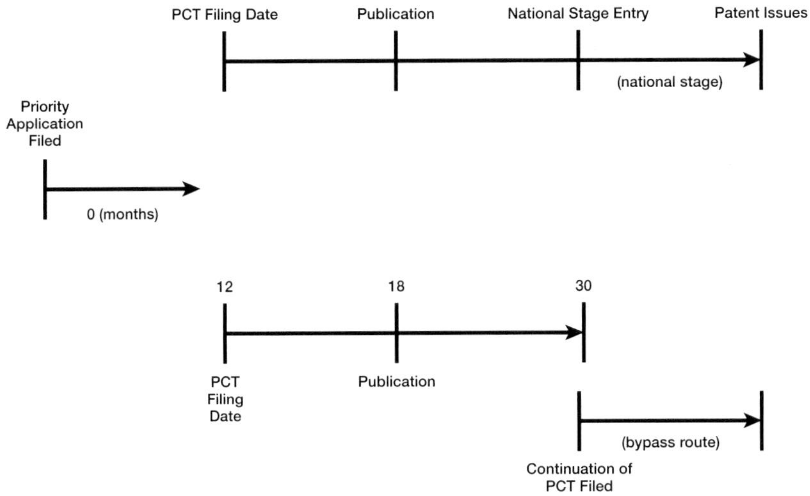

Figure 7.1
National Stage versus Bypass Route

Regardless of the route you use, entry into the national phase must occur by 30 months from the earliest priority date, as set forth in 37 C.F.R. § 1.495. You are free, however, to commence the national phase early, as set forth in § 371(f) of the Patent Act.

Typically, upon entry into the United States, either as a national stage application or as a bypass application, you need to meet certain requirements, including:

- paying fees,
- filing a declaration or oath,
- designating a "pedigree," namely, an explanation of the route your application has taken to enter the United States, and identifying any priorities you may be claiming, and
- submitting the necessary documents.

The next sections of this chapter will discuss each of the four requirements for national stage entry under § 371 and then for the bypass continuation entry under § 120. The benefits and concerns of using each route will follow.

2. National Stage

2.1 Fees

The following fees are required when you take advantage of the national stage route under § 371 of the Patent Act: the basic national fee, the search fee, the examination fee, and additional fees for excess claims, multiple dependent claims, and excess sheets.[2] Although the basic national fee is a fixed amount, the amount of the search fee depends upon which ISA you used and what the outcome of the international search and/or preliminary examination may have been. For example, if you chose the USPTO as your ISA (ISA/US), you will receive a substantial reduction in the national stage search fee. Moreover, if the results of the U.S. international search or international preliminary examination reveal that all of your claims satisfy the requirements of novelty, inventive step, and industrial applicability, the national stage search fee will be waived entirely.

You will receive a small reduction even if the international search report (ISR) was prepared by an ISA other than the U.S., so long as the USPTO was provided a copy of the report or a copy had previously been communicated to it by the International Bureau. For all other situations, for example, if the ISA determines that no search report can be issued or fails to issue a report on time, you will have to pay the full search fee.

In contrast to the search fee, the examination fee is subject to only one possible reduction. If the U.S.-prepared written opinion (WO) of the international searching authority or the international preliminary examination report (IPER) indicates that all claims are novel, have inventive step, and industrial applicability, you need not pay an examination fee. In all other situations, you must pay the fee.

As with so many other USPTO fees, the national fee, search fee, examination fee, and other national stage fees—including excess page and claim fees, a fee for filing multiple dependent claims, and a

2. The fees can be found in 37 C.F.R. § 1.492(a)–(i).

surcharge for late filing or late payment—are subject to a 50 percent reduction for small entities.

Finally, there are no exceptions for payment of the basic national fee. It must be paid within 30 months. Failure to do so will result in abandonment of the application.

2.2 Oath or Declaration

Section 115 of the U.S. Patent Act[3] requires that in almost all cases inventors execute an oath or declaration of inventorship attesting that the invention was made or authorized to be made by them and that they believe themselves to be the original inventors or joint inventors of the claimed invention. As described in Chapter 2, Box VIII of the PCT request form contains a declaration that meets all the requirements of U.S. law (in fact, it was created in order to meet those requirements). To the extent feasible, applicants should include a completed declaration with their application, or they should file a declaration with the International Bureau, preferably within 16 months of the priority date but at least before the International Bureau has completed the technical preparations for publication of the application. In those cases, the International Bureau will send a copy of the declaration of inventorship to the USPTO when the application enters the national stage, and no new oath or declaration will be required.

Submission of an inventor's oath or declaration is a requirement of early entry into the U.S. national stage. But in all cases, it should be considered a best practice to file the oath or declaration before the 30-month national stage deadline.[4] If you have failed to file it on time, however, all is not lost. Under the provisions of the America Invents Act, you may postpone filing the oath or declaration until your application is in condition for allowance, so long as you have filed a patent application

3. 35 U.S.C. § 115, as amended by the America Invents Act.

4. In the event that there are multiple inventors, each inventor can sign an individual declaration that names only her or him, provided that each individual declaration is filed together with a patent application data sheet (ADS) that names all the inventors. Without the accompanying ADS, the declarations will be considered defective.

data sheet (ADS) that identifies each inventor by his or her name and provides a mailing address for each inventor if different from the application mailing address. You will then have to file the oath or declaration within the time period set forth in the Notice of Allowability that you will receive from the USPTO. You must nevertheless pay a surcharge for any declaration that you file beyond the 30-month deadline.

There are times when inventors cannot sign the oath or declaration because they are deceased, are legally incapacitated, cannot be reached, or have simply refused to execute the document. In such cases, you can replace the oath or declaration with a substitute statement. In addition, an assignment can sometimes take the place of an oath or declaration if it was executed by the inventor, contains all the required statements and information, and has been recorded in the USPTO's assignment database.

2.3 Documents Required

When you enter the national stage pursuant to § 371, the International Bureau will furnish the USPTO with most of the documents it requires, including a copy of the PCT application as originally filed; a copy of the ISR, together with an English translation if the report was not issued in English; a copy of any amendment to the claims (and/or statement) submitted under PCT Article 19; and a copy of any declaration of inventorship filed under PCT Rule 4.17(iv).

In addition, the International Bureau will furnish copies of the following:

- the priority application where the application was not filed in the USPTO;
- the International Preliminary Report on Patentability (Chapter I) (IPRP I) and any informal comments the applicant may have filed when the applicant did not seek international preliminary examination; or

- if the applicant did seek international preliminary examination, a copy of the International Preliminary Report on Patentability (Chapter II) (IPRP II), including any annexes, as well as an English translation of the report if it was not issued in English (but not an English translation of any of the annexes).

So what is left for the applicant to submit? In fact, very little: the applicant's responsibility is limited basically to two categories of documents: translations and sequence listings. As for translations, if the international application was, for example, filed and published in a language other than English, the applicant must supply an English translation of the entire application as well as translations of Article 19 amendments or annexes to the IPRP that are not already in English. Similarly, with respect to sequence listings, where a PCT application discloses one or more nucleotide and/or amino acid sequences, the applicant will need to furnish a sequence listing in electronic form that complies with the internationally accepted standard provided in the WIPO Administrative Instructions—unless the USPTO already has access to the sequence listing. Note that if an applicant does not submit the above items by the 30-month date, the USPTO will specify the deadline for submission, in most cases in a Notice of Missing Requirements. In response to such a notice from the USPTO, the applicant usually will have to pay a surcharge for any documents submitted after the 30-month date.

There is an exception, however, for English translations of Article 19 amendments, which must be submitted by the 30-month date; otherwise, the amendments will be considered as cancelled. However, even if the amendments have been cancelled and it is past the 30-month period, the amendments may still be inserted into the national stage application by means of a preliminary amendment.

A summary of the documents furnished by the International Bureau and the documents the applicant has to furnish is shown in Figure 7.2.

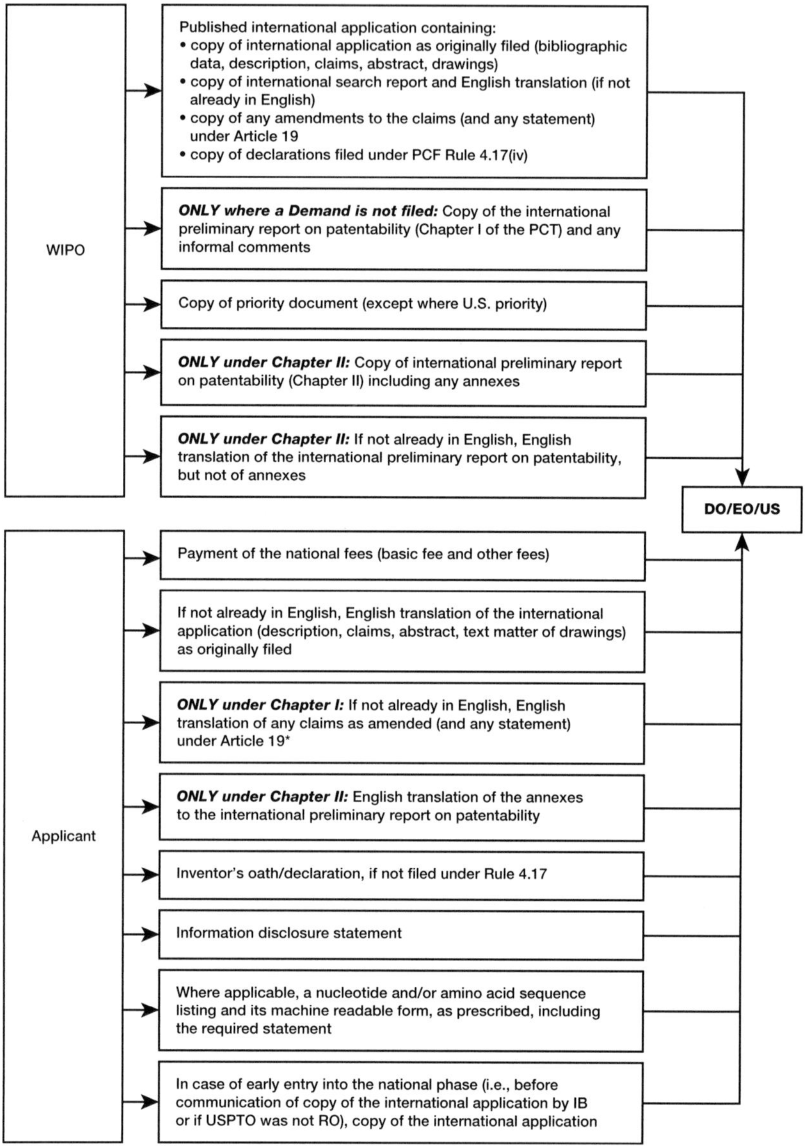

*See also PCT Applicant's Guide, National Phase, National Chapter (US)

Figure 7.2
Entry into the National Phase under Chapters I and II before the USPTO as DO/EO/US (within 20/30 months from the priority date)

2.4 Pedigree

Recall that your application's "pedigree" is based on the path it has taken to enter the national stage in the United States and any priorities that you may be claiming. For an application to be able to enter the national stage, there are two events in the PCT timeline you must identify and acknowledge to claim the pedigree, but you must do so at the proper time and in the proper manner. The first event occurs when you file the PCT application. At that time, you must properly identify and note any priorities you may be claiming. The second event occurs upon entry into the national phase, when you must make any additional pedigree statements that may be needed.

Although a national stage application under § 371 is the same application as its PCT counterpart, any earlier priority, either foreign or U.S., that you claimed when the PCT application itself was filed must be claimed again to be entitled to the pedigree. You must, in other words, recite the benefit of any earlier U.S. or foreign priority at the time of entry into the national stage. A PCT application may claim benefit to different types of priority applications, and the following checklist will help ensure that you claim the benefit correctly.

Priority benefit may be claimed in a PCT application to

- a provisional application under the provisions of 35 U.S.C. § 119(e);
- a nonprovisional application under the provisions of 35 U.S.C. § 120;
- an international application designating the United States under the provisions of 35 U.S.C. § 365(c); or
- a foreign application under the provisions of 35 U.S.C. § 119(a)–(d).

Claiming Foreign Priority

Upon Filing the PCT Application

As discussed in Chapter 2, a claim for foreign priority must have been made in Box No. VI of the PCT request form or within the time limit set forth in PCT Rule 26*bis*[5] to claim such foreign priority. A claim for foreign priority cannot be added during the national stage.

Upon Entering the National Stage

List the foreign priorities as recited in the request in the ADS document.

Note that if you made use of the declaration of inventorship provided in Box VIII(iv) of the request form when you filed the PCT application, no new declaration is required. Also note that in the declaration of inventorship form, no foreign priority is listed, since the priority claim was indicated in the request form, and that indication itself is adequate.

No first paragraph requiring foreign priority information is required in the U.S. specification.

As previously mentioned, since the International Bureau already provides a copy of the foreign application, you are not required to submit one.

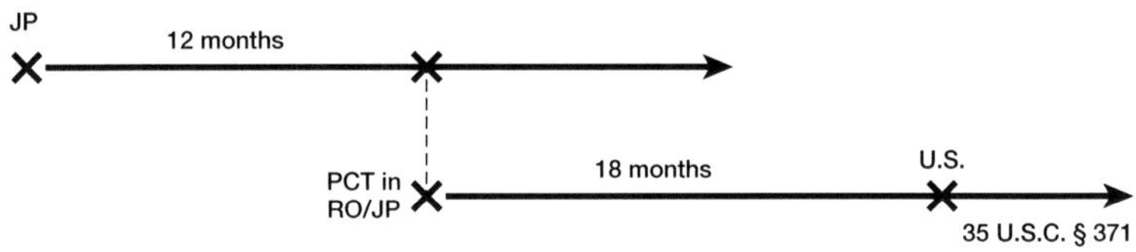

- Declaration
  - Can file Box No. VIII(iv) declaration of inventorship sheet of the request form during the international phase or a U.S. declaration at national entry for § 371 national phase entry
- "Pedigree"
  - Must include an ADS and list foreign priority applications that were indicated in the request
  - No first paragraph required in U.S. specification
- Fees
  - Must pay basic fee on entry

Figure 7.3
National Stage Entry (35 U.S.C. § 371) Claiming Foreign Priority

5. PCT Rule 26*bis*.1(a) provides that the time limit for correcting or adding a priority claim is "16 months from the priority date or, where the correction or addition would cause a change in the priority date, 16 months from the priority date as so changed, whichever 16-month period expires first, provided that such a notice may be submitted until the expiration of four months from the international filing date."

Claiming Priority to a U.S. Provisional Application

Claiming the benefit of a provisional application for filing a PCT application is provided for under 35 U.S.C. § 119(e) and is considered as an internal priority for the United States.

Accordingly, the following is required for appropriate "pedigree" identification.

Upon Filing the PCT Application

The priority information on the request form in Box VI should include the U.S. priority information. Incidentally, this will also satisfy the necessary priority claims for entry in foreign countries under the Paris Convention.

Upon Entering United States National Stage

The priority information is inserted into the Application Data Sheet.

Claims to the benefit of an earlier-filed application can still be made within the later of 4 months from the date on which the national stage is entered under 35 U.S.C. § 371(b) or (f), or 16 months from the filing date of the earlier filed application.

It should be noted that claims for U.S. priority should also be listed in the ADS.

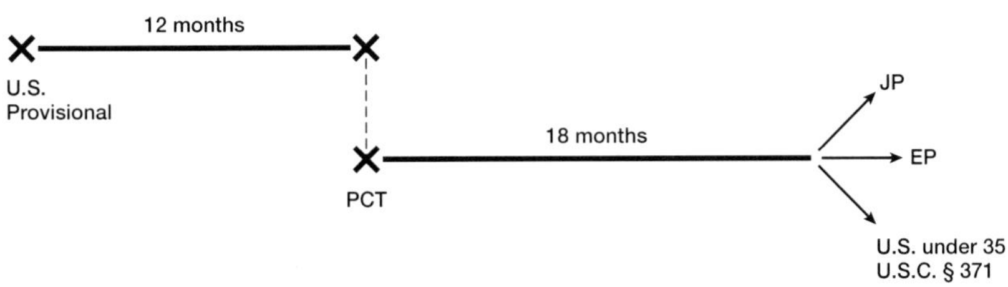

- Declaration
  - Can file Box No. VIII(iv) declaration of inventorship sheet of the request form during the international phase or a U.S. declaration at national entry for § 371 national phase entry
- "Pedigree"
  - Must refer to earlier applications in Application Data Sheet
  - No first paragraph required in U.S. specification
- Fees
  - Must pay basic fee on entry

Figure 7.4
National Stage Entry (35 U.S.C. § 371) Claiming a U.S. Provisional Priority

Claiming the Benefit of a U.S. Nonprovisional

When filing a PCT application claiming the benefit of a previous U.S. nonprovisional application, the PCT application is essentially a continuation, or may even be a continuation-in-part (CIP) of the earlier nonprovisional U.S. application. Such PCT application is therefore being filed under § 120 of the Patent Act, 35 U.S.C. § 120. In foreign countries, the benefit of the U.S. nonprovisional is a priority claim under the Paris Convention; however, for the United States, it is a continuation (or CIP) priority claim.

At the Time of Filing the PCT Application

Essentially, there is no claim that needs to be made at this point for getting the benefit of the earlier nonprovisional application. Filling out the Request Form Box VI with the U.S. priority information is only useful for Paris Convention priorities or internal priorities under § 119(e). It does not refer to any claim for a benefit under § 120 and therefore does not address the claim for the nonprovisional priority. Such a claim will only be made later, upon entry into the national stage.

Entering the National Phase

At this point, a claim must be made to the earlier nonprovisional application. The claim must be made in the Application Data Sheet.

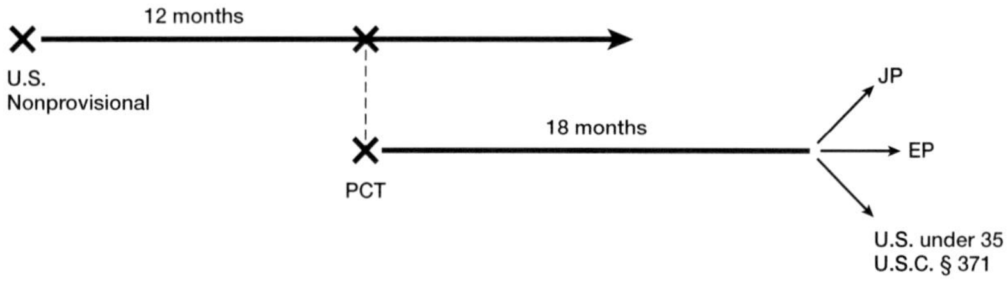

- Declaration
  - Can file Box No. VIII(iv) declaration of inventorship sheet of the request form during the international phase or a U.S. declaration at national entry for § 371 national phase entry
- "Pedigree"
  - Must refer to earlier applications in Application Data Sheet
- Fees
  - Must pay basic fee on entry

Figure 7.5
National Stage Entry (35 U.S.C. § 371) Claiming U.S. Nonprovisional Priority

2.5 Filing Dates in a National Stage Application

When filing a § 371 national stage application, there are a number of filing dates to be aware of; they are set forth on the application.

International Filing Date

Because a PCT application during its international phase is considered a pending national application, the international filing date is considered to be the effective filing date for that application when it ultimately enters the national stage under § 371.

35 U.S.C. § 371(c) Date

Another date will be listed as the "filing date" in the United States. This is the date of the completion of all of the items listed under § 371(c)(1) and (2), which includes payment of the basic national fee and the submission of an application. This is referred to as "the filing or 371(c)" date on the filing receipt.

2.6 Restriction Practice in the United States and PCT

The PCT requires that a PCT application "shall relate to one invention only or to a group of inventions so linked as to form a single general inventive concept."[6] This requirement is known as "unity of invention." In the USPTO, unity, which is known generally as restriction practice, is determined based on the definition provided in the Patent Act, 35 U.S.C. § 121. Section 121 states that an application must not claim "independent and distinct" inventions. As interpreted by the USPTO, unity is generally deemed lacking any time a separate classification or separate search might be required by the examiner. As a result, examiners very often view method and apparatus claims in the same application as violating unity, and they will issue a restriction requirement mandating the separation of the two sets of claims (which are considered to be two independent and distinct inventions) into two separate applications. Under the PCT standard of unity of invention, however, method claims, apparatus claims, method of use claims, method of manufacture

6. Rule 13.1 of the Regulations under the PCT.

claims, and so forth may all be maintained in a single application if all of the claim sets are linked to a single inventive concept that is the main feature of the invention.

Since a national stage § 371 application is an ongoing prosecution of the international phase of the same application, the examiners in the USPTO must apply the PCT unity of invention standard to national stage applications, rather than the usual restriction practice standard that they apply to all other applications. Accordingly, entering the national stage under § 371 provides a good opportunity to maintain more types and categories of independent claims in the same application than entering under the bypass route.

2.7 Failure to Meet the 30-Month Deadline

If for any reason you have failed to enter the national stage by 30 months, you need to keep in mind that your international application is a pending U.S. application. Accordingly, it may be possible to revive your "pending" U.S. application under both the unintentional and unavoidable abandonment standards that are available for all abandoned applications under the provisions of 37 C.F.R. § 1.137. You will have to file the necessary petition for revival, pay the associated fees, and furnish the accompanying documents, as is normally required for such petitions, but you will obtain the benefit of a filing date.

3. Bypass Application under 35 U.S.C. § 111(a)

As mentioned, an alternative to entering the national phase from a PCT application is to file a bypass application. Essentially, the bypass application is a continuation or continuation-in-part (CIP) of a PCT application. You have the right to file a bypass application because a PCT application designating the United States is considered a pending U.S. application; therefore, just like any pending U.S. application, you may file a continuation application or CIP from it.

It must be remembered that this option is unique to the United States. Foreign countries do not have continuation practice, and, as a result, the only way to enter the national phase in foreign countries is through normal national phase entry from the PCT application.

3.1 Fees

One of the benefits of using the bypass route is that you do not have to pay any fees upon filing. Of course, you will have to pay the fees later when you receive a Missing Requirements Notice, at which point you will also have to pay a surcharge. The bypass route can be particularly advantageous, for example, if an applicant has not provided an advance of the fees to the attorney and the attorney is not willing to lay out the fees on behalf of the applicant. Using the bypass route allows the attorney to file the application and provides the applicant with an opportunity to pay the fees later.

3.2 Oath or Declaration

Because a bypass application is a new application, a new U.S. declaration must be filed. The declaration can be submitted at the time of filing or upon receiving a Missing Requirements Notice, but it can still be filed up to the time of receiving a Notice of Allowability.

3.3 Documents Required

Similarly, since using the bypass route results in a new application, you must submit a new, full application at the time of filing, including any required formal drawings. But since the application is new, it provides some added flexibility. For example, if you need to include new matter in the application, you can file the application as a CIP. Or, in addition to claiming the benefit of the PCT application, you may be able to add a claim to a foreign priority that you might have omitted in the PCT application. Yet another advantage concerns the situation where the inventive entity named in the international application may have changed or been incorrect, and you did not correct it during the international phase. In such cases, you can rectify matters by filing a bypass application and simply naming the correct inventive entity in the declaration, thereby avoiding the usual procedure to change inventorship or delete or add an inventor. You need to keep in mind, however, that there must be at least one inventor in common with the previous PCT application since you are claiming the benefit of the earlier application.

Finally, because a bypass application is new, it is easier to make changes in the text, modify the claims, and prepare a full application without requiring numerous amendments. With the § 371 national stage route, you must add any Article 19 (or Article 34) amendments at the time of filing, as well as any additional preliminary amendment that you wish to make, all of which can become very confusing. Using the bypass route, you simply file a new set of claims. Also, by using the bypass route, it is not necessary to file a literal English translation of a non-English language PCT application, which is required for the national stage route, and it is therefore possible to clean up a translation in an easy way.

One disadvantage of the bypass route, however, is that if any foreign priority has been claimed in the filing of the PCT application, it is your responsibility to file a certified copy of the foreign priority document with the USPTO.

3.4 Pedigree

Just as is required for the national stage route, you must claim the application's "pedigree" at the time you enter the United States. However, you need to lay the groundwork for the pedigree when you file the PCT application to ensure easy bypass route entry. You can claim the benefit of both foreign and U.S. priority applications, as the following checklist will describe.

Claiming a Foreign Priority

At the Time of Filing the PCT Application

The foreign priority application must be listed in the request form in Box VI.

If you have not listed it, you can submit the claim in the bypass application to correct the failure to have claimed it in the PCT request form. In either case, you must submit the information in the Application Data Sheet.

You must also submit a certified copy of the foreign priority application. The one exception to this requirement is if the patent office for the priority application participates in WIPO's Digital Access Service/Priority Document Exchange (DAS/PDX), which is described in some detail in Chapter 10.

Finally, you must make reference to the PCT application in the Application Data Sheet.

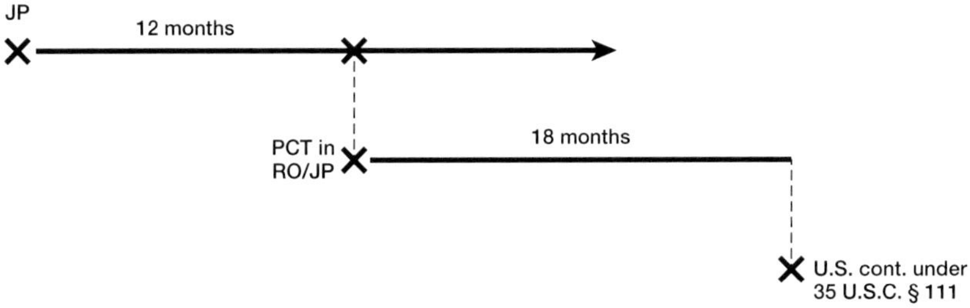

- Declaration
  - Must use a new U.S. declaration when filing the § 111(a) application
- "Pedigree"
  - Must claim Foreign Priority under 35 U.S.C. § 119(a)–(d) in Application Data Sheet
  - Must file a certified copy of foreign patent application (unless office of priority country is a DAS/PDX Participating Office)
  - Must refer to earlier international application in Application Data Sheet
- Fees
  - Can be delayed

Figure 7.6
Bypass Application Using Foreign Priority

Claiming Priority to a Provisional Application

At the Time of Filing the PCT Application

Since the PCT application claiming the benefit of a provisional application is filed under § 119(e), you must submit the filing date and number of the provisional application in Box VI of the request form. Doing so will allow you to satisfy claims to both U.S. internal priority to the provisional application and foreign priority under the Paris Convention.

At the Time of Filing the Bypass Application

In the Application Data Sheet, you must refer to the application as a continuation of the PCT application, and you must also indicate that the application claims the benefit of the U.S. provisional application. Both must be indicated.

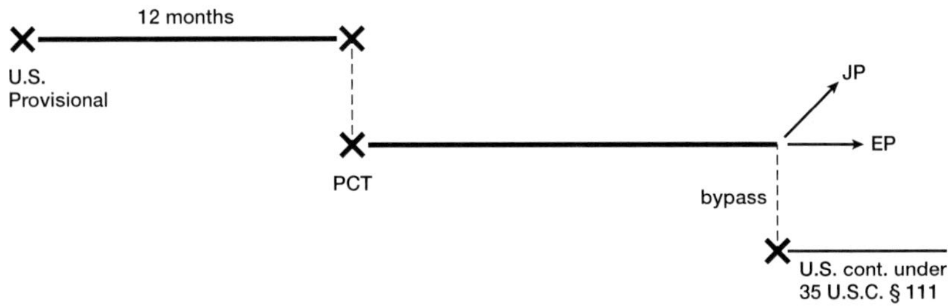

- Declaration
    - Must file the declaration when filing the § 111(a) application
- "Pedigree"
    - Must refer to earlier applications in Application Data Sheet
- Fees
    - Can be delayed

Figure 7.7
Bypass Application Claiming U.S. Provisional Priority

U.S. Nonprovisional as Priority

It must be remembered that the original PCT application itself was a continuation of the U.S. nonprovisional under 35 U.S.C. § 120. Thus, the bypass, which is a continuation of the PCT application, is therefore a second continuation.

At the Time of Filing the PCT Application

You should have filled out Supplemental Box III[7] of the PCT request form in order to ensure that there is a continuity in the intervening PCT case in order to claim the benefit of the original nonprovisional priority.

7. Supplemental Box III provides the opportunity "to make an indication of the wish that the international application be treated, in the United States of America, as a continuation or continuation-in-part of an earlier application: in such case, write 'United States of America' or 'US' and the indication 'continuation' or 'continuation-in-part' and the number and the filing date of the parent application. . . . "

At the Time of Filing the U.S. Application

You must refer to the earlier applications in the Application Data Sheet referring to this application as a continuation of the PCT international application as well as the PCT application itself being a continuation of the original nonprovisional application.

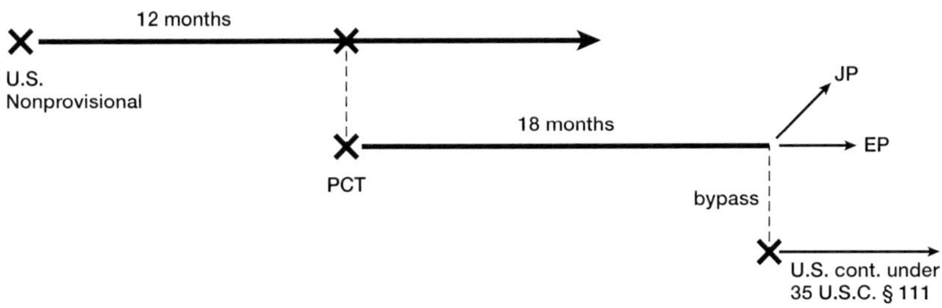

- Declaration
  - Must file a new U.S. Declaration when filing the § 111(a) application
- "Pedigree"
  - Must refer to earlier applications in Application Data Sheet
  - Must have filled out Supplemental Box 3 when filing PCT
- Fees
  - Can be delayed

Figure 7.8
Bypass Application Using Nonprovisional Priority

3.5 Restriction Practice

Because a bypass application is a new application, the usual restriction practice applied to regularly filed U.S. applications will apply to the bypass application. The benefit of the PCT unity of invention standard is not applicable in the case of bypass applications.

How to Claim the Benefit

To an Earlier Foreign Application:

- on the Application Data Sheet

To an Earlier U.S. Domestic Application (Provisional or Nonprovisional):

- on the Application Data Sheet

Benefit of an Earlier U.S. Filing Date

Should be made in a PCT Request Form:

- Claiming a nonprovisional U.S. priority: complete supplemental Box 3
- Claiming a provisional U.S. priority: complete Box No. VI

3.6 Failure to Meet 30-Month Deadline

If for any reason you have failed to file the bypass application by 30 months, it must be remembered that the bypass is similar to the filing of any other continuation application. If the parent has gone abandoned, a continuation may still be filed by reviving the parent. Accordingly, it is possible to revive the PCT parent, which is a "pending" U.S. application under both unintentional and unavoidable abandonment standards as prescribed in 37 C.F.R. § 1.137, and still obtain the benefit of a filing date for the bypass application by filing the necessary petition for revival and the associated fees, together with all of the accompanying documents, as normally required for such petitions.

The following table compares the benefits and disadvantages of national stage entry and bypass continuation.

	NATIONAL STAGE 35 U.S.C. § 371 APPLICATION	BYPASS 35 U.S.C. § 111(a) APPLICATION
Fees	National fee by 30 months	Can pay all fees later
Documents	a. Application is submitted by WIPO b. English translation must be exact of the international application c. Must submit Article 19 amendments with English translations when filing d. Further amendments submitted by preliminary amendment	Must submit new application on filing and can be flexible in translation to file in good English

Figure 7.9
Comparison of National Stage Entry versus Bypass Continuation

	NATIONAL STAGE 35 U.S.C. § 371 APPLICATION	BYPASS 35 U.S.C. § 111(a) APPLICATION
New Matter	Must be same as PCT application	Can add new matter and file as CIP ·
Priority Document	WIPO provides	Applicant must provide certified copy of any foreign priority
Unity	PCT Unity of Invention Standard	USPTO Restriction Practice
Declarations	Can use PCT Rule 4.17(iv) declaration or new declaration	Must submit new declaration
Change in inventive entity	Requires petition	Just name correct inventors

Figure 7.9 *(continued)*

Helpful Hints for U.S. National Phase

To ensure consideration of references cited at the international phase on the ISR, SISR, or IPRP (Chapter I or II):

- List them on an IDS
- Provide copies of any non-U.S. patent documents
  - Foreign patent documents
  - Non-Patent Literature (NPL)
- Copies of references are not communicated to the USPTO by the IB or any international authority

Clearly ask for early processing where filing prior to 30 months with all 35 U.S.C. § 371(c) requirements:

- Supply the declaration, additional fees, translations, etc., as soon as possible
  - Filing receipt and notification of acceptance will be issued more quickly

CHAPTER 8

Entry into the National Phase in Europe, China, and Elsewhere

1. Entering the European Regional Phase

The European Patent Convention (EPC) is a multilateral treaty that provides a unified means for the grant of a European Patent (EP patent) by the European Patent Office (EPO). The deadline for initiation of the regional phase before the EPO is 31 months, one month more than the standard deadline provided for in the PCT. Although the actual process of entering the regional phase is relatively simply, it usually requires the use of a European associate admitted to practice before the EPO. After an EP patent issues, the patent must be validated in each of the countries within the EPC where the applicant seeks protection.

The EPC entered into force on October 7, 1977, with just seven members. Today the EPO consists of 38 member countries and two extension countries (countries that recognize European patents but that are not members of the EPO).

Country	Date	Country	Date
Belgium	07-Oct-77	Turkey	01-Nov-00
France	07-Oct-77	Bulgaria	01-Jul-02
Germany	07-Oct-77	Czech Republic	01-Jul-02
Luxembourg	07-Oct-77	Estonia	01-Jul-02
Netherlands	07-Oct-77	Slovakia	01-Jul-02
Switzerland	07-Oct-77	Slovenia	01-Dec-02
United Kingdom	07-Oct-77	Hungary	01-Jan-03
Sweden	01-May-78	Romania	01-Mar-03
Italy	01-Dec-78	Poland	01-Mar-04
Austria	01-May-79	Iceland	01-Nov-04
Liechtenstein	01-Apr-80	Lithuania	01-Dec-04
Greece	01-Oct-86	Latvia	01-Jul-05
Spain	01-Oct-86	Malta	01-Mar-07
Denmark	01-Jan-90	Croatia	01-Jan-08
Monaco	01-Dec-91	Norway	01-Jan-08
Portugal	01-Jan-92	Former Yugoslav Republic of Macedonia	01-Jan-09
Ireland	01-Aug-92	San Marino	01-Jul-09
Finland	01-Mar-96	Albania	01-May-10
Cyprus	01-Apr-98	Serbia	01-Oct-10

Figure 8.1
Current List of EPC Contracting States
Extension States: Bosnia & Herzegovina, and Montenegro

Figure 8.2
Current Map of the EPC

A common misconception is that the EPO is part of the European Union (EU) and that the EPC is an EU-governed treaty. In fact, the EPO is self-governing and is unrelated to the EU. The two bodies maintain productive relations, however, and have worked together for years in the quest to establish a unitary European patent (a patent that would not need to be validated in individual countries).[1] PCT applicants benefit in at least one significant way from the independence of the EPO:

---

1. At the time of drafting this chapter, movement toward the creation of a unitary European was closer than ever, but final agreement had not yet been achieved.

EPO membership includes countries that are not members of the EU. Albania, Croatia, Iceland, Liechtenstein, Macedonia, Monaco, Norway, San Marino, Serbia, Switzerland, and Turkey are all members of the EPC, but not of the EU.

1.1 What Is Required

As mentioned above, entering the regional phase in Europe is a simple matter. All your European associate needs is a PCT application or publication number, on the basis of which the associate completes and submits a form entitled "Entry into the European Phase (EPO as designated or elected Office)" (EPO form 1200, a copy of which is contained in the annex to this chapter). There is no need to submit a copy of the application, unless the applicant is also submitting preliminary amendments to the application (known in European parlance as "voluntary amendments"). As long as the PCT application was published in English, French or German, the official languages of the EPO, there is also no need to submit a translation. For applications published in PCT languages other than the EPO languages (for example, Japanese, Russian, or Chinese), the deadline for submitting a translation into an EPO language is the same as the deadline for regional phase entry (that is, 31 months from the priority date). Finally, the applicant also needs to pay European regional phase fees.

1.2 Fees

The following fees are due upon entry into regional phase:

- A filing fee, including an excess page fee for each page of an application above 35 pages. On-line filers receive a reduction in the filing fee;
- A search fee, which varies depending upon the patent office that served as the ISA (see more below);
- A designation fee, which gives an applicant the right to validate an EP patent in the EPO member countries, and extension fees if the applicant seeks to validate the patent in extension countries;

- An examination fee, which is due on entry into regional phase unless the ISR in question was published by the International Bureau of WIPO after 25 months from the priority date. If the ISR was published after 25 months, the applicant has six months from the publication date both to request examination and pay the examination fee. (see more below); and
- A renewal fee, in the rare case (for example, the PCT application is the first-filed application) that the regional phase entry date occurs after the end of the month in which the second anniversary of the PCT application falls.

In addition, excess claims fees, where applicable, must be paid within one month of entry into regional phase (see more below).

The current (as of July 2012) EPO schedule of fees can be accessed at http://archive.epo.org/epo/pubs/oj010/03_10/03_sup10.pdf, or at http://www.wipo.int/pct/guide/en/gdvol2/annexes/ep.pdf. Changes in the fees are announced in the EPO Official Journal, in the PCT Applicant's Guide, and in the PCT Newsletter.

Search Fee

The EPO carries out only a top-up search in the regional phase if the EPO was the ISA in the international phase. As a result, there is no need to pay the search fee if the EPO was the ISA. If the ISA in the international phase was any of the other ISAs that U.S. applicants are free to use (Australia, Korea, Russia, or the United States), the search fee is subject to a 20 percent reduction.[2] And the search fee is reduced by €890 if the ISR was prepared by Austria, Finland, the Nordic Patent Institute, Spain, or Sweden—ISAs from countries that are members of the EPO.

Examination Fee

Applicants who have sought international preliminary examination under Chapter II of the PCT and who selected the EPO as the International Preliminary Examining Authority are entitled to a 50 percent reduction in the examination fee (which is distinct from the search fee).

2. The 20 percent reduction also applies to applications that were searched by Japan Patent Office and the State Intellectual Property Office of China when they serve as ISA.

This reduction is to account for the extensive examination that the EPO has already performed in the international phase.

Excess Claims Fees

The EPO has imposed very expensive excess claims fees in order to encourage applicants to limit the number of claims they file. The first 15 claims are "free," and reflect the EPO's view that there are few applications that require more than 15 claims. The current excess fee for each claim from the 16th to the 50th is €210, and for each claim beyond 50, the fee is a mind-boggling €525. An applicant who enters regional phase in Europe with an application containing 100 claims would therefore owe the EPO €33,600 in excess claims fees, payable within one month of the regional phase entry date. In order to avoid such predicaments, applicants should consider filing preliminary amendments to their PCT applications upon entry into regional phase to:

- Use multiple claim dependencies to reduce the number of claims
- Cancel duplicative or inconsequential claims
- Possibly incorporate some claim language into the description.

(See more in the chapters on tips and strategies.)

2. Practice upon Entry into the European Regional Phase

The EPO introduced a number of rules in 2010 that impact the practice and procedure of entry into regional phase.

2.1 Filing of Amendments

In accordance with Rule 137(2) and (3) of the Implementing Regulations to the Grant of European Patents, applicants who did not file preliminary amendments within the 31-month time limit for entry into regional phase may still do so, but only within a strict deadline. That deadline is one month from the communication from the EPO that all the regional phase filing requirements have been met. Amendments not filed within that deadline will not be taken into consideration by the EPO in any supplementary search that the EPO may have to perform.

Applicants nevertheless have two other opportunities to file amendments. The first is following receipt of a supplementary search report (assuming one has been established) and before the first communication (i.e., office action) from the EPO examining division. The second is after receipt of, and in response to, the first communication from the examining division. An applicant may only submit other amendments at the discretion of the examining division. In addition, pursuant to Rule 137(4), an applicant is required to identify and indicate the basis for all amendments in the original specification, in the same manner as the requirement to identify and indicate the basis for amendments under PCT Articles 19 or 34.

2.2 Mandatory Response to the IPRP

The EPO treats as the equivalent of a first office action any IPRP that it prepared in its capacity as an international searching or international preliminary examining authority. Consequently, applicants who have sought international search or international preliminary examination from the EPO must, pursuant to Rule 161, respond to any deficiencies cited in the EPO-issued IPRP following entry into regional phase. The deadline for submitting a response to the IPRP, which should also include all desired amendments to the description, claims, or drawings, is six months from the date of the EPO communication inviting the applicant to correct deficiencies (which is issued shortly after the regional phase entry date). Failure to meet the deadline results in the application being deemed withdrawn. Furthermore, any subsequent amendments that the applicant submits and that are not in response to specific objections raised by the examiner are admissible only at the discretion of the EPO Examining Division. Therefore, if you want to initiate amendments that are not in response to examiner objections, the only time to be sure you can do it under Rule 161 is in response to the EPO communication.

Applicants who do not use the EPO as ISA do not need to respond to the IPRP, since it was prepared by another office. The EPO will still send the communication under Rule 161, however, and will give applicants a six-month opportunity to amend their applications. More importantly, the EPO will carry out a supplementary search on all applications that it did not search in the international phase, and it is therefore important that you conform your claims to EPO requirements at the time of entry into regional phase (see the next two topics). Following the supplementary search, the EPO will prepare an Extended European Search Report (EESR), and, just as in the case of the IPRP, applicants must file a response to the search opinion or their applications will be deemed withdrawn. The deadline for filing a response to the EESR is six months from the EPO communication. Just as in the case of applicants who must respond to an IPRP, it is important to note that your last opportunity to file voluntary amendments is with your response to the search opinion. Further amendments are at the discretion of the Examining Division.

Despite the seeming cumbersomeness of the mandatory response procedure, you can accelerate processing, if you wish, by expressly waiving the right to receive the communication under Rule 161, paying all excess claim fees that may be due, and if there was an IPRP, filing the mandatory response to it. If you take those steps, your application will proceed immediately to the preparation of the search report or to examination.

2.3 Opportunity to Respond to Objection that No Meaningful Search Can Be Carried Out

In accordance with Rule 65 of the EPC Regulations, if the EPO determines that the claims in an application are so unclear that a meaningful search of the application cannot be carried out, or that the application fails in other ways to allow a meaningful search, the examiner will communicate with the applicant and provide a two-month period for the applicant to file a statement clarifying the claims or correcting the deficiency. If the examiner determines that the statement still does not resolve the matter, he or she may either carry out a partial search on the basis of the claims that are understandable or issue a statement that no meaningful search is possible. If the examiner determines that he or she can only carry out a partial search, he or she will invite the applicant to restrict the claims accordingly.

2.4 Restriction on Search of Multiple Independent Claims

Article 43(2) of the EPC provides that a European application may not have more than one independent claim in the same category (product, process, apparatus, or use). In the event that your application contains more than one independent claim, Rule 62a authorizes the examiner to order you to elect the one independent claim on which you want the search to be carried out. You have a two-month period to select the claim. If you do not respond within the two months, the examiner will search only the first independent claim in each category, and substantive examination will only be carried out on searched claims. You will need to delete any unsearched claims, but you may possibly pursue them by filing a divisional application (see below for rules on filing divisionals).

In view of this limitation, it is important that you either draft no more than one independent claim per category, or, more realistically, amend the claims by creating multiple claim dependencies and canceling duplicative or unessential claims when entering European regional phase. By copying the canceled claims into the description, you can often preserve them for future use.

Claims Drafting Tip: Draft no more than one independent claim per category, or amend the claims by creating multiple claim dependencies. Cancel duplicative or unessential claims when you enter the European regional phase. Copy the canceled claims into the description to preserve them.

3. EPO Divisional Practice

The EPO has put rules into place that limit the opportunity applicants have to file divisional applications. An applicant may only file a divisional application when the application to be divided is still pending, and only from the later of:

- 24 months from the examiner's first communication—either the examination report or the notice of intention to grant under Rule 71(3)—in respect of the earliest related application; or
- 24 months from any examiner's communication raising a specific lack of unity objection for the first time.

The first 24-month period is considered a voluntary divisional, and the second a mandatory divisional.

If divisional practice is important because, for example, you wish to obtain independent protection for different features in the same claim category, it may be wise to voluntarily divide your application in a timely manner and perhaps consider drawing additional unity issues in your divisional application in the hope that the examiner will raise a lack of unity objection, which will enable you to divide again.

4. Additional Practice Tips

4.1 Delaying Entry into Regional Phase

Although it will be costly, you have the possibility to delay entry into European regional phase if you need more time to decide whether to pursue a European patent. It is a rather straightforward procedure. Upon expiration of the 31-month entry deadline, the EPO will issue you a letter noting "loss of rights." You have two months following the date of that letter to enter regional phase—without loss of rights. You will have to pay a 50 percent surcharge on all fees, however.

4.2 Accelerating Entry into Regional Phase

You may also accelerate entry into regional phase by completing the requirements early and requesting early processing. On entry into the regional phase or together with your response to the WO, IPRP or SISR, you may request accelerated examination. You are not required to provide a reason. Following receipt of your request the EPO Examining Division will make every effort to issue the first examination communication within the following three months and all subsequent communications within three months or your response to the preceding communication.

4.3 Making Prosecution More Efficient

You can streamline prosecution by including filing full and complete responses to the IPRP or search opinion and by providing the detailed basis for all amendments by clearly indicating where in the description support for the amended claim can be found. In addition, you may consider making "auxiliary requests," that is, to file an auxiliary set (or sets) of claims with the examiner.

4.4 Auxiliary Requests

Auxiliary requests come into play when examiners invite applicants to correct deficiencies in the application. Assuming that applicants find the deficiencies to be justified, they will need to file amended claims to overcome the examiners' objections. Applicants generally will want to maintain claims that are as broad as possible, but they may have difficulty deciding how much of the original claim content they can preserve. In such cases, applicants may choose to file the most broadly worded set of claims as the main request and one or more sets of more limited claims as auxiliary requests. Applicants who are unsure as to how to frame the auxiliary requests should make contact and speak with the examiner—a good and worthwhile technique in any event. Examiners will look to the auxiliary requests only if they believe the main request is unacceptable.

4.5 Problem and Solution Approach to Overcome Inventive Step Rejections

Still another technique in the event of a rejection on grounds of lack of inventive step (i.e., rejection on the grounds of obviousness) is to use the "*problem and solution*" approach to argue the rejection. The problem and solution approach is the technique the EPO uses to examine for inventive step, and it is consequently language and methodology with which examiners are most familiar.

The problem and solution approach requires the examiner to select the closest prior art to the claimed invention, in other words, to identify a single prior art reference that is directed to a similar purpose, effect, or use as the claimed invention and that would constitute the best hypothetical starting point for creating the invention. Once selected, the examiner needs to determine the extent to which, and if so how, the invention's technical features can be distinguished, either in terms of structure or function, from the technical features of the closest prior art. The objective technical problem consists in determining the modifications or adaptations necessary to provide the closest prior art with the distinguishing technical features embodied in the invention—in other words, filling the gap. In the final stage of assessing inventive step, once the examiner has arrived at the technical problem by comparing the invention and the closest prior art, the examiner needs to answer the question—whether there is any teaching in the prior art as a whole that would have prompted the skilled person, faced with the objective technical problem, to modify or adapt the closest prior art while taking account of that teaching, thereby arriving at something falling within the terms of the claims, and thus achieving what the invention achieves. When the answer to the question is negative, the invention is deemed to possess inventive step.

The problem and solution approach is illustrated in the flowchart in Figure 8.3.

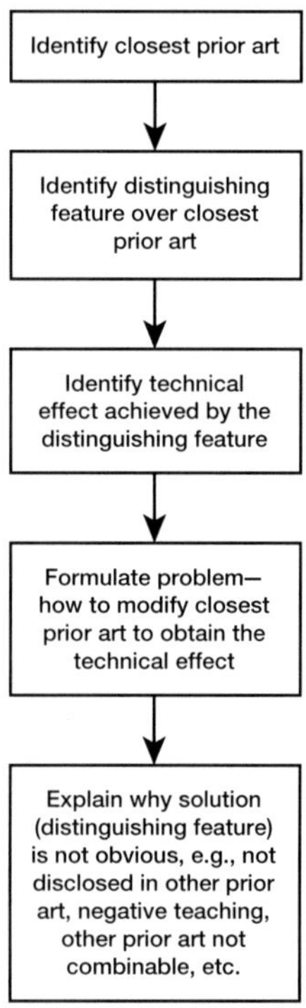

Figure 8.3
Problem and Solution Argumentation: Five Steps to Non-Obviousness

5. Validation after Grant

5.1 Validation Rates

As previously mentioned, once an EP patent issues of the patent must be validated in each country in which specific patent rights are sought. Figure 8.4, which dates from 2007, provides an estimate of the percentage of granted European patents that are validated by applicants in each of the 16 leading EPO member countries:

Country	Validation Rate
Germany (DE)	95%
France (FR)	88%
United Kingdom (GB)	86%
Italy (IT)	53%
Spain (ES)	32%
Switzerland (CH)	26%
Belgium (BE)	25%
Netherlands (NL)	24%
Austria (AT)	23%
Sweden (SE)	18%
Ireland (IE)	12%
Denmark (DK)	10%
Finland (FI)	9%
Luxembourg (LU)	8%
Portugal (PT)	8%
Greece (GR)	7%

Figure 8.4
Estimate of Percentage of Granted European Patents Validated by Applicants in the 16 Leading EPO Member Countries in 2007

As can be seen, applicants consistently validate European patents in Germany, France, and the United Kingdom, but they get significantly more selective when it comes to validating in the other EPO member countries. The process for selecting the countries in which to validate your European patent is basically the same as the process for selecting the countries in which you want to enter the national phase.

5.2 Translations

As originally conceived, the EPC required owners of European patents to translate the entire specification (description and claims) into the national language of every country in which the owners desired validation. The entry into force in 2008 of the London Agreement greatly eased the burden of translation. Under the terms of the agreement, countries may choose not to require the translation of a European patent into the country's national language, or it may opt to require only the translation of the claims. The following countries are party to the London Agreement and have chosen not to require a translation or to require a translation of the claims only:

No Post-Grant Translation Required	Translation of Claims Only
United Kingdom	The Netherlands
Germany	Iceland
France	Latvia
Switzerland	Croatia
Liechtenstein	Slovenia
Monaco	Denmark
Luxembourg	Sweden
	Lithuania
	Hungary
	Finland

Figure 8.5
London Agreement Countries and Their Translation Requirements

The remaining countries, which are not bound by the London Agreement, still require translations of the description and the claims.

National Route and Closing the National Route
As mentioned above, 11 EPO member countries have closed the national route. In other words, those countries have declared that the only way to obtain a national patent using the PCT is first to enter the European regional phase and to receive a European patent. Those 11 countries are: Belgium, Cyprus, France, Greece, Ireland, Italy, Latvia,

Malta, Monaco, the Netherlands and Slovenia. But for all the other countries, the PCT permits applicants a choice: obtain national protection via the European regional route; or obtain protection by entering the national phase directly in the country concerned. If you require protection in only one or two European countries that permit direct national phase entry (for example, the UK and Germany), it may make strategic and economic sense to obtain protection using the direct national route.

6. National Phase Entry in China

6.1 Chinese Emergence

China has emerged as a leading PCT nation. According to statistics compiled by WIPO,[3] in 2010 China ranked in fourth place among the top countries of origin for the filing of PCT applications. Only the United States, Japan, and Germany surpassed China in the number of PCT applications filed. Even more notable, the number of Chinese applications filed in 2011—16,406—represented a 33.4 percent increase over the number of applications filed in 2010 (12,296), and two Chinese applicants—ZTE and Huawei—were among the top three PCT filers in 2011 based on the number of applications published. Just five years earlier in 2006, China came in eighth place among PCT countries of origin, with only 3,942 applications.

Equally dramatic are the statistics relating to entry into the national phase in China. In 2010, the State Intellectual Property Office of China (SIPO) received 62,317 PCT national phase applications, making China the third biggest recipient of national phase applications after the European Patent Office and the USPTO. Of those 62,317 applications, the largest number—17,649—were filed by U.S. applicants. In addition to its rank among designated offices for PCT applications, SIPO now ranks as the fourth largest receiving office and the fourth largest International Searching Authority. China's growing importance within the

3. World Intellectual Property Organization, *PCT: The International Patent System, Yearly Review (Developments and Performance in 2010)*, 2011.

PCT system does not necessarily mean that the country should always be on the list of national phase countries, but it does mean that China should not be ignored.

When an international filing strategy includes considerations to file for protection in China, it is helpful to consider the following items.

6.2 Relationship to Hong Kong

If you wish your Chinese patent rights to extend to Hong Kong, it is important to note that obtaining a patent in China does not automatically provide patent protection in Hong Kong. China established the Hong Kong Special Administrative Region in 1997, and Hong Kong maintains its own Patent Registry, which operates under its own Patent Ordinance. Patents granted by SIPO therefore do not automatically extend to Hong Kong, but they can form the basis for Hong-Kong–granted patents. By virtue of having designated China on your PCT request form and entered the national phase in China, your right to obtain a patent in Hong Kong will be preserved.

There are nevertheless certain procedural formalities that you will need to follow. One of those formalities is that you will have to file a request, using a standard form, to record your application. The deadline for filing the request is six months from the date your international application was published in China. You will also need to send a copy of your international application to the Hong Kong Patents Registry as well as a copy of the Chinese translation of your application as published by SIPO (unless you filed your application in Chinese) and any other published information about your application, and you will need to pay fees. Provided it is not refused, your request to record will be published by the Hong Kong Registry. Once SIPO has granted your patent, you will have six months to request the registration and grant of a patent in Hong Kong. There is again a standard form that you may use; in addition, you will need to submit a verified copy of the granted patent as published by SIPO, and you will have to pay filing and advertisement fees within one month of filing the request for registration. Registration will accord you full patent rights in Hong Kong.

6.3 Two Types of Protection Offered

China provides for the grant of utility models (see below) in addition to standard patents, which are called "invention patents" in China. Utility models generally protect structures or fixed shapes, have a lower inventive step threshold, carry a term of protection of ten years, and are not subjected to a prior art search and examination before grant. Utility models are a particularly popular and effective form of protection in China (the largest damage award granted to date was for the infringement of a utility model[4]), but they have tended to be little used by foreign applicants. They are nevertheless especially useful if you want quick protection. If you wish to obtain a utility model on the basis of your international application instead of an invention patent, you may do so, but you must indicate your choice when you enter the national phase. Once you have made your choice, you may not switch.[5]

The national phase requirements for utility models are basically the same as for patents except:

- The fees are lower;
- You need to furnish a drawing; and
- Your application will not be subject to substantive examination.

You will quickly be armed with a utility model registration that you can enforce as you would a standard patent. Following a parallel process as mentioned above for patents, you may also register your utility model (referred to as a short-term patent in the Hong Kong Ordinance) in Hong Kong.

4. The case was *Chint v. Schneider*, in which the Wenzhou Intermediate People's Court ordered defendant Schneider to pay the plaintiff Chint RMB 330 million in damages.

5. If you want to pursue both forms of protection, you would need to file a utility model application on the same day as you file a PCT application.

6.4 Terminology

One warning about terminology: Because we use the term "utility patent" to refer to a standard patent, the term can be confusing to Chinese practitioners, for whom the word "utility" signals utility model. You should therefore try to avoid using the word "utility" when communicating with Chinese associates, except when you mean to refer to a utility model. Although semantic, Chinese practitioners often experience confusion due to the different meanings of the terms.

6.5 Fees

The Chinese national phase entry fees for patents and utility models, applicable in July 2012, are listed in Figure 8.6. They must be paid in order for national phase entry to be valid. Any modifications in the fees will appear in the PCT Applicant's Guide.

Fee	**Currency: Yuan Remnibi (CNY)**
For a patent:	
Filing fee:	CNY 900
Additional filing fee:	
— for each sheet of the description in excess of 30 sheets	CNY 50
— for each sheet of the description in excess of 300 sheets	CNY 100
— for each claim in excess of 10	CNY 150
Application publication fee:	CNY 50
Fee for priority claims, per priority:	CNY 80
For a utility model:	
Filing fee:	CNY 500
Additional filing fee:	
— for each sheet of the description in excess of 30 sheets	CNY 50
— for each sheet of the description in excess of 300 sheets	CNY 100
— for each claim in excess of 10	CNY 150
Fee for priority claims, per priority:	CNY 80

Figure 8.6
Chinese National Phase Entry Fees

It should be noted that China has both excess page fees and excess claim fees. Moreover, China calculates the excess claim fees in a way that most non-Chinese applicants find particularly annoying. While most offices will calculate the excess claim fees on the basis of the number of claims as filed in the national office on the date of national phase entry, SIPO calculates the excess claim fees on the basis of the number of claims filed with the PCT application on the international filing date. Therefore, attempts to reduce the number of claims upon entry into the national phase will be to no avail. Since U.S. practice tends favor a multitude of claims, U.S. PCT applicants can pay a heavy price when entering the national phase in China.

When entering the national phase in China, keep in mind that China calculates excess claim fees on the basis of the number of claims filed with the original PCT application, not on the number of claims filed on the national phase entry date. If minimizing filing costs is important, try to avoid duplicative or unnecessary claims in your PCT application.

6.6 National Phase Entry Form

Like many countries, SIPO makes available a form for entering the national phase. It is not necessary to make use of the form, but your foreign associate will certainly do so when paying the fees and furnishing the copies of the Chinese translation of your international application.

6.7 Deadline for National Phase Entry

China is a particularly generous country. Although the national phase entry deadline is 30 months from the priority date, China automatically grants a two-month extension upon payment of a surcharge for late entry. The two-month extension is particularly helpful in light of the need to prepare a Chinese translation of the PCT application.

6.8 Translation

You must file two copies of the translation of the request form, description, claims, any text matter in the drawings, and the abstract. If any of those parts have been amended, they must be translated both as originally filed and as amended. In accordance with the normal PCT rules, the translation must be provided when entering the national phase. In most cases, your foreign associate will provide translation services. Because of the difficulty entailed in producing a Chinese translation, if errors are discovered, SIPO permits them to be corrected to accurately reflect the text of the international application as filed.

6.9 Amendments and Requesting Examination

You may amend your application when you request examination and within three months after receiving notice that the substantive examination process has begun. You will be able to file further amendments in response to opinions issued during examination.

SIPO is one of the offices that does not examine your application until you have officially requested examination and paid the examination fee (currently CNY 2,500). A request for examination must be effected within three years from the priority date.

6.10 Assignments

Some U.S. practitioners have encountered obstacles in satisfying the Chinese requirements for assignments when a new applicant was added to the international application or there was a change in applicant, and the international application claimed priority to a U.S. provisional or nonprovisional application. In cases where there has been a change in ownership, SIPO requires an instrument of assignment not only for the PCT application but also for the priority application, and it will not add or effectuate a change in applicant until all assignments are recorded in the USPTO and certified copies provided to SIPO.

In general, SIPO does not require an instrument of assignment in the case of a PCT application if the applicant is a business entity and the application is for an invention made by an employee of the entity. It does require the filing of an assignment after the application has been filed, whenever there is a change in the person of the applicant. At the time of drafting this chapter, the new provisions of the America Invents Act that permit the filing of an application in the name of the business entity had not yet entered into force. It will be interesting to see whether the new provisions alleviate the obstacles that the U.S. applicants have encountered.

7. National Phase Entry in Other Countries

In 2010, the most popular national phase destinations for U.S. PCT applications after the EPO and China were Japan, Canada, Korea, India, and Australia.

Figure 8.7 indicates the top 20 national phase entry destinations for PCT applications filed by U.S. applicants in 2010:

National Phase Entries by U.S. Applicants	Number
EPO	23,708
China	17,649
Japan	15,040
United States	14,070
Canada	12,538
Korea	9,960
India	8,087
Australia	8,050
Brazil	6,800
Mexico	5,719
Russia	3,100
Singapore	2,932
Israel	2,643
South Africa	1,939
New Zealand	1,831
Philippines	1,061
Germany (direct national route)	974
Vietnam	814
Ukraine	740
Eurasian Patent Organization	562

Figure 8.7
2010 National Phase Entries for U.S. Applicants
Source: WIPO, 2012 PCT Yearly Review

The exact process for entering the national phase differs for each country. Additionally, the laws and procedures in each country are subject to continuing change. Accordingly, and as mentioned above, for national phase prosecution outside the United States you will need to rely on a foreign associate; in fact, in many countries it is required. In addition, it is always helpful to refer to the relevant national chapter in the PCT Applicant's Guide.

8. Other Types of Protection Available via PCT—Utility Models

When we think of the PCT, we tend to think of it as a tool to obtain patent protection. But the PCT can also be used to obtain a type of protection that is widespread in many part of the world but little known in the United States. That type of protection is commonly known as a utility model. Utility models differ by country, but in general they are looked to to protect mechanical inventions and they require a lower threshold of inventive step. Moreover, they will either not be subject at all to a substantive examination, or the substantive examination will be less stringent than for a standard patent. A utility model can be obtained much faster than a patent and at a lower cost. The downside, however, is that utility models are usually only available for limited subject matter and their term of protection is shorter, ranging from seven to ten years. Therefore, utility model applications may be appropriate where you need quick protection, where your application may be unlikely to overcome the inventiveness requirement of a patent application, or where you want some form of protection during the period of examination of the corresponding patent application.

Utility models are available in a significant number of countries, including China, Germany, Korea, Russia, Ukraine, Japan, Spain, Brazil, Czech Republic, and Australia. While China by far leads the world in the grant of utility models, the German utility model (the *Gebrauchsmuster*) may be the oldest and is considered the "dean" of utility model systems worldwide.

The PCT can be used to file applications for utility models in the national phase. However, since you can usually only enter the national phase to pursue either a patent or a utility model, you may wish to consider filing a utility model application through the Paris Convention at the same time as you file your PCT application so that you may pursue both forms of protection at the same time. If the technology is protectable through a utility model, a grant will give you protection until the patent issues, at which point you will need to abandon the utility model to avoid double patenting.

Germany is an exception to the rule stated in the above paragraph, however. Germany provides for the grant of utility models, and it permits applicants to enter the national stage in Germany for a utility model at the same time as the applicants enter regional stage in the EPO to pursue a European patent based on the same PCT application. This "double dipping" of sorts can be extremely useful if Germany is a strategically important country for protection and you do not want to wait until the European patent issues and you register the patent in Germany.

When to think about filing a utility model application: where you need quick protection; where your application may be unlikely to overcome the inventiveness requirement of a patent application; or where you want some form of protection during the period of examination of the corresponding patent application. Utility models are a much overlooked tool. They can be very beneficial.

The number of utility model applications is growing globally, but the growth is due almost entirely to the significant increase in utility model applications in China, and that growth has been driven by large increases in resident filings. In 2010, 409,839 utility applications were filed, but only 2,598 were non-resident applications, of which 892 were filed by U.S. applicants. Considering the growing domestic market in China and China's advantages in production and research and development, it may be that utility models are undervalued by U.S. applicants. A Chinese utility model does not require substantial examination and can usually be obtained in a year and a half, at most. Utility models have been successfully enforced and have resulted in large monetary damages awards up to $48 million. Where appropriate, a Chinese utility model grant enables U.S. applicants an easy means of enforcement for up to ten years, while the invention patent is undergoing examination, or it provides alternative protection for products with a short product lifecycle.

Figure 8.8's graphs indicate the offices that grant utility model protection and the number of applications that have been filed at them. As can be seen, with the exception of China, utility model protection may be an underused tool.

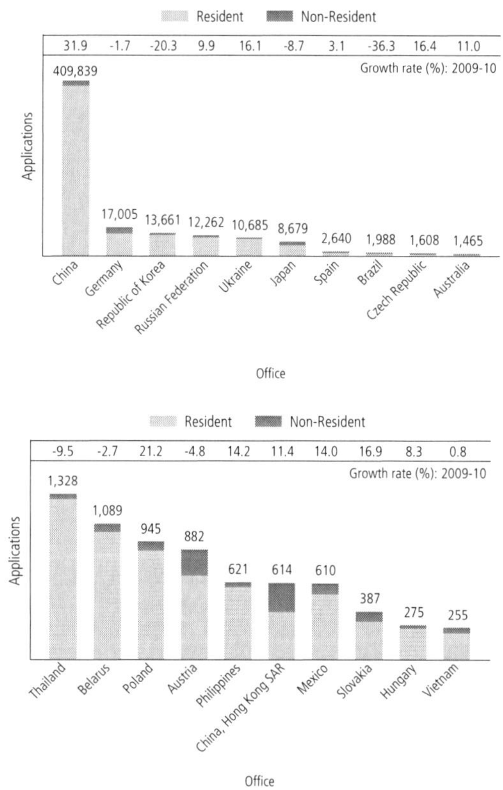

Figure 8.8
Utility Model Applications by Office: Top Offices, 2010
Source: WIPO Statistics Database, October 2011

And finally, Figure 8.9 indicates the type of protection available in each PCT member country.

Types of Protection Available via the PCT in PCT Contracting States (status on 1 October 2012)								
	National patent	ARIPO patent (AP)	Eurasian patent (EA)	European patent (EP)	OAPI patent (OA)	Utility model **instead of** national patent	Utility model **in addition to** national patent	Other
AE	X					X		Patent of addition
AG[1]	X							
AL	X			X[2]		X		Extension of EP patent[3,4]
AM	X		X			X		
AO	X					X		Certificate of addition
AT	X			X		X	X	Patent of addition
AU	X							Patent of addition
AZ	X		X			X		
BA	X							Consensual patents, extension of EP patent[3]
BB	X							
BE				X				
BF					X	OAPI utility model		OAPI certificate of addition
BG	X			X		X	X	
BH	X						X	
BJ					X	OAPI utility model		OAPI certificate of addition
BN[1,5]	X							
BR	X					X		Certificate of addition
BW	X	X				ARIPO utility model	ARIPO utility model	Utility model certificate
BY	X		X			X		
BZ	X					X		
CA	X							
CF					X	OAPI utility model		OAPI certificate of addition
CG					X	OAPI utility model		OAPI certificate of addition
CH + LI	X			X				
CI					X	OAPI utility model		OAPI certificate of addition
CL	X					X		
CM					X	OAPI utility model		OAPI certificate of addition
CN	X					X		
CO	X					X		
CR	X					X		
CU	X							Patent of addition, inventor's certificate, inventor's certificate of addition
CY				X				
CZ	X			X		X	X	
DE	X			X		X	X	Patent of addition
DK	X			X		X	X	
DM[1]	X							
DO	X					X		

[continued on next page]

Page 1

Figure 8.9
Types of Protection Available in PCT Member Countries

Types of Protection Available via the PCT in PCT Contracting States (status on 1 October 2012)								
	National patent	ARIPO patent (AP)	Eurasian patent (EA)	European patent (EP)	OAPI patent (OA)	Utility model **instead of** patent	Utility model **in addition to** patent	Other
DZ	X							Certificate of addition
EC	X					X		
EE	X			X		X	X	
EG	X					X		
ES	X			X		X		Patent of addition
FI	X			X		X	X	
FR				X				
GA					X	OAPI utility model		OAPI certificate of addition
GB	X			X				
GD[1]	X							
GE	X					X		
GH	X	X				ARIPO utility model	ARIPO utility model	Utility certificate
GM	X	X				ARIPO utility model	ARIPO utility model	
GN					X	OAPI utility model		OAPI certificate of addition
GQ					X	OAPI utility model		OAPI certificate of addition
GR				X				
GT	X					X		
GW					X	OAPI utility model		OAPI certificate of addition
HN	X					X		
HR	X			X				"Consensual patent"
HU	X			X		X		
ID	X							
IE				X				
IL	X							Patent of addition
IN	X							Patent of addition
IS	X			X				
IT				X				
JP	X					X		
KE	X	X				National or ARIPO utility model	ARIPO utility model	
KG	X		X			X		
KM[1]	X							
KN[1]	X							
KP	X					X		Inventor's certificate
KR	X					X		
KZ	X		X			X		Innovative patent
LA[1]	X							
LC	X							
LI (see CH)								
LK	X							
LR	X	X				ARIPO utility model	ARIPO utility model	
LS	X	X				National or ARIPO utility model	ARIPO utility model	

[continued on next page]

Figure 8.9 *(continued)*

Types of Protection Available via the PCT in PCT Contracting States
(status on 1 October 2012)

	National patent	ARIPO patent (AP)	Eurasian patent (EA)	European patent (EP)	OAPI patent (OA)	Utility model **instead of** patent	Utility model **in addition to** patent	Other
LT	X[6]			X				
LU	X			X				
LV				X				
LY	X							Patent of addition
MA	X							Certificate of addition
MC				X				
MD	X		X[7]					Short-term patent
ME	X							Extension of EP patent
MG	X							Certificate of addition
MK	X			X				
ML					X	OAPI utility model		OAPI certificate of addition
MN	X							
MR					X	OAPI utility model		OAPI certificate of addition
MT				X				
MW	X	X				ARIPO utility model	ARIPO utility model	Patent of addition
MX	X					X		
MY	X							
MZ	X	X				National or ARIPO utility model	ARIPO utility model	
NA	X	X				ARIPO utility model	ARIPO utility model	
NE					X	OAPI utility model		OAPI certificate of addition
NG	X							
NI	X					X		
NL				X				
NO	X			X				
NZ	X							Patent of addition
OM	X					X		
PA[1,8]	X							
PE	X					X		
PG	X							
PH	X					X		
PL	X			X		X		
PT	X			X		X	X	
QA[9]	X							
RO	X			X		X	X	
RS	X			X[10]				Patent of addition, petty patent, extension of EP patent[3, 11]
RU	X		X			X		
RW	X[12]	X[13]				National or ARIPO utility model	ARIPO utility model	
SC	X							
SD	X	X				ARIPO utility model	ARIPO utility model	
SE	X			X				

[continued on next page]

Figure 8.9 *(continued)*

Types of Protection Available via the PCT in PCT Contracting States (status on 1 October 2012)								
	National patent	ARIPO patent (AP)	Eurasian patent (EA)	European patent (EP)	OAPI patent (OA)	Utility model **instead of** patent	Utility model **in addition to** patent	Other
SG	X							
SI				X				
SK	X			X		X	X	
SL	X	X				National or ARIPO utility model	ARIPO utility model	
SM	X							
SN					X	OAPI utility model		OAPI certificate of addition
ST	X							
SV	X					X		
SY	X							Certificate of addition
SZ		X				ARIPO utility model	ARIPO utility model	
TD					X	OAPI utility model		OAPI certificate of addition
TG					X	OAPI utility model		OAPI certificate of addition
TH	X							Petty patent
TJ	X		X			X		
TM	X		X					Provisional patent
TN	X							
TR	X			X		X		Patent of addition
TT	X							Utility certificate
TZ	X	X				ARIPO utility model	ARIPO utility model	
UA	X					X		
UG	X	X				ARIPO utility model	ARIPO utility model	Utility certificate
US	X							
UZ	X					X		
VC	X							Utility certificate
VN	X							"Patent for utility solution"
ZA	X							Patent of addition
ZM	X	X				ARIPO utility model	ARIPO utility model	Patent of addition
ZW	X	X				ARIPO utility model	ARIPO utility model	Patent of addition

1 Information regarding any other type of national protection is not yet available.
2 Only for international applications filed on or after 1 May 2010.
3 A request for an extension may be made at the time of entry into the regional phase before the European Patent Office, provided that the designations of EP and/or of the State concerned have not been withdrawn. See the *PCT Applicant's Guide*, International Phase, paragraphs 4.026 and 5.054, and National Phase, National Chapter (EP) for further details as to the procedure to be followed.
4 Only for international applications filed before 1 May 2010.
5 Only for international applications filed on or after 24 July 2012.
6 Lithuania will close its national route via the PCT on 4 September 2014
7 Only for international applications filed before 26 April 2012.
8 Only for international applications filed on or after 7 September 2012.
9 Only for international applications filed on or after 3 August 2011.
10 Only for international applications filed on or after 1 October 2010.
11 Only for international applications filed before 1 October 2010.
12 Only for international applications filed on or after 31 August 2011.
13 Only for international applications filed on or after 24 September 2011.

Figure 8.9 *(continued)*

CHAPTER 9

PCT Strategies and Recommendations

1. First Filing Your Application

Filing a PCT application inherently includes the filing of a U.S. application. However, the main reason applicants file PCT applications is that they are considering filing in other countries. As a result, the filing of PCT application should be considered as a foreign filing. With that in mind, applicants must take into consideration the different laws of countries outside the United States and must be sure to comply with those laws at the time of filing the PCT application.

Additionally, as there are numerous ways to obtain the benefits of a PCT application, it is important to be aware of those ways and make use of them in a strategic manner that fits each particular application.

Each individual application should be analyzed, and the appropriate methodology used to file the application should be chosen based upon the technology involved, the importance of the invention, its potential use, and other considerations.

2. Different Laws in Different Countries

In order to be sure that your PCT application will be a viable application in foreign countries, care must be given to the various laws in foreign countries that may be different from those in the United States. In many cases the patent laws of many countries have been harmonized, but there are still differences, and these must be considered.

For many years, the United States remained the only country with a first-to-invent system, while the rest of the world adopted first-to-file systems. Having harmonized U.S. law so that the United States is now also a first-inventor-to-file country, U.S. applicants should give appropriate consideration to getting their applications filed as soon as possible and, hopefully, will no longer rely on the date of invention.

However, other differences still exist, for example, with respect to grace period. The United States still has a one-year grace period, as do some other countries of the world. Some countries have only a six-month grace period, while in most countries, including member countries of the European Patent Convention (and the EPO), no grace period exists at all. And in countries with a grace period, the right to invoke it may differ significantly. As a result, it is too late to consider the differences in national and regional patent laws only at the time of filing a PCT application. It is important that applicants contemplating international protection consider those differences even before they file their priority application and, in the case of the availability of a grace period, that they take precautions not to disclose their inventions prior to filing, especially if protection is desired in Europe.

3. Various Ways to Obtain the Filing of a PCT Application

In filing a PCT application, an applicant may typically claim the benefit of an earlier filed national application. When doing so in the United States, that earlier filed application can be a provisional application, a nonprovisional application, or another PCT application. There are also instances where an applicant may want to file a PCT application first without claiming the benefit of any previously filed national priority application. There are strategic reasons for choosing each of these routes. There may be greater up-front costs associated with one of these routes as compared to the others. Some routes may provide the ability to obtain earlier search results before making strategic and costly decisions. Some routes may provide the ability of obtaining earlier protection in the United States. Decisions should be made on a case-by-case basis as to which route is more appropriate for an application.

Once a particular strategic route is chosen, an applicant must be knowledgeable in how to properly claim the benefit of the priority application, assuming that there is at least one priority claim. Applicants must be aware that there are differences in filling out the request form that reflect the different types of priority applications upon which they may rely. Knowing how to properly claim the benefit of a priority application is an important part of the PCT application process.

3.1 Using a U.S. Provisional Application as Priority for the PCT Application

One strategy is to initially file a U.S. provisional application, and at the end of the year, file a PCT application claiming the benefit of the provisional application. With respect to the U.S. protection, two options are then available. One is simply to rely on the PCT for any U.S. filing and not file a nonprovisional application at the end of the year, thereby permitting the U.S. provisional application to lapse. The other possibility is to file both the PCT application and a U.S. nonprovisional application at the end of the one year.

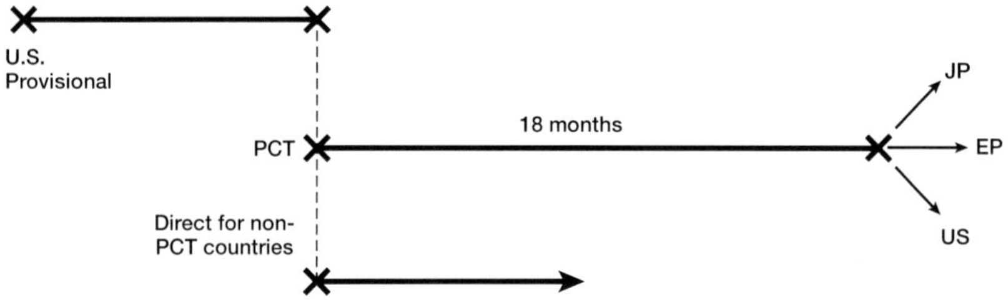

Figure 9.1
Using a Provisional Application as Priority for a PCT Application

Basing the PCT application on the U.S. provisional application has strategic benefits as well as drawbacks. To the extent that only the PCT application is filed and no nonprovisional application is filed in the United States, as shown above, initial up-front costs will be considerable lower since only the preparation of the U.S. provisional application is required. There will be the cost of preparing the PCT application, though that is delayed one year from the filing of the provisional application, so the initial entry into the system is at a lower cost. The applicant can then choose when to enter into the United States from the PCT application. Thus, the applicant gets the benefit of a search and written opinion before any large investment is required in either the United States or foreign countries.

In the United States, patents expire 20 years from the filing date of a nonprovisional application or the international filing date of a PCT application. The 20-year term does not start from the filing of a provisional application. Accordingly, in the example shown above, the applicant also gets the benefit of an extra year term of protection in the United States since the U.S. patent will expire at the same time as the foreign patents. Both for the United States and foreign countries, the 20-year term will begin with the filing of the PCT, which is the international filing date.

One of the drawbacks, however, is that a delay may occur in beginning the prosecution of the U.S. application since entry into the United States will not yet have taken place. However, to the extent the international search report (ISR) and written opinion (WO) indicate the possibility of getting patent protection, the applicant does not have to wait until the end of the 30 months to file a U.S. national phase application, but may, at any point earlier, request national entry. Furthermore, to the extent there is an indication of "allowable" claims in the PCT search report, the applicant can request expedited prosecution of that U.S. application under the PCT-PPH process.

Another strategy is to base the PCT application on a U.S. provisional, but the applicant also files a nonprovisional application in the United States simultaneously with the filing of the PCT application.

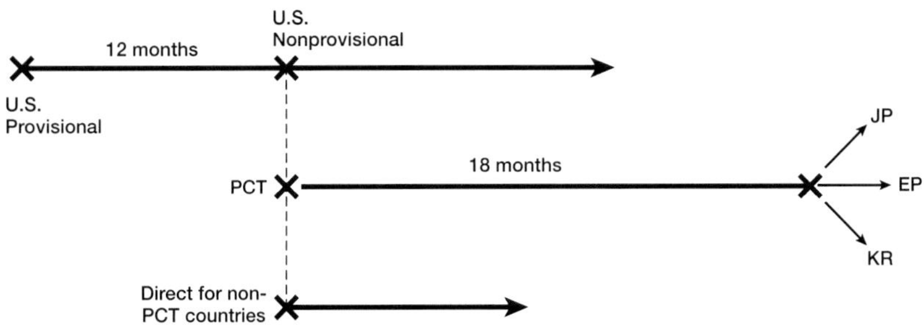

Figure 9.2
Using a Provisional Application as Priority, but Also Filing a Nonprovisional

This strategy likewise has benefits as well as drawbacks. Although there are limited front-end costs in that the applicant files only a provisional application, the cost of filing a U.S. nonprovisional application will come only 12 months later, before the international search report or written opinion has issued. However, if the international search reveals that claims are allowable and U.S. prosecution has not yet begun, the applicant can file a request for PCT-PPH to expedite processing of the U.S. nonprovisional application. Also, since the U.S. nonprovisional will ultimately receive a U.S. search, the applicant can choose an ISA other than the USPTO to carry out the international search in order to get the benefit of a foreign search report in addition to the U.S. search report. All of the applications will expire at the same time since the U.S. term will begin with the filing of the nonprovisional application, which will be the same day as the day on which the PCT application was filed.

Filing a PCT application in the United States using a provisional as priority falls under the provisions of § 119(e) of the Patent Act, 35 U.S.C. § 119(e), and will be considered a domestic priority filing. For all of the foreign countries, it will be considered a Paris Convention filing.

In filing the PCT application, the priority claim information must be inserted on the request form for both the United States and foreign countries. The priority claim should be filled out in Box VI, as indicated in Figure 9.3.

Box No. VI PRIORITY CLAIM AND DOCUMENT

The priority of the following earlier application(s) is hereby claimed:

Filing date of earlier application *(day/month/year)*	Number of earlier application	Where earlier application is:		
		national application: country or Member of WTO	regional application: regional Office	international application: receiving Office
item (1) 26 January 2005 (26.01.2005)	60/394,014	US		
item (2)				
item (3)				

☐ Further priority claims are indicated in the Supplemental Box.

Furnishing the priority document(s):

☐ The **receiving Office** is requested to prepare and transmit to the International Bureau a certified copy of the earlier application(s) *(only if the earlier application(s) was filed with the receiving Office which, for the purposes of this international application, is the receiving Office)* identified above as:

☐ all items ☒ item (1) ☐ item (2) ☐ item (3) ☐ other, see Supplemental Box

☐ The **International Bureau** is requested to obtain from a digital library a certified copy of the earlier application(s) identified above, using, where applicable, the access code(s) indicated below *(if the earlier application(s) is available to it from a digital library)*:

☐ item (1) access code ______ ☐ item (2) access code ______ ☐ item (3) access code ______ ☐ other, see Supplemental Box

Figure 9.3
Including Priority Claim Information in the PCT Request

3.2 Using a Nonprovisional U.S. Application as Priority for the PCT Application

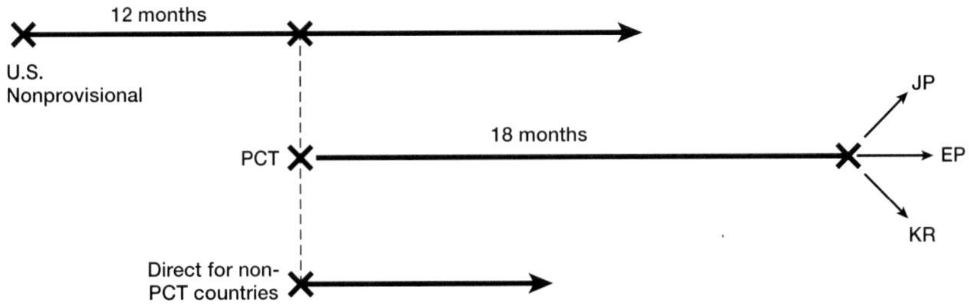

Figure 9.4
Using a Nonprovisional Application as Priority for a PCT Application

In this case, the initial filing is a U.S. nonprovisional application. Within one year, the PCT application is filed claiming the benefit of the U.S. nonprovisional application. From a strategic viewpoint, initially filing a U.S. nonprovisional and thereafter within one year filing the PCT application has both benefits and drawbacks. The filing of the PCT will result in an ISR which may occur before the U.S. application gets searched. That might give the applicant the benefit of the results of the search in order to modify the U.S. claims. To the extent this search has "allowed" claims, the applicant can also use that search to expedite prosecution under the PCT-PPH so long as prosecution has not begun on the nonprovisional application. It also permits selection of a different international searching authority than the USPTO, thereby getting the benefit of a foreign search and a U.S. search. Additionally, there is the possibility of using the international (PCT) application for filing a second U.S. application in addition to the one being used for priority.

However, the cost will be significant, because this strategy will involve both the preparation of a U.S. nonprovisional application as well as the cost of the PCT. Also, the termination of the U.S. patent will be one year earlier than the termination of all of the foreign patents since the U.S. term begins with the filing of the nonprovisional application, which is one year before the international filing date, while the term for foreign applications will begin with the filing of the PCT application.

It should be recognized that when using a nonprovisional U.S. application as priority for a PCT application, such PCT application is actually a "continuation" application under U.S. law, and the claim for the benefit of the earlier U.S. nonprovisional application is under 35 U.S.C. § 120. For foreign countries, however, the PCT filing is a Paris Convention filing.

With respect to claiming priority for foreign countries, it is necessary to include the priority information on the request form in Box VI, as indicated in Figure 9.5.

Box No. VI PRIORITY CLAIM AND DOCUMENT

The priority of the following earlier application(s) is hereby claimed:

Filing date of earlier application *(day/month/year)*	Number of earlier application	Where earlier application is: national application: country or Member of WTO	regional application: regional Office	international application: receiving Office
item (1) 26 January 2005 (26.01.2005)	11/349,014	US		
item (2)				
item (3)				

☐ Further priority claims are indicated in the Supplemental Box.

Furnishing the priority document(s):

☐ The **receiving Office** is requested to prepare and transmit to the International Bureau a certified copy of the earlier application(s) *(only if the earlier application(s) was filed with the receiving Office which, for the purposes of this international application, is the receiving Office)* identified above as:

☐ all items ☒ item (1) ☐ item (2) ☐ item (3) ☐ other, see Supplemental Box

☐ The **International Bureau** is requested to obtain from a digital library a certified copy of the earlier application(s) identified above, using, where applicable, the access code(s) indicated below *(if the earlier application(s) is available to it from a digital library)*:

☐ item (1) access code ______ ☐ item (2) access code ______ ☐ item (3) access code ______ ☐ other, see Supplemental Box

Figure 9.5
Including Priority Information in the PCT Request to Designate Priority in Foreign Countries

However, for the United States, since the PCT application is a continuation under 35 U.S.C. § 120, no specific designation is required at that time. The designation will be made upon entry into the national phase in the United States.

Nevertheless, in order to preserve the rights—should the applicant want to enter the United States at the end of the international phase and utilize a bypass route (as was previously discussed)—it is necessary that this intermediate application (i.e., the PCT application) must include continuation information.

For that reason, the applicant should include the priority information in Supplemental Box III, Item 3, where the PCT is to be treated as a continuation or a continuation-in-part of an earlier U.S. nonprovisional application.

Supplemental Box III, Item 3 on the request form should then indicate that the applicant is claiming the benefit of a U.S. application and should specify whether this is a continuation or a continuation-in-part application and should also include the application number and the filing date. Such indication is shown in Figure 9.6.

3. *If the applicant intends to make an indication of the wish that the international application be treated, in the United States of America, as a continuation or continuation-in-part of an earlier application: in such case, write "United States of America" or "US" and the indication "**continuation**" or "**continuation-in-part**" and the number and the filing date of the parent application (Rules 4.11(a)(ii) and 49bis.1(d)).*	U.S., continuation-in-part, 10/999,888, 4 November 2008 (04.11.2008)

Figure 9.6
Indicating Priority Information in the Supplemental Box When the PCT Application Will Be Treated as a Continuation or CIP of the Nonprovisional.

3.3 PCT First

Another strategic approach is to file the PCT application first without the benefit of any priority. In such cases, no priority is claimed on any request form in the PCT application.

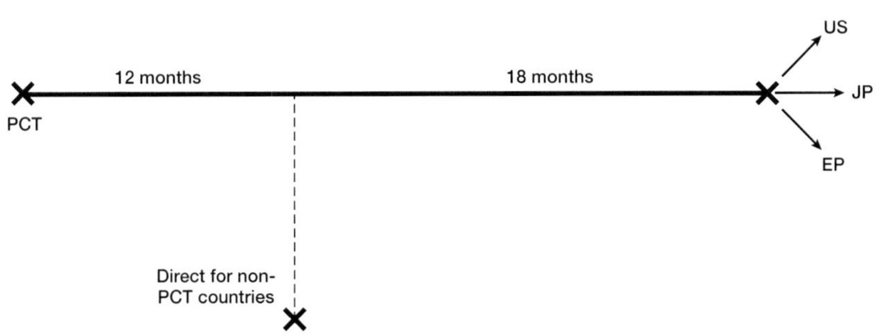

Figure 9.7
Filing the PCT Application First

One of the benefits of this route is that you will get an ISR before any real cost investment is required. This also gives you the longest time for amending the claims within the international phase. It is a relatively inexpensive way to get started since no national filing fees are incurred. It gives you the ability to file U.S. cases as well as any foreign cases, at any time during the international phase since there is no need to wait until the end of the 30 or 31 months before filing or entering into any national country.

Of course, the termination will be one year earlier than with other routes because for all countries the term will start at the international filing date and continue for 20 years thereafter.

In each of the above scenarios, it must be remembered that in addition to filing the U.S. application and the PCT application, for those countries that are not members of the PCT, direct Paris Convention filing must occur within one year of any initial filing to the extent that protection is desired in those non-PCT countries.

Helpful Recommendations

- For an individual inventor or a small start-up company, it is suggested to file a provisional application and one year later file a PCT. The year for the provisional application provides an opportunity to see if the applicants can raise funds, license the invention, pursue tests or evaluations, and so forth.
- For significant high-tech inventions, filing PCT first would be recommended. The extent of an early search and examination can be achieved before decisions are made concerning filing and the particular type of claims to be pursued. Immediately after the search and written opinion, national entries should be done without waiting the 30/31 months. Although there will be a year less in the duration of the patent, the loss of the year at the end of the term is not always significant for high-tech cases, which move rather fast because of evolving technology.
- For pharmaceutical inventions, which take time to develop and also need longer term, filing multiple provisionals as developments occurs would be recommended. At the end of the year from the first provisional, all of the material should then be collected and a PCT application filed.

4. Selecting Countries for National Filing

Filing of a PCT application preserves the right to file an application in all of the member states of the PCT. Currently, 146 countries are member states, and by filing a PCT application, you preserve the rights to file an actual national application in all of those 146 member states. However, at some point, whether at the end of the 30 or 31 months or earlier if the applicant so decides, the applicant will have to choose into which of those 146 countries a national phase application will be filed. Accordingly, at some point, the applicant must address the question: where do I want to foreign file?

4.1 Factors to Consider in Determining Where to Foreign File

Technology

The type of technology is often one factor in determining how many countries to choose for foreign filing. By way of example, an important high-tech invention may be filed in only four or five countries. On the other hand, a pharmaceutical or biotech invention may be filed in 120 countries or even more. In some industries, such as computer architecture, one patent in a major country such as in the United States may be sufficient. If the product cannot be sold in the United States, it probably isn't going to be made at all since major markets in the United States often dominate global sales of a product.

In addition to the type of technology, other considerations in determining where to foreign file include an appreciation of the significance of the invention and where it fits within the overall business of the applicant. Likewise, the type of applicant must also be taken into consideration. Universities have different considerations for filing abroad than do large corporations. Similarly, a single inventor may have a different set of interests than does a corporation.

Cost

A critical aspect to the decision of where to foreign file is the cost involved. Although it is desirable to have patent coverage in as many countries as possible, the cost may be prohibitive. Costs for filing in foreign countries far exceed the costs for U.S. filing. For example, it has been estimated that the cost of U.S. prosecution and maintenance (not including the actual preparation of the application) may be in the neighborhood of $25,000 for the life of the patent. In Europe, these costs—including translations, national fees, and maintenance fees—may be in the neighborhood of $150,000, and in Japan, those costs may be in the neighborhood of $75,000. Accordingly, a cost-benefit determination must be made for each invention as to where to foreign file.

It is therefore clear that in order to determine where to foreign file, the applicant, or sometimes the patent attorney, must evaluate the significance of the invention, evaluate the cost and benefit for each country involved, appreciate the technology, and understand the type of applicant involved as well as the available budget.

4.2 Evaluation of the Invention

A determination of where to foreign file must be made on a case-by-case basis. In doing so, the applicant or the patent attorney must provide an analysis of the invention. This will typically include answers to the questions: What problem is being solved? What were previously suggested solutions? How does the invention solve the problem? What are the distinguishing features of the invention?

Additionally, it is important to determine the type of invention that is being evaluated. For example, it must be determined whether this is considered a basic invention or an improvement invention over technology that has already been covered. The analysis should also determine whether this is just one of numerous alternate embodiments to an existing problem.

Furthermore, not only must the invention be analyzed, but also a determination must be made as to the relationship between the invention and the client's business. For example, is it directly or peripherally related, or possibly unrelated, to the applicant's core business? Sometimes the invention is more significant to a competitor's business than to the applicant's own business. Furthermore, you must take into account the amount of time and money that was invested into producing the invention. In some way, invention protection should be considered similar to insurance. If there is a very expensive piece of property, you don't mind paying a larger amount of insurance to protect the property. Likewise, if there was a great investment of time, effort, and money in producing an invention, greater consideration should be given to broader filing protection. Likewise, an analysis should be made as to the anticipated life span of the invention.

A determination should also be made as to the purpose of obtaining the patent. In some cases, the purpose is to protect the technology from being used by keeping competitors away. Sometimes the purpose is to improve the marketing position of the client. In other instances, the reason for patenting may be for defensive purposes in order to block others from obtaining patents in certain technological areas.

In some situations, as for example with universities, occasionally patent filing is for recognition in order to establish a reputation for the inventor, the laboratory, or the university itself.

Sometimes the filing may be used for business relationships such as joint ventures or licensing purposes. In other cases, there may be existing licenses, and the filing may be in support of those existing licenses.

No matter the reason, the applicant or the attorney must answer the question: if you don't get a patent in a particular country, so what? Often focusing on this question and seeking a convincing answer will help to determine the significance of the invention and its relationship to filing in a particular country.

4.3 Evaluating Countries for Filing

Not only is it significant to understand the invention and its relationship to the applicant, but in order to make a proper determination and selection of the countries in which to file, there must also be a good understanding of the country itself and especially of the patent laws in the country.

For example, countries must be analyzed based upon their population, market potential, and the potential growth of the country, and also on the client's activity within that country and whether it is an emerging or industrialized country.

For example, in connection with pharmaceuticals, a cost analysis should be made as to the potential sales of the particular pharmaceutical in that country, and a determination should be made about whether the potential sales in the country are sufficient to cover the cost of the patenting plus profit and investment.

In addition, a good understanding is needed of the patent laws and the patent protection offered by a country. One must review the standards of patentability in a country to determine the prospect of obtaining a patent. Likewise, the cost of patenting in that country and the type of patents available in the country all must be taken into consideration. Enforceability of the patent in the country is likewise significant.

In certain economically emerging countries, it may be politically important for a company to have some basic patents in order to show support of the local laws and the local economy. In some countries where enforcement is difficult, or sometimes almost impossible, the presence of the patents may still be important to demonstrate the presence of an applicant in a particular country.

4.4 Guidance Tools

Many corporations, especially larger corporations with different product lines, have come up with guidance tools for selecting countries for foreign filing. These may typically be in the nature of groupings of countries in order of importance. For example, for a particular product line, they may have Group A countries, which are the basic countries that are always selected. For more important inventions in that product line, they may have an additional set of B countries that can be added on. For the very significant inventions, they will have an additional set of C countries. When each invention is analyzed, it is rated for the A, B, or C level of technology, and the importance of the invention and the country filings is then determined based upon such guidance tools.

While such guidance tools are helpful, they must be updated on a regular basis since laws change, technologies changes, and markets change, and unless these tools are updated annually or biannually, they tend to deteriorate and are not very useful and may only result in a waste of funds. Furthermore, these tools must be tailored to the particular product line since different products may have different lists of countries.

4.5 Suggestions on Prioritizing Countries

Based upon experience and analysis, the following suggestions may be useful, although by no means is this to be considered an exclusive list. Though these are general guidelines, it should be appreciated that numerous situations could cause variations from these recommendations.

The initial filing recommendation is always to protect local manufacture. To the extent a company has investment in property, plants, and personnel in a particular country, there should be great consideration for putting patent protection in that country. For many products, employees tend to leave a company and may very well move across the street to start their own competitive business. To the extent patents are in place, this provides "insurance" against loss of technology and potential employees becoming competitors, and it protects the investment in both plant, personnel, and property in a particular country.

To the extent a particular company is aware of identified competitors existing in specific foreign countries, patents should be placed in those competitors' countries. For example, if a major competitor is in Denmark, a number of basic patents should be placed in that country. It is often better to enforce patents against infringers in one country where they are manufacturing a product rather than to have to enforce it in multiple jurisdictions where the competitor may be selling in the market place.

If identification of a particular competitor's home country is difficult or if there are too many countries to cover, then placing patents in the major markets is significant. For example, Germany is considered the linchpin of Europe. Having a patent in Germany is significant, since it is often difficult to sell products in Europe if they are not going to be sold in Germany. Therefore, it might be easiest to stop a competitor in a major market country like Germany, which dominates a broader region economically.

Likewise, in South America, Brazil is considered a major hub, and to the extent you can stop sales in Brazil, you can probably do so for most of South America.

The last recommendation is to cover export sales. Although a company may be selling exports to a particular area, those exports change frequently, and next year they may be selling somewhere else. Because a patent has a 20-year lifetime, it is often impossible to predict where these export sales may be in the future, and only if there is adequate funding for a patent filing should you consider covering export sales.

Again, it should be appreciated that these recommendations are broad and can be varied and changed based upon the particular product and particular unique situations that may exist.

Helpful Recommendations for Foreign Filings

• Type of Invention/Product	• Recommendation
◦ System, assembly, complex machine	◦ Limited filing in industrialized countries
◦ Components and materials	◦ Broad filing in all major countries
◦ High-technology product	◦ Limited filing in industrialized countries and sourcing countries
◦ Worldwide consumer product	◦ Broad filing in major market countries
◦ Industrial product	◦ Limited filing in industrialized countries
◦ Pharmaceutical/chemical products	◦ Broad filing, especially where product is easily producible
◦ Labor-intensive product	◦ Low-cost manufacturing countries

5. Drafting a Global Patent Application

International patent protection is becoming more important to U.S. applicants. However, the tremendous increase in international patent costs places severe restrictions on the ability to obtain adequate patent coverage around the world. A major cost in obtaining foreign patent protection is the expense of filing and prosecution of the patent application. By properly preparing the initial U.S. application as a "global" application, considerable cost savings can likely be achieved in a foreign filing program.

5.1 The Need for a "Global" Patent Application

U.S. patent applications tend to be the lengthiest applications of those in any country in the world. One reason for this is the desire to be complete in order to fulfill all of the requirements of 35 U.S.C. § 112 concerning the written description, enablement, and best mode clauses. As a result, many features are inserted into the application; the description is repeated numerous times, frequently with different wording for each element, and many parts of the peripheral environment of the invention are described in great detail.

The applications prepared in the United States also tend to include many independent claims because of the literal interpretation of claims in the United States and the need to infringe every element of the claim, as well as the cases of *Festo Corp. v. Shoketsu Kinzoku Kogyo Kabushiki Co., Ltd.*,[1] *In re Bilski*,[2] and others. Accordingly, the same invention may be claimed with numerous claims, each taking a different approach in the hopes of obtaining adequate protection and stopping competitors from producing the invention with minor variations.

A number of corporations tend to "farm out" the preparation of applications, and some attorneys may believe that the greater the length of the application, the more significant the application will be to the corporation. Similarly, in preparing an application directly for a private client, many attorneys believe that the greater the length of the application, the more impressive it will be to the client and the greater the billing that can be passed on to the client.

While the length of the U.S. patent application will not dramatically affect the cost of U.S. filing and prosecution, such lengthy text can be a serious cost factor in an effective foreign patent filing strategy. For example, currently, the translation and typing costs for filing an application in Japan is about $300 per page; in Denmark it is about $225

1. 535 U.S. 722 (2002).
2. 545 F.3d 943, 88 U.S.P.Q.2d 1385 (Fed. Cir. 2008).

per page; and in Germany it is about $200 per page. The excess claim fee over 15 claims is about $300 per claim in Europe, $150 per claim in Denmark, and $50 per claim in Japan after the first claim.

Reducing the text of a patent specification by five pages and reducing the number of claims from 20 to 10 with filing in five translation countries can result in an approximate savings of at least $15,000 on a single filing. Further savings will occur when requesting examination of the application and later on, upon issuance, when there is a charge for printing and claim fee. If a company files 50 cases a year, this can amount to approximately a million dollars of savings annually. Based upon the size of the application, these savings can be at least 25 percent of foreign filing costs.

Many attorneys try to reduce such excessive foreign filing costs by revising the U.S. text shortly before foreign filing. Though this can lessen the costs somewhat, the revisions normally take place toward the end of the priority year, at which time the attorney may have forgotten much of the application and/or the attorney who originally wrote the text may no longer be available for the revisions. Therefore, additional time and expense is required for these revisions when they are done subsequent to the original filing. Also, once the application has been filed in the United States, attorneys are often hesitant to eliminate items from the text that was originally filed.

Furthermore, many national offices require translation of the priority document in addition to a translation of the filed application. Therefore, the revisions may save some of the cost, but the translation of the lengthy priority document may still be necessary. For example, when filing under the PCT, the countries in which the application is being perfected require a translation of the full original text, not the revised version that may be filed when entering the national phase.

Other problems resulting from later revisions may relate to the question of getting the benefit of the priority date if certain aspects of the invention have been eliminated from the text during the revision. Furthermore, under the Patent Law Treaty (PLT), "reference filing," which will permit a foreign filing based upon the date of the priority document, is availability, and this will require the translation of the full original text.

In addition to the costs generated by a lengthy text and a large number of claims, the particular type of language used, the style, and the approach taken in a typical U.S. patent application may often cause difficulties in prosecuting the corresponding application in foreign countries. The U.S. patent application probably could be easily modified so that it will still satisfy U.S. law while at the same time providing reduced cost, easier prosecution, and a better application for foreign filing. It is therefore recommended that at the time a U.S. application is written, it should be written as a "global" application, which is suitable both for U.S. and foreign filing.

5.2 General Recommendations for a "Global" Application

Describe the Invention Only Once

Typically, a U.S. patent application describes the invention at least four, and possibly, even five times. For example, in writing the Summary of the Invention, the attorney will generally go into detail describing the invention with all its embodiments. This is the first time the invention is described. Thereafter, in the Brief Description of the Drawings, rather than being "brief," the description of each figure frequently goes into detail explaining how that figure participates in the overall invention and what that particular figure shows in connection with the invention. This effectively provides a second description of the invention.

In the body of the specification referred to as the Description of the Invention, the attorney will describe the invention at least once more in connection with a general explanation and, perhaps, a further time when describing a particular best mode. If those three or four descriptions are not enough, it is often found that at the end of the specification, the attorney summarizes the invention and provides yet another description of the entire invention.

While such multiple descriptions may make interesting reading and a thorough application and may impress the client, it provides for a substantial translation cost when foreign filing. One wonders whether the U.S. examiner bothers to re-read the description of the invention so many times in the same application. Furthermore, often, each description varies from the others causing inconsistencies and possible enforcement problems.

Accordingly, in writing the U.S. application, it is best to describe the invention only once—specifically, in the section called Description of the Preferred Embodiment—and, if possible, to describe it that one time in connection with the best mode.

Limit Number of Pages in the Specification

It is not often easy to be concise. However, if corporations, senior attorneys, and those handling the supervision of the work insist on brevity, attorneys will comply. It may in fact require more time and effort to be concise, but doing so will improve the quality of the application and reduce foreign costs.

Use Language that Will Address a "Global" Audience

Many words in English are ambiguous in meaning and may lead to an erroneous translation. For instance, with the term "the current system," it is unknown whether this is a reference to an electrical circuit or to the present time. Likewise, it may be unclear whether a reference to something contained in a "bracket" refers to a parenthesis or a clamp.

Indefinite language such as "low" and "effective amount" presents problems in foreign countries. In addition, many foreign countries may raise specific objections to the use of such vague terms. Likewise, generalizations such as "any," "all," and other similar terms should be avoided.

Reference to Pending Applications

Cross-referencing and incorporation by reference to pending U.S. applications should be avoided. Foreign countries do not permit incorporation by reference. Furthermore, a pending U.S. application cannot form part of the prior art in foreign countries. Likewise, such a pending U.S. application cannot be used for an enabling disclosure. If the material of the pending application is required for an understanding of the invention, it must be recited in detail. If it is not needed, reference to such pending application should be avoided.

5.3 Writing a "Global" Patent Application

Abstract of the Invention

At the time of preparing the abstract of the invention, reference numerals should already be included in the abstract. These reference numerals can be left in for the U.S. application because the abstract does not form part of the invention and therefore does not provide any limitation. However, at the option of the attorney, such reference numerals may be deleted for the U.S. filing. Nevertheless, they should already be included for later foreign filing.

If an application is sent for foreign filing without reference numerals in the abstract, a foreign agent may have to spend time reading the entire specification in order to be able to insert those reference numerals. Likewise, reference numerals are required for a PCT filing.

The length of the abstract should also be kept to a minimum. Many foreign countries have length limitations for the abstract, and there is little to be gained by making the abstract excessively long.

Background of the Invention

First, one should remember that it is not a requirement to teach the technology. The patent application is addressed to one skilled in the art. Even the examiner is an individual who is skilled in the art. Therefore, in the background of the invention, it is not necessary to go through many references and describe them and distinguish over each of them. In fact, doing so might actually "misdescribe" one of these references, or might not go into enough detail of every aspect of the cited reference, and this may actually cause trouble during litigation in the United States.

Accordingly, only one prior art reference should be mentioned, if any, when writing the background of the invention. If one is included, it should be the closest reference. If it is desired to mention other references, these should be put into an Information Disclosure Statement (IDS) and submitted separately with the application when filing in the USPTO. This is important since foreign countries generally ask only for the closest reference. Furthermore, if prior art is described in the background of the invention, a U.S. examiner is not required to cite those references. The references should be submitted separately in the IDS and not placed as part of the specification where it will require translation.

When describing the closest prior art, it is not necessary to redescribe the entire prior art invention. It is only necessary to briefly state what the invention was about, point out a problem or deficiency with the referenced invention, and use that as a basis to describe the solution provided by the new invention. It is recommended to include a copy of this closest reference for the examiner in each country in which the application is being filed and let the examiner read the reference to learn about it, rather than include a description of that prior art, which will also require a translation.

In distinguishing over references, it should be remembered that most foreign countries do not have a grace period. Therefore, you must also take into consideration those references that have been published within one year of the U.S. filing date.

A preferable way of presenting the invention is to use the "problem/solution approach." The prior art should be described with its deficiencies, and then the approach taken by the new invention to solve those deficiencies should be presented. At least one definite advantage of the present invention should be included since many foreign countries require it.

Summary of the Invention

The Summary of the Invention should be just that, a summary. Basically, you should paraphrase Claim 1 or your broadest claim of the invention since some countries require a "consistory statement" of the invention. To the extent that you may have different aspects of the invention, you may include a short statement that other embodiments of the invention are feasible and then simply list them.

Avoid reciting excessive objectives for the invention; avoid puffing; avoid recitation of numerous benefits. U.S. attorneys have a tendency to go on and on with numerous objectives and advantages. Not only is it costly for translation, but also many foreign countries will require that every issued claim be able to provide support for every single one of the objects and advantages recited in the specification. This could be devastating to the invention.

Drawings

The Brief Description of Drawings should be exactly that—namely, just the listing of the figure numbers and a one-line explanation of what each figure represents.

It is important to use A-4 sized paper for the drawings. These are accepted in the USPTO and are required by almost all foreign countries. Using A-4 paper will prevent the costly problem of re-drawing, reducing, recopying, modifying the drawings, and so on. It is a good idea to use the PCT guidelines for such things as drawing margins, heading room, and numeral sizes when initially preparing a set of "global" drawings. This will save cost and time later on when it is necessary to foreign file the application. Use computerized drawings to facilitate drawing changes. Also, if there are block diagrams, have one set with blank boxes without any words or text and use these for foreign filing to avoid translation in the drawings.

In preparing the drawings, focus on the specific invention. Limit drawings of the peripheral environment as much as possible. If the invention relates to a vehicle door handle, it is not necessary to show the vehicle, or even the entire door. Furthermore, even if it is important to show the door, it should be shown only generally, without any major description or detail.

Avoid using descriptive words in the drawings wherever possible since these will require translation when foreign filing, which will add to the cost of the filing.

Description of the Invention

As previously explained, you should describe the invention only once. Such description should come in the section "Description of the Invention" and, preferably, in connection with a description of the best mode. However, each time a particular item or material is mentioned, alternatives can be given. For example, if you are dealing with a jewelry item and are describing a gold chain, at the time you mention that it is made out of gold you can also indicate that other precious metals such as silver, platinum, and rhodium could be utilized. The description should be done briefly and succinctly and should focus in on the specific invention. The peripheral environment needs only a brief statement of description without much detail.

In describing elements, you should be consistent. Specifically, it is helpful to keep a parts list. As you go through each part, you should list it on a sheet of paper along with the numeric reference associated with it. That way, you can be consistent when referring to the same part with the same term throughout. However, you need not file the parts list itself.

Certain limiting language should be avoided unless such limitations are actually intended. Use of the words "must," "requires," "necessary," and so forth may force you to actually limit your claims to those amounts and values. Thus, unless a limitation is intended, such words should be eliminated.

Values should already be stated in SI units. If you must use U.S. units, include both U.S. and SI units, for example, 2.2 lbs. (1 kg.).

Use of Examples

The use of examples is extremely important for both U.S. and foreign filings. Nevertheless, the number of example and the extent to which they are included may be limited in order to reduce costs. Though it is always necessary to give more than one example, the type of examples that are used should be generic. For example, use a single example to describe each of a group of species.

In addition to examples, use generic language where appropriate. Also, use summary lists wherever possible without repeating details of similar examples.

When a particular range is recited, the examples should be adequately dispersed to cover the scope of the broadest claimed range. An example should be given at the low end, the high end, and the midrange. Furthermore, where values are critical, you must give examples out of the range to show lack of inventive benefits for those values. These will serve as a control to prove the inventiveness of your critical range.

In foreign countries—especially Europe, China, and Japan—full support is needed for any claimed range. Accordingly, if you indicate a range as 1 to 10, you will only be able to claim that full range in many foreign countries. In the United States, you may be able to reduce the claimed range and claim a portion of it in order to avoid prior art; foreign countries, however, may not permit claiming a sub-range unless there is full support for it in the specification. Therefore, in addition to claiming a full range of values, you may want to claim sub-ranges for potential support in later claiming.

Prophetic examples are also useful. However, although those examples may not have actually been carried out, they should be based upon adequate factual support and evidence so that if challenged, there is sufficient technical support for predicting the results from the examples.

When "means" are being recited, you should provide examples of the various types of "means" that can be used as well as an extensive list of possible alternatives that would satisfy the desired function.

Claims

Claims are the most difficult to globalize because of the differences in claim requirements and claim interpretation around the world. The basic rule is that you should limit the number of claims. Even if your U.S. application has many claims, limit your foreign filing to only 10 to 15 claims. A PCT application also should be limited to 10 to 15 claims because ultimately, those claims are the ones that will be used for translation purposes in perfecting the PCT application nationally. A good approach is to write your U.S. claims so that the first 10 to 15 claims can be used for foreign filing.

Remember that in most foreign countries there is a Unity of Invention rule rather than Restriction Practice, as in the U.S. Accordingly, you can include more than one type of claim in the same application—for example, method, apparatus and use claims—so long as they refer to a single inventive concept. In Europe, only one independent claim can be used for each claim type—specifically, only one independent method claim, one independent apparatus claim, one independent use claim, and so on.

Europeans like functional language, as do the Japanese. Though they like using "means," it is recommended that you write the claims with other functional language and do not necessarily include the "means" clause because it is often misunderstood in other foreign countries. South American countries specifically do not like the use of the term "means."

In connection with dependent claims, most foreign countries limit dependent claims to novel features. Thus, do not include dependent claims for common knowledge features. Also, in foreign countries, use multiple dependencies wherever possible to reduce the number of claims.

All of the rest of the U.S. claims not used for foreign countries can be added at the end of the specification itself as embodiments of the invention.

Since many foreign countries ask for reference numerals in the claims, at the time the original "global" claims are being prepared, it would be helpful to include reference numerals in those claims. Those reference numerals can be deleted for filing in the United States but will already be available for foreign filing. This will save considerable time for otherwise having to revise the claims when foreign filing.

Conclusion

For many years, U.S. patent attorneys have been writing very lengthy and detailed U.S. patent applications. So long as cost was never a factor, there was no limitation on space. However, with tremendous increases in U.S. and foreign filing costs and expensive translation costs, U.S. attorneys should restrain themselves and write more concise, more specific, and less wordy applications for both U.S. and foreign filing. Preferably, the initial preparation of the application should be done in a manner so that the application can be utilized for U.S. and foreign filing. Attempts should be made to initially prepare such a "global patent application" whenever possible.

- Helpful Recommendations for a Global Application
  Describe the invention only once
- Don't teach the technology
- Avoid objects, puffing, and numerous benefits
  - Use nonconfusing words and sentences
  - Use PCT format

6. Routes to Faster Acceptance: The Patent Prosecution Highway

There are various techniques available to accelerate the prosecution process of a patent application. Through a procedure referred to as the Patent Prosecution Highway (PPH), an applicant can make use of the ISR and WO of a PCT application to expedite prosecution of related national applications.

Other accelerated procedures are also available and will be discussed below.

6.1 Purpose of PPH

The concept of the Patent Prosecution Highway is to permit examiners in one patent office to make use of the work previously done during a search and examination in another patent office. Specifically, when claims are determined to be allowable in one office, a corresponding application with corresponding claims in another office would be fast-tracked for examination. The concept is that the later office can utilize the earlier search and examination results from another officer, thereby avoiding duplication of work and expediting the examination process in the later office.

6.2 Three Generations of PPH

Although the PPH is relatively recent, three "generations" or types of PPH have already been developed. The first generation of PPH is referred to as the Paris Route PPH. It makes use of the results of only a national country's examination of a national application. It requires that a determination for at least one allowable claim be made in the Office of First Filing (OFF), and then a corresponding application with corresponding claims in an Office of Second Filing (OSF) would be fast-tracked for examination.

The second generation is referred to as the PCT-PPH. In this case, the work product is that of an international authority—either the International Search Authority or International Preliminary Examination

Authority, or the final IPRP. Use is made of the ISR and WO of a particular international authority. Although there are no allowable claims in the PCT, so long as at least one claim is determined to have novelty, inventive step, and industrial applicability, those results can be used in other countries to expedite the examination process during the national phase of a corresponding application.

The third generation, known as PPH Mottainai, improves upon the Paris Route PPH. The term Mottainai refers to a Japanese term meaning "a sense of regret concerning waste when the intrinsic value of an object or resource is not properly utilized." In this case, very often a search and examination occurs, but not necessarily from the Office of First Filing. Typically, Europeans may initially file a priority application in one of the national countries, such as Austria. They use that for a subsequent EPO filing. They may, in fact, drop their national Austrian priority filing. The search and examination work is done by the EPO. However, the EPO is not the Office of First Filing. Under the original Paris PPH system, the use of the search and examination of the EPO would not be available in any subsequent office since EPO was not the Office of First Filing.

This was felt to be a resource not properly utilized. Therefore, instead of an Office of First Filing, the definition is modified in the Mottainai PPH to refer to an Office of Earlier Examination (OEE), and so long as that OEE finds at least one allowable claim, a request can be made in an Office of Later Examination (OLE) to expedite the examination process based upon the results of the OEE.

The three systems—the Paris PPH, the PCT-PPH, and the Mottainai PPH—can be demonstrated in Figure 9.8, 9.9, and 9.10.

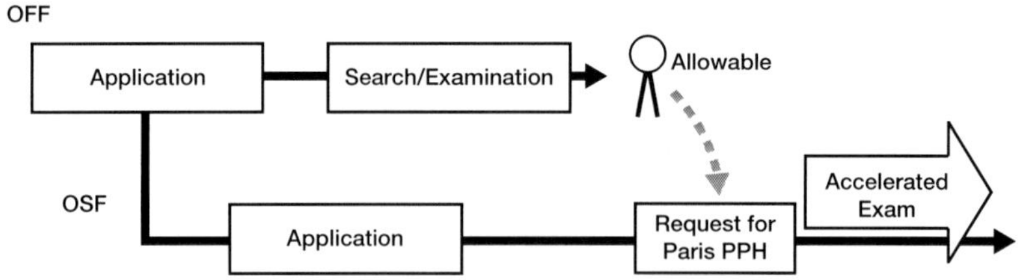

Figure 9.8
Paris PPH

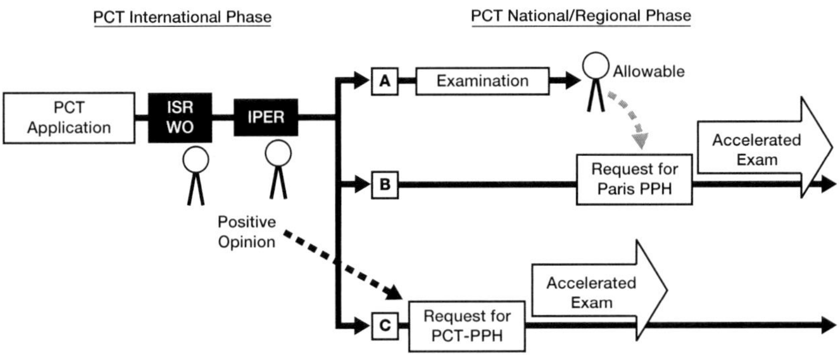

Figure 9.9
PCT-PPH

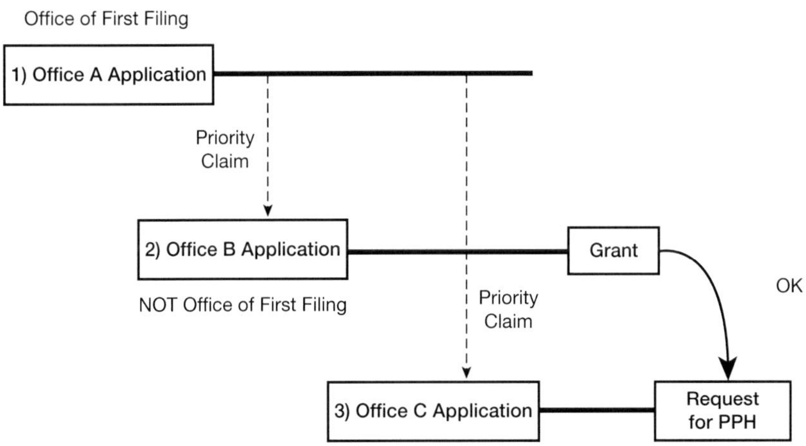

Figure 9.10
Mottainai PPH System

It should be noted that in the Mottainai PPH, the actual Office of First Filing does not have to be one of the Mottainai PPH member countries. This process can be used so long as the Office of Earlier Examination and the Office of Later Examination are both parties to a Mottainai PPH agreement.

6.3 Requirements for Use of the PPH

In order to make use of the PPH, there must be a direct relationship between the application having claims allowable and the application on which you are filing the request for the PPH. However, such correspondence can be any relationship provided that there is a common priority traceable through the applications.

In order to make use of the PPH, a petition for expedited examination under the particular PPH type must be filed in the country where you are seeking expedited examination. Furthermore, a correspondence chart must be submitted showing the correspondence between claims that have been allowed in the earlier search and examination and the claims that are being submitted with the request for PPH. The prior art must be submitted and, for USPTO, translations of foreign language references are required as well. Likewise, copies of all of the prosecution history (for PPH, it is the international prosecution papers) must be submitted, and for USPTO, translations must also be submitted.

The only claims that are eligible for PPH examination are those that have been found allowable. Minor changes can be made to accommodate for stylistic or formal requirements from country to country. However, changing from one category to another is not permissible. Thus, for example, if you have method claims allowed, you cannot file a petition for PPH for apparatus claims. A key requirement is that substantive examination has not begun in the office in which you are requesting the PPH.

It should also be noted that although a PPH request can be filed in connection with those claims that have been allowed, it is possible to file a divisional or, in the case of the USPTO, a continuation application to try to get broader claims or to try for claims that were not allowed in the previous search and examination. A separate request for PPH must be filed in the divisional and/or continuation since the original PPH request only applies to the specific application in which the request has been filed.

6.4 Country Participation

As of January 2013, the countries listed in Figure 9.11 have one or more PPH agreements with the USPTO:

PPH Agreements with USPTO		
Paris PPH	**PCT-PPH**	**Mottainai PPH**
Australia	Australia	Australia
Austria	Austria	Canada
Canada	China	Finland
China	European Patent Office	Japan
Colombia	Finland	Russia
Czech Republic	Japan	Spain
Denmark	Korea	United Kingdom
European Patent Office	Nordic Patent Institute	
Finland	Russia	
Germany	Spain	
Hungary	Sweden	
Iceland	United States	
Israel		
Japan		
Korea		
Mexico		
Norway		
Russia		
Singapore		
Spain		
Taiwan		
United Kingdom		

Figure 9.11
Countries with One or More PPH Agreements with the USPTO

6.5 Statistics

Use of the PPH continues to increase greatly with both the PPH Paris (with improved Mottainai capabilities) and the PCT-PPH. Though the PPH program only guarantees expedited prosecution of the application in the national patent office, statistics have shown that the allowance rate of applications using the PPH is substantially higher than the allowance rate of non-PPH applications. Of course, to some extent, this is to be expected since the claims that are being used for the PPH are those that have been allowed in other countries. Such allowance of claims means that either those claims inherently were limited over the prior art and/or were amended to provide patentable limitations over the prior art. It is therefore to be expected that there would be a higher allowance rate.

Thus far, some of the statistics show that the allowance rate for Paris PPH cases is almost twice as high as for non-PPH applications. PCT-PPH applications have shown an even higher allowance rate. Currently, the non-PPH allowance rate in the USPTO is just under 50 percent.

Likewise, the number of actions per disposal is reduced. For non-PPH cases, there is an average of about 2.5 office actions per disposal. For Paris-PPH, this is down to about 2.3, and for PCT-PPH, it is about 1.6.

The average time to a first office action from the filing of an application for non-PPH cases is approximately 27 months. For PPH cases, the time from the grant of the Paris-PPH request to the first office action is approximately 6 months, and for PCT-PPH cases, the first office action from grant of the PPH request is approximately 3 months.

It should also be appreciated that as a result of a reduced number of office actions per disposal, there is a considerable cost savings. If an average amount of money is assigned to an office action response, by reducing the office action responses by approximately 60 percent, as is done by PPH, the cost for the prosecution phase of a PPH case can probably result in a 60 percent reduction. This includes attorneys' fees, government fees, and related expenses as well as the time and effort associated with it.

6.6 Strategic Use of PCT-PPH

Although there are many scenarios in which PCT-PPH can be used to expedite prosecution in national phase countries, only some examples will be provided.

Example 1

An applicant initially files a U.S. application (provisional or nonprovisional) and a year later files a PCT application. When the applicant receives the ISR and WO, if allowable claims are found, they can be retained in the applicant's files. When the applicant enters the national phase, the applicant can file a PCT-PPH request and obtain expedited examination in PCT-PPH partner countries. This is in Figure 9.12.

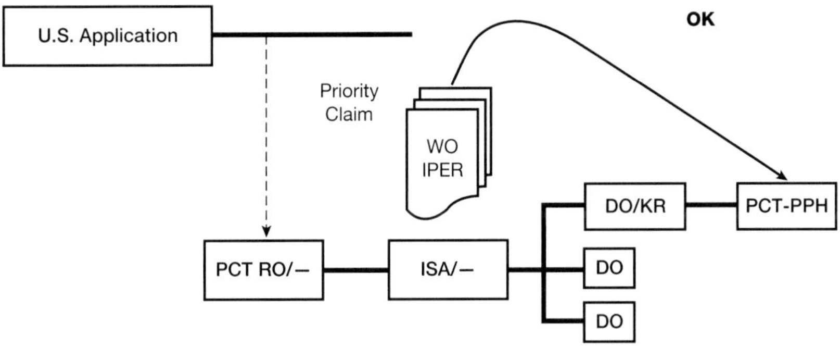

The applicant can use the PCT search results for PPH treatment in other PPH-PCT partner countries

Figure 9.12
Using PCT-PPH for Foreign Applications

Example 2

In addition to using the favorable PCT-PPH search and written opinion results for other countries, the results can actually be used in any domestic U.S. priority application. For example, an applicant files a U.S. application (provisional or nonprovisional) and a year later files a PCT application. Assume the applicant continues with the U.S. nonprovisional application simultaneously with the PCT application. Typically, the applicant will get the ISR and WO before the U.S. application will be examined. Should there be allowable claims in the WO, the applicant can make use of those claims in the corresponding nonprovisional priority application, which is pending in the USPTO. Conforming the claims to those allowed in the WO, the applicant can file a PCT-PPH petition in the U.S. patent office. This will expedite prosecution in the corresponding U.S. application, as shown in Figure 9.13.

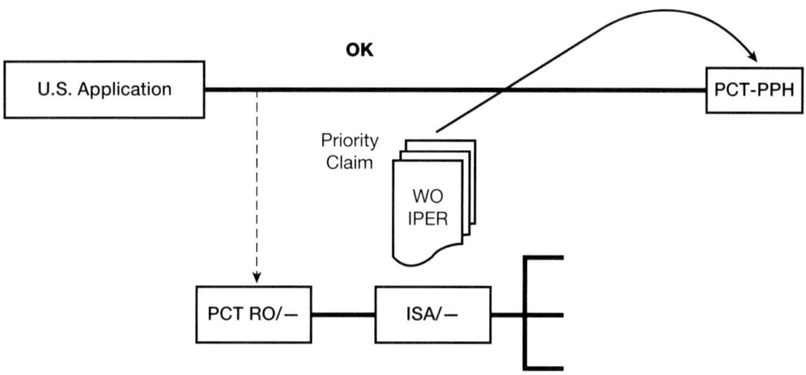

Can use PCT Results in domestic U.S. Priority Application

Figure 9.13
Using PCT-PPH Also for a Domestic Application

Example 3

It is also possible to use both the PCT-PPH and the Paris-PPH together. In the example below, after getting the ISR, the applicant files a PCT-PPH request for expedited examination in the corresponding U.S. application. Of course, the applicant can also use the PCT-PPH request for other national phase countries that are members of the PCT-PPH. However, once a U.S. priority application is allowed, the allowance can then be used in a Paris PPH (or Mottainai PPH) in other countries that are not members of the PCT-PPH. This is shown in the example in Figure 9.14.

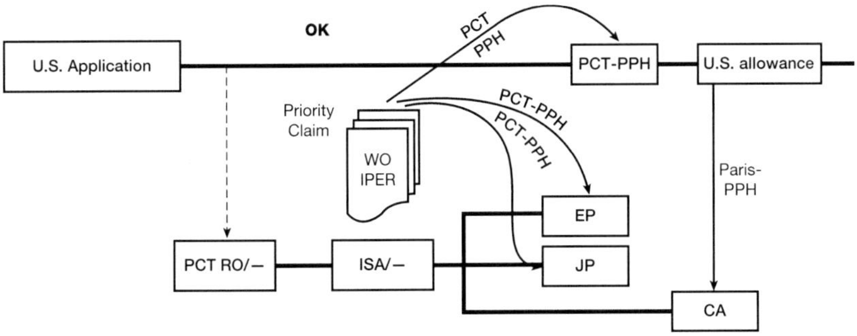

Figure 9.14
Combining PCT-PPH and Paris (or Mottainai) PPH

6.7 Benefits of PPH

By using the PPH, and especially the PCT-PPH, it is possible to reduce duplication of effort because patent offices can use the work product done by another patent office. So long as the applicant is satisfied with the claim coverage, it will probably increase the grant rate. It definitely reduces pendency and legal uncertainty and brings about compact prosecution with reduction of costs.

The availability of the Paris-PPH and PCT-PPH generally provides increased patent strategy flexibility to the client. It provides the ability to get patents faster when speed and flexibility are important.

It should be remembered, however, that not every client in every technology area or for every application is always interested in getting a faster patent. However, to the extent that it is important to get a patent allowed, the PCT-PPH route has proved to be extremely successful.

6.8 Cautions with PPH

It is important to remember that the results of the Office of First Filing or Earlier Examination are not binding on the subsequent patent office. Examiners are still obligated to conduct their own search and examination and often do find additional references. It must also be remembered that the claim correspondence must be maintained. Although additional limitations can be added—and in the United States these are added in sub-claims—you cannot change the scope of the examination from one subject matter to another during the course of a PPH prosecution.

In using PCT-PPH, note that in addition to the claim correspondence, it is important to also address all of the observations identified in Box VIII in the written opinion. These are typically related to matters covered by 35 U.S.C. § 112. However, all of those items must be addressed as part of the petition for PPH; otherwise, the petition will be rejected. Also note that each country may determine unity of invention differently. Even with respect to PCT application national phase where the U.S. patent office presumably applies the PCT unity of invention standard, experience has shown that foreign patent offices determine unity differently than U.S. examiners. Therefore, applying a series of claims that have been allowed in an ISR and WO with a claim correspondence chart entering into the national phase in the United States, the U.S. examiner may request further divisionals. It will be of little assistance to allege that the ISR did not require dividing the claims. The U.S. Patent Office examiner will make his or her own independent determination and will force divisionals should he or she feel it is necessary, despite what was determined on the international phase.

7. Other Accelerating Programs

In entering into the U.S. national phase from a PCT application, if you have used the United States as the International Searching Authority or the International Preliminary Examination Authority, and if you do get allowed claims from the U.S. Search or Examination Authority, 37 C.F.R. § 1.496 permits your case to be "advanced out of turn for examination." Again, this will only apply to claims that have been allowed.

While this is a form of expedited examination, it is not as beneficial as the PCT-PPH program. First, Rule 496 works only for a national stage file, while PCT-PPH works for any corresponding case.

Additionally, Rule 496 only applies to the first office action. PCT-PPH applies throughout the prosecution history of the case, and even on appeal, it will obtain an expedited basis.

8. Selecting and Working with Foreign Counsel

Every patent office in the world requires the use of a patent practitioner who is registered to practice before that office. Some also require a local mailing address. As a result, in entering the national phase of your PCT application, you will have to work with a local counsel to handle the patent application before the local patent office.

In connection with the PCT international application, you do not have to select the foreign counsel you will be dealing with until you are about to enter into the national or regional phase. However, if you are planning to enter into a particular national phase, you would be well advised to look into selecting foreign counsel a few months before the end of the 30- or 31-month deadline.

8.1 Types of Foreign Counsel

In the United States, patent attorneys are lawyers who, in addition to passing the legal bar, have also passed the patent bar, which requires a technical background. However, in foreign countries, generally the foreign counsel will be the equivalent of a patent agent in the United States; in other words, they will have a technical background, but they will not possess a law degree. In just about all foreign countries, there is no need for a patent practitioner to be a lawyer. In fact, some foreign countries have distinct and separate titles for their patent practitioners as compared to lawyers. For example, in Japan, the patent attorney is a "bengoshi," while a regular lawyer is a "benrishi." In Germany, a patent attorney is a "patentanwalt," while a lawyer is a "rechtsanwalt." In England, the patent practitioner is referred to as a patent attorney, while the lawyer is either a solicitor or a barrister. In some cases, a particular individual may have been suitably trained and have both titles, but this is rare. Additionally, in many countries, not everyone who handles patent matters will even be a patent attorney. In Japan, the patent attorney exam is extremely difficult, and only a small percentage pass the exam and become a patent attorney. Therefore, many Japanese firms have a number of engineers but only a few patent attorneys. However, it is the patent attorneys who ultimately sign off on every document to be filed in the Japanese patent office.

The particular training and requirements to become a patent practitioner in foreign countries also varies. In countries such as Japan, UK, EPO, and others, a practitioner must pass a difficult exam before he or she can become a patent attorney. In other countries, there may not be an exam, but there is a required apprenticeship for a number of years before one can practice. Yet other countries require little if any exam or apprenticeship, and practice is based only upon experience.

The European Patent Office provides a training program as well as an exam. Individuals from any of the member countries can enroll in the training program and take the exam, and regardless of which country they are from, they have equal rights in practicing before the EPO once they pass the exam.

8.2 Finding a Foreign Counsel

Often, the best way to select a foreign counsel is by means of a reference. Inquiring among U.S. colleagues for the name or names of patent counsel in foreign countries and asking for recommendations as to their capabilities is probably the best way to make a selection.

Nevertheless, if you cannot get a recommendation, or if it is a particularly remote country into which you must file, a number of listings are available. The international AIPPI (International Association for the Protection of Intellectual Property) has a membership list by country that covers most, if not all, countries that you may encounter. Searching the Internet for patent attorneys in particular countries may also provide listings. Some patent firms, including some from remote countries, advertise in patent magazines, such as *Managing Intellectual Property* and other international patent magazines. Additionally, a patent bar association in a particular country might provide you with listings of the patent firms in that country.

8.3 Selection Criteria for Patent Counsel

Once you have listings or recommendations of various patent counsel and patent firms in a particular country or region, you must then select the particular firm or counsel, and this can be done based upon various criteria.

The size of the patent firm should be taken into consideration. Historically, foreign patent firms were generally small, but over the years, mergers, acquisitions, and internal growth generally have resulted in some of these foreign firms being almost as large as some U.S. law firms. Some of these patent firms straddle various foreign countries, and in many cases, some of them have even established branch offices in the United States. Nevertheless, there are still many smaller offices situated around the world that handle patent matters.

A smaller firm might be able to devote more attention and time to your case, especially if you have a substantial patent portfolio and you are willing to offer to them a large number of cases. On the other hand, the larger firms may have more resources and more political clout within the country and within the patent office, and they have experience with a greater variety of technologies. However, a large firm may be able to give you the attention of some of the senior staff and more experienced attorneys, especially if you have only a small portfolio to provide to them.

Technical competence is always an important factor in selecting foreign counsel. Some firms—especially the smaller ones—may only specialize in specific technical areas, such as high tech or biotech, and they may not have a wide variety of technical capabilities. Of course, if your cases are focused in only a narrow area of technology, a small dedicated law firm may actually be the better choice if they are capable of addressing your particular area of technology. On the other hand, if you have a broad spectrum of technologies, the smaller law firm may not have competence in all these areas. However, to the extent you only have a few cases and these span across numerous areas of technology, there is no reason you cannot use more than one small law firm so long as each one specializes and is dedicated to the particular area that you need for that case and you can get their attention, and especially the attention of a more experienced individual in such small law firm.

Although conflicts are a major issue with U.S. law firms, in general, outside of the United States, conflicts are of less concern. Nevertheless, foreign firms are becoming more sensitive to this issue, especially if they handle major local corporate clients. Those clients may not want that law firm to represent competitors. In some countries, where a particular company is dominant, you may find that most if not all of the law firms there are somehow involved in getting work from that single major corporation. For example, it may be difficult to find a law firm in Finland that does not handle some amount of work for the company Nokia. If your client is agreeable, at least retaining a particular attorney within such a law firm who does a competitor's work and maintaining a "protective wall" between the attorney handling your case and the other attorneys might be the best you can achieve in such situations.

Of course, one issue that must be addressed when selecting a firm is the fee structure. In some countries, the local patent bar association may have a uniform fee schedule, and the patent law firms from the country try to adhere to that fee schedule. However, patent law firms are not under any obligation to maintain such a fee structure, and they generally can offer fee reductions and other fee arrangements, especially for a commitment of work or on a reciprocity arrangement. Most foreign firms have their own fee schedules for paralegal services and work on an hourly basis for attorney involvement. However, some of them will agree to fixed fee arrangements, especially for a volume of work.

It is always recommended to request a printed fee schedule from a firm before beginning to work with them and to always compare fee schedules among firms, because fees for patent work can vary greatly.

One area of charges that must be monitored continuously is the cost for translations. In many cases, the patent law firm may not be doing the translations themselves but may be contracting them out to translators and substantially marking up the actual translation costs. It is thus important to request and compare fee schedules for translations between one firm and another firm as this often represents the bulk of the costs in filing foreign cases.

The question arises about where translations should take place, i.e., in the United States or in the foreign country. It is generally recommended to do the translation in the country in which you are will be filing. Local translators have a better understanding of the grammar, the idioms, and the technical uses of terms in their own country, and since it is the foreign translation that must be used in enforcement, experience has shown that you get a better translation in the local country itself.

Where the same translation can be used in multiple countries, it may be advisable to determine whether a particular law firm has branch offices and/or subsidiaries in the other common language countries and to have that firm do the translation for an entire group of countries. Using a common translation may be cost effective.

For instance, if you are filing in Spain and also various Spanish-speaking Central and South American countries, be aware that many Spanish law firms have offices in Central and South America and will arrange for the use of the same translation in their other countries at a cost saving. Likewise, among the Arab-speaking countries, a single law firm may have offices in multiple Arab countries, and cost savings may be available through the use of a common translation, although minor changes may be needed for the individual countries.

A significant factor to be taken into consideration is the country into which a filing will be made. For example, a distinction should be made whether it is a "prosecuting-type country" or a "registration-type country." When entering into the national phase in a country like Japan, Korea, or the region of Europe, you must take into consideration that additional prosecution will be needed even after the international search may have taken place. Each of these countries carries out its own additional search and its own examination. Accordingly, the technical competence of the patent firm may be of prime importance. Especially when dealing with sophisticated technology, you would want to be sure that you get a highly skilled and experienced individual who will be able to prosecute your case and get the broadest possible claim coverage in that particular country. As such, you may give great attention to some of the smaller firms that have technical competence in your particular field of technology and where you can personally deal with an experienced senior practitioner in that firm.

On the other hand, in registration-type countries where essentially little if any substantive prosecution will take place, the technical nature of the firm may not be as significant. For example, Singapore, some of the South American countries, or some countries in Southeast Asia do not provide significant substantive prosecution on PCT applications to bring them into their national phase. However, there are often delays, administrative issues, and other details that may postpone the issuance of the patent in that country. As a result, in those countries, you may look more toward patent law firms that have a larger presence with greater political involvement and/or have patent attorneys who previously were officials in the patent office of that country but have retired or transferred. These individuals and their law firms may have contacts within the patent office in those countries and may be able to expedite matters should problems arise.

Helpful Recommendations for Selecting Foreign Counsel

- For examination countries, consider using smaller firms that are experienced in your technical field, where you can make use of a senior individual who will give your cases his personal attention.
- For nonexamination countries, consider using a large, well-connected firm and having retired patent office personnel who would be available to expedite any administrative complications that may arise.

8.4 Working with Foreign Counsel

Once you have selected your foreign counsel, you must establish a working relationship with that counsel. To the extent there is going to be ongoing prosecution of that national phase within that country or region, it is helpful to know who you are dealing with. Personal relationships are always important in dealing with foreign counsel. If you can arrange a visit to that country, be sure to do so and spend time, even on a social basis, getting to know the individual who is handling and prosecuting your cases. If that is not possible, at the very minimum, establish a telephone relationship with that individual. It is important to get to know not only the firm but also the particular individual or individuals in that firm who are working on your specific cases.

There is always a question of how much work the U.S. attorney should do in handling the foreign case and how much reliance should be given to the foreign counsel. The U.S. attorney should try to do as much of the work as possible and provide detailed instructions, and in some instances, he or she should even propose claims to the foreign associate. Typically, the U.S. attorney will have experience in prosecuting and handling the corresponding U.S. case. You will have better direct contact with the client and thus appreciate the types of claims, business needs, and strategies of the client. You will also have a better opportunity of seeing an overall picture of corresponding cases in other countries. As such, you will be in the best position to direct the type and scope of claim coverage worldwide. Limitations introduced in one country may be useful in other countries where similar references are being cited.

In fact, it is often helpful for the U.S. attorney to examine what is happening in other countries each time you receive an office action from a prosecuting country. Because the prosecution does not always take place uniformly from country to country, experience from his or her U.S. prosecution may be helpful in Europe and thereafter may be helpful in Japan. You should check the claims and their references from country to country as you continue to prosecute each new country. In prosecuting in new foreign countries, it may be necessary to go back and look at the claims in the issued U.S. patent to be sure that no newly cited references affect the issued U.S. claims; it may be necessary to file a reexamination in the United States should references affect the scope of the claims.

Accordingly, the U.S. attorney is in the best position to control worldwide prosecution of the particular foreign counterparts to the U.S. case. It should therefore be up to the U.S. attorney to provide the necessary arguments and recommended claims to be used in each particular foreign prosecuting country.

At the same time, because there are nuances and differences from country to country, the local attorney should be able to review the claims and suggest modifications and improvements based upon the local foreign practice, which the foreign counsel is much more familiar with. It is thus important to develop a dialogue and working relationship with your foreign counsel where he or she recognizes what you bring to the prosecution process, and you appreciate what the foreign counsel contributes toward obtaining the best claims in that country.

Helpful Recommendations for Working with Foreign Counsel

- Keep related cases with the same foreign counsel.
- Provide arguments and claims for foreign counsel to keep consistency and uniformity of corresponding prosecution throughout the patent family.
- Give foreign counsel permission to review and possibly revise those claims for local practices.
- Get to know your foreign counsel personally.

CHAPTER 10

WIPO Resources

In addition to providing a system for filing PCT applications, WIPO provides a number of other patent services. Some of these are used by the national offices, while other services are for users. These are services that are typically Internet based and are easily accessible.

1. Priority Document Exchange and Digital Access Services

Both the Priority Document Exchange (PDX) and Digital Access Services (DAS) systems are intended to facilitate the furnishing of electronic copies of priority documents filed in an Office of First Filing to an Office of Second Filing. The priority documents are transferred electronically, thereby eliminating the need to send certified paper copies of the priority documents. There is no cost to applicants to use the systems.

Under the PDX system, there is an automatic "pull" of the priority document by the Office of Second Filing from the Office of First Filing. The PDX system is bilateral in nature and is currently limited to arrangements among the European Patent Office (EPO), the Japan Patent Office (JPO), and the Korean Intellectual Property Office (KIPO). The WIPO DAS system requires the applicant in the Office of First Filing to register the priority document from that office into the WIPO DAS system. The applicant must then also request the Office of Second Filing to retrieve a copy of the priority document through the system.

As priority documents are typically required by an Office of Second Filing before an application will be published at 18 months, it is necessary in both systems to provide authorization for sending priority documents or for permitting a participant office to retrieve the documents before the 18 months. The USPTO has currently provided a checkbox on the declaration/oath for the purpose of providing such authorization.

1.1 PDX System

As mentioned above, the USPTO currently has agreements under the PDX System with the European Patent Office (EPO), the Japan Patent Office (JPO), and the Korean Intellectual Property Office (KIPO) to both obtain and provide priority documents.

For applications filed in the United States claiming priority from the EPO, JPO, or KIPO, simply reciting the claim for foreign priority on the Application Data Sheet will cause the USPTO to automatically retrieve the document from any of those other offices.

Moreover, the arrangements with the EPO and JPO permit the USPTO to automatically retrieve not only a European or Japanese priority document, but also a priority document from a nonparticipating country in the EPO or JPO database. For example, if an applicant filed a U.S. application that claimed priority to a French application, and the EPO already possessed a certified copy of the French application because the copy is included in the electronic record of a European application, the USPTO would be able to retrieve a copy of the French application and include it in the electronic record of the U.S.

application.[1] Likewise, the EPO and JPO can automatically retrieve not only U.S. priority documents but also non-U.S. priority documents contained in U.S. applications.

The PDX arrangement with KIPO is currently more restricted, however. The U.S. is authorized to retrieve only Korean priority applications from KIPO, and KIPO can retrieve only U.S. priority applications.

It nevertheless must be remembered that ultimate responsibility for obtaining a copy of the priority document remains with the applicant. While the participating offices will usually succeed in retrieving the priority documents, it is advisable to monitor the USPTO's Patent Application Information Retrieval (PAIR) system to confirm that the document was retrieved. When the system fails, you will probably be notified in an office action from the USPTO or in a notice of allowance that no priority document was submitted. That notice should serve as a "red flag" for you to manually obtain a hard copy of the priority document. Of course, the hard copy will have to be certified for submission to the USPTO.

1.2 WIPO DAS System

In addition to the PDX system, which is a bilateral system and is limited to certain countries, WIPO has established a Digital Access Services (DAS) system for filing and retrieving priority documents.[2] While the system is available for all WIPO member countries, currently only certain states participate in this program. Under the program, an Office of First Filing deposits the priority document within the WIPO DAS system, and Offices of Second Filing can then access that priority document electronically from the DAS system. Currently, the following countries are involved in the WIPO DAS system in addition to the PDX countries: Australia, Denmark, China, Spain, Finland, United Kingdom, Sweden, and PCT applications filed in the Receiving Office (RO)/International Bureau (IB).

---

1. All of this is conditioned upon compliance with the requirements of 37 C.F.R. § 1.55(d), which deals with claims for foreign priority.

2. Additional information on the DAS system can be found at http://www.wipo.int/das/en/.

In order to make U.S. priority documents available for accessibility to the Office of Second Filing through the DAS, applicants must be sure to permit the USPTO to send out their priority documents before the 18-month publication date. This can be done by checking the appropriate box on the Application Data Sheet. Alternately, a separate form PTO/SB/39 can be used. Applicants will then have to register their priority applications with DAS from the DAS portal website, https://webaccess.wipo.int/priority_documents/services/jsp/user/entry.jsp.

Applicants will need to provide the U.S. application number and the access code, which, for a U.S. application, is the confirmation number of the U.S. application and can be found on the EFS-Web Electronic Acknowledgement Receipt document and the filing receipt. Applicants will then have to manage the list of patent offices that may access their U.S. priority documents using the Access Control List (ACL) in DAS.

Figures 10.1, 10.2, and 10.3 show the various steps involved in utilizing WIPO's PATENTSCOPE in order to make use of WIPO's DAS service for those countries that are currently DAS accessing offices and depositing offices.

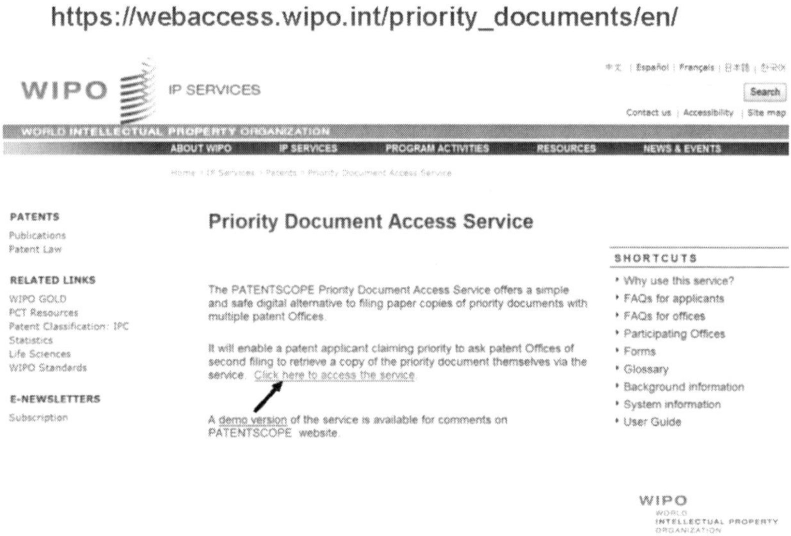

Figure 10.1
Accessing the WIPO Priority Document Access Service (DAS)

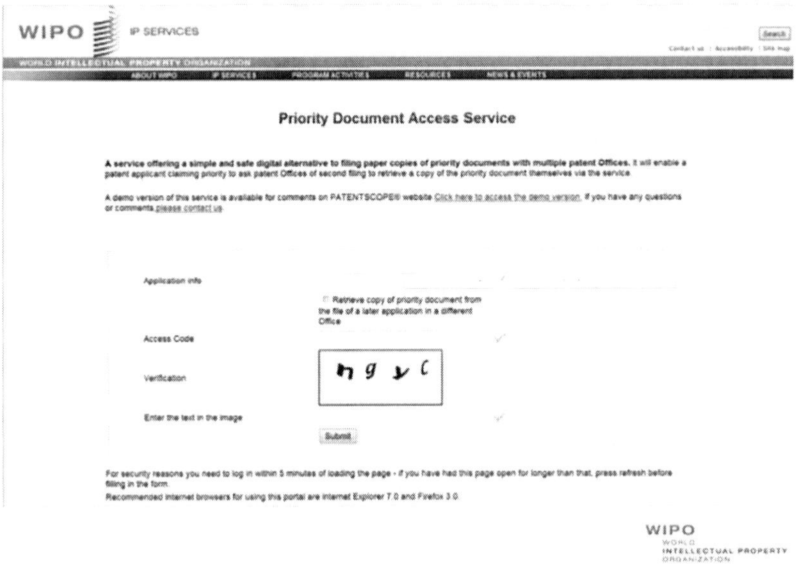

Figure 10.2
Getting Online to DAS

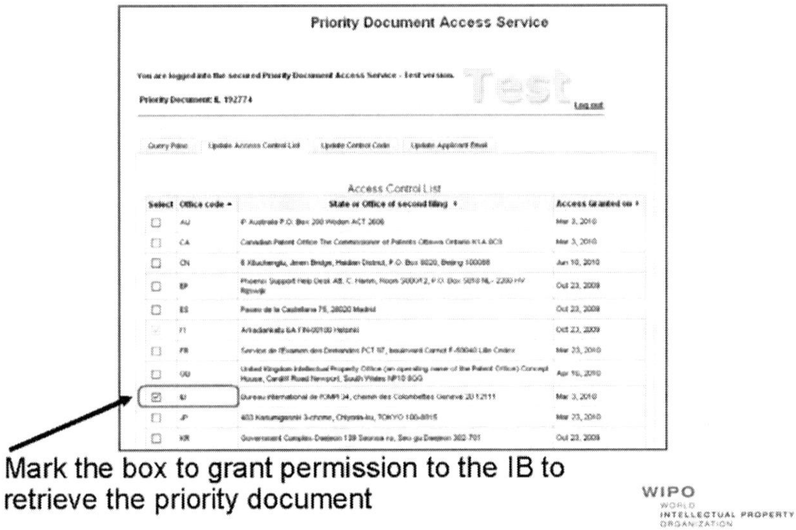

Figure 10.3
DAS—Granting Access Permission

2. Use of PDX and WIPO DAS with a PCT Application

The previous sections describe the use of the PDX and WIPO DAS systems in general, and specifically in connection with Paris Convention cases, but it is also important to understand how to make use of the systems with PCT applications.

First, it is important to remember that when filing a PCT application based upon a previous national priority, under Rule 17 of the PCT Regulations, the applicant has an obligation to submit a copy of the priority document. The IB then has the obligation, at the specific request of a designated national office, to provide a copy of the document to that national office. Accordingly, when an applicant enters the national phase of any PCT member country with a PCT application, a copy of the certified copy will be provided by the IB, so long as the IB has received it.

2.1 When Claiming a U.S. Priority

For PCT applications claiming priority to a U.S. application and filed with the RO/US, the USPTO will automatically prepare and transmit electronically a certified copy of the priority U.S. application, provided priority is claimed in Box VI of the request form. Once the International Bureau receives the document, it will satisfy the requirement provided by Rule 17 to furnish a copy to any designated office.

2.2 When Claiming a Foreign Priority

For PCT applications entering the United States and claiming a foreign priority, the procedure for obtaining priority documents would depend on how the U.S. national phase was entered. If entry was by the usual national phase route from the international phase under Section 371, the priority document would normally be made available by the International Bureau under Rule 17 of the PCT. However, when the bypass route is used, a certified copy of the original priority document will be needed. If the priority country is an EPO member country, Korea, or Japan, simply using the PDX system will automatically permit the U.S. to access the priority document electronically. The WIPO DAS system would be available for other countries that are DAS affiliated. However, to use DAS, the earlier application of which priority is claimed would have to be filed with a WIPO Depositing Office and the application successfully entered into the WIPO DAS system. Furthermore, the access control list would have to be updated to give access to the application by the IB. Furthermore, the IB would have to be requested to obtain a copy of the earlier application from a digital library using Box VI on the request form.

What if there are multiple priorities? If there is more than one priority application and the priority applications were filed in different countries, it may be necessary to retrieve the applications with different retrieval systems, but still using Box VI on the request form to make the priority claims. For example, if a PCT application were to be filed with the RO/US claiming both a U.S. and a United Kingdom priority, you would ask the USPTO to furnish a copy of the U.S. application, and, since the United Kingdom is a member of the WIPO DAS system, you would ask the IB to retrieve a copy of the United Kingdom application from the digital library. Of course, the United Kingdom application would have to be registered in DAS, and the access control list would have to give appropriate access. Box VI on the request form (form PCT/RO/101, available at http://www.wipo.int/export/sites/www/pct/en/forms/request/ed_request.pdf) would be filled out as indicated in Figure 10.4.

Box No. VI PRIORITY CLAIM AND DOCUMENT

The priority of the following earlier application(s) is hereby claimed:

Filing date of earlier application *(day/month/year)*	Number of earlier application	Where earlier application is:		
		national application: country or Member of WTO	regional application: regional Office	international application: receiving Office
item (1) 12 February 2011 (12.02.2011)	61/999,888	US		
item (2) 10 September 2011 (10.09.2011)	1118765.4	GB		
item (3)				

☐ Further priority claims are indicated in the Supplemental Box.

Furnishing the priority document(s):

☒ The **receiving Office** is requested to prepare and transmit to the International Bureau a certified copy of the earlier application(s) *(only if the earlier application(s) was filed with the receiving Office which, for the purposes of this international application, is the receiving Office)* identified above as:

☐ all items ☒ item (1) ☐ item (2) ☐ item (3) ☐ other, see Supplemental Box

☒ The **International Bureau** is requested to obtain from a digital library a certified copy of the earlier application(s) identified above, using, where applicable, the access code(s) indicated below *(if the earlier application(s) is available to it from a digital library)*:

☐ item (1) access code ______ ☒ item (2) access code ______ ☐ item (3) access code ______ ☐ other, see Supplemental Box

Figure 10.4
Using DAS with the PCT: Making the Request on the PCT/RO/101 Form

A similar request could be made in PCT-SAFE as indicated in Figure 10.5. Information on the PCT-Safe can be found at http://www.wipo.int/export/sites/www/pct/en/forms/request/ed_request.pdf.

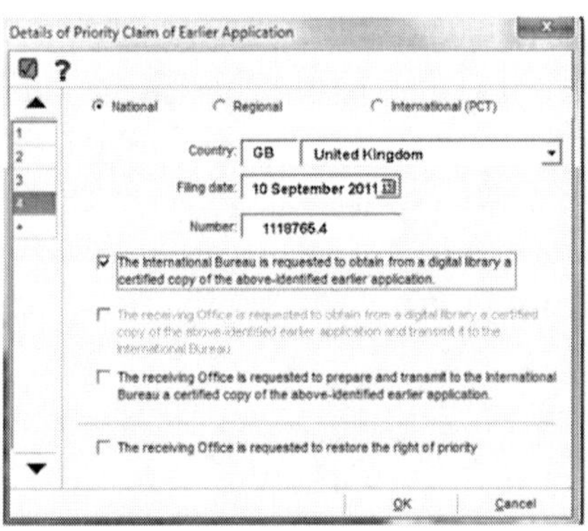

Figure 10.5
Using DAS with the PCT: Making the Request in PCT-SAFE

3. WIPO Publications

WIPO provides numerous publications both on the Internet and in printed form. Most are available free of charge and provide useful information about WIPO and, more specifically, about the PCT system. A list of the free publications can be found on the web at http://www.wipo.int/freepublications/en/. Among the publications are WIPO official documents, treaties, information in general on the PCT system, and documents about downloading published patent applications. Particularly helpful are various patent landscapes by product and country, country profiles, regular statistical updates, and a guide for using PATENTSCOPE, which is the main searching tool provided by WIPO.

A page from the WIPO website devoted to PCT Resources is shown in Figure 10.6 and provides an indication of the many items available to access or download from WIPO relating to the PCT. It is available at http://www.wipo.int/pct/en/.

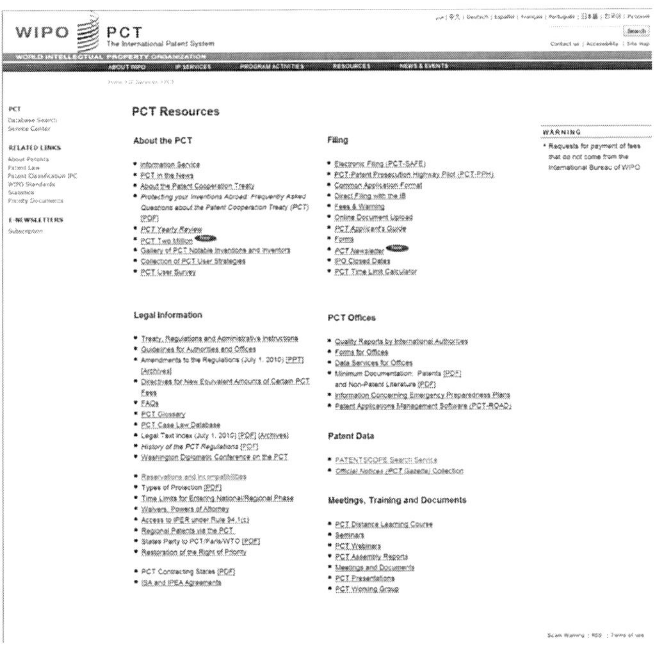

Figure 10.6
PCT Resources

3.1 WIPO Internet Resources

PCT-related information available from WIPO on the Internet includes the following:

- PCT Treaty and Regulations, as in force from July 1, 2012: www.wipo.int/pct/en/texts/
- PCT Administrative Instructions, as in force from July 1, 2012: www.wipo.int/pct/en/texts/
- PCT Newsletter (monthly): www.wipo.int/pct/en/newslett/
- Legal Text Index, providing references to PCT articles, rules, administrative instructions, forms, and various PCT guidelines: www.wipo.int/pct/en/texts/pdf/legal_index.pdf
- Official Notices (PCT Gazette) Collection: www.wipo.int/pct/en/official_notices/index.html
- PCT Receiving Office Guidelines: www.wipo.int/pct/en/texts/gdlines.htm
- PCT International Search and Preliminary Examination Guidelines: www.wipo.int/pct/en/texts/gdlines.htm
- WIPO Standards: www.wipo.int/scit/en/standards/standards.htm
- PCT Minimum Documentation, Patents, and Non-Patent Literature: www.wipo.int/scit/en/standards/pdf/04-01-01.pdf and www.wipo.int/scit/en/standards/pdf/04-02-01.pdf
- Agreements between International Bureau of WIPO and International Searching and/or Preliminary Examining Authorities: www.wipo.int/pct/en/access/isa_ipea_agreements.htm

WIPO also provides a free weekly e-mail updating service highlighting the latest PCT-related information.

Of all the information highlighted above, one of the most basic and useful tools is the PCT Applicant's Guide.

3.2 PCT Applicant's Guide

The PCT Applicant's Guide, which is updated regularly, is a web-based publication that is available free of charge at http://www.wipo.int/pct/en/appguide/index.jsp. The guide includes an international phase section, which provides general information about the PCT and detailed information concerning practice before every receiving office, international searching authority, and international preliminary examining authority. There is also a national phase section, which includes information on all acts that must be or may be performed before each of the individual national and regional offices. It includes the time limits in each of these offices and the fees involved, and sometimes provides blank national forms for use.

3.3 PATENTSCOPE

PATENTSCOPE is the essential database supported by WIPO for searching all PCT publications, as well as for providing access to 28 searchable national patent collections. The following countries' collections are included: Argentina, Brazil, Chile, Colombia, Costa Rica, Cuba, Dominican Republic, Ecuador, El Salvador, Guatemala, Honduras, Israel, Japan, Kenya, Korea, Mexico, Morocco, Nicaragua, Panama, Peru, Russian Federation (including USSR data), Singapore, South Africa, Spain, Uruguay, Vietnam, ARIPO, EPO, and LATIPAT (a collection of patent documents in Spanish and Portuguese from Latin America that are published on the EPO's Espacenet database).

Additionally, information on national phase entry into 44 countries/regional offices is also monitored, and that information is contained within PATENTSCOPE. Searches can be made on any of the bibliographic data included on the front page of a patent document, and the search results are well organized. Using the cross-lingual expansion tool (CLE), search queries in one language can be translated into several other languages using special software developed by WIPO. Additionally, access to GOOGLE TRANSLATE permits users to obtain English-language translations of patent applications filed in any PCT language.

3.4 Other PCT Resources Available on the Internet

- PCT distance learning course
- PCT webinars
- PCT case law database
    - Available at www.wipo.int/pctcaselawdb/en
    - Contents of this text searchable database:
        - Decisions from national courts

    - Decisions from regional administrative bodies
    - Abstracts and legal references added by IB
  - Any comments or submissions for addition can be sent to the IB at pct.legal@wipo.int

3.5 Really Simple Syndication (RSS) Feeds

Search results in PATENTSCOPE can now be retrieved using any standard RSS feed. Additionally, other WIPO RSS feeds include searching on general news, WIPO press releases, upcoming conferences, meetings and seminars, treaty notifications, and even the PCT newsletter. Using RSS feed on the PATENTSCOPE website, you can set up searches that will be reported on a regular and continuous basis. You can set up RSS feeds, for example, to retrieve all PCT applications handled by your own firm or company, to receive notice of competitors' PCT publications, or to be notified of all PCT publications in a particular area of technology.

4. PCT Licensing Feature

In January 2012, WIPO launched a new feature whereby applicants who are interested in licensing their inventions contained in the international application can ask the International Bureau to make this information available on its PATENTSCOPE website.

Applicants who are interested in licensing their inventions may submit PCT form PCT/IB/382 or send a letter indicating that the claimed invention is available for licensing. They may also include further licensing terms. It is possible to submit such licensing indications at any time beginning from the filing of the international application until the expiration of the 30-month time period.

Such licensing indications will be reflected in the bibliographic data relating to the particular application on PATENTSCOPE. However, it will not be part of the published international application itself. A link is available between the licensing statement on the bibliographic data page and the particular form or letter, allowing third parties to go directly to its content.

CHAPTER 11

Afterword—The Future of the PCT

When the PCT first began operations in 1978, it was a vastly different system than it is today. The PCT then was entirely paper based. You had to enter the national phase at 20 months from the priority date unless you requested international preliminary examination. You individually designated the countries in which you wanted protection when you filed your PCT application by checking lots of boxes on the request form, and you had to pay designation fees. The PCT had far fewer member countries, and U.S. applicants had the choice only of the USPTO or the EPO as an ISA. And those are just a few of the differences. One of the major accomplishments of the PCT is that it has been able to embrace and adapt to changing technologies and changing times. With that history of change in mind, the PCT member countries and the International Bureau are continuing to look to the future to find ways to improve the system. The current focus of attention is on ways to increase efficiency and quality by promoting worksharing among offices, leveraging the work of the ISAs, and taking advantage of advances in the electronic filing and processing of PCT applications worldwide. Here are a few of the changes under discussion that may soon become part of the PCT.

1. Publishing the Written Opinion

When the PCT member countries considered the proposal for ISAs to establish a written opinion (WO) along with the International Search Report (ISR) for every PCT application, representatives of the PCT user groups, including the ABA-IPL and the AIPLA, supported the WO proposal but opposed the publication of the WO until entry into the national phase. They felt at the time that making the WOs publicly available risked damaging the competitive situation of the PCT applicants. The user groups participated as observers in the WIPO meetings that deliberated the proposal, and their presence exerted a great influence on the decision of the PCT member countries to keep the WO confidential until entry into the national phase. Now, almost ten years later, both user groups and patent offices are reconsidering the decision, and the United Kingdom has introduced a proposal, which the USPTO and the International Bureau support, to make the WO available on PatentScope at the same time as the international application and ISR. If the proposal is adopted, the publication of the WO will bring the PCT into line with most national systems, which make examination documents available, and will benefit national offices by enabling them to use the results of the WO in processing equivalent national applications.

2. Collaborative Search and Examination

Several years ago, IBM, a major user of the PCT system, suggested that the quality and reliability of the ISR and WO could be improved if two or more offices collaborated in the preparation of the search documents. IBM also developed experimental software that would support the collaboration. The idea caught on, and at the time of drafting this chapter, the USPTO, KIPO, and the EPO had initiated two pilot projects to evaluate the feasibility of collaborative search and examination. Under the pilots, a first examiner from one of the three offices takes the lead on a file, but that examiner is assisted by an examiner from each of the other offices. The role of the other examiners is to improve the first examiner's search strategy and to find citations that the first examiner may not have identified. The objective of collaborative search is at least twofold and would benefit both applicants and national offices. It would give applicants a clearer and more thorough view of the likelihood of success in the national phase as well as more precise information on which to base prosecution strategies. It would also give national offices a stronger basis for relying on the ISR and WO during the national phase and minimize the need for any national phase procedure other than a top-up search. Although collaborative search would thereby greatly increase the value of the resulting ISRs and WOs, the downside is that the cost of collaborative search is likely to be two to three times the current cost, according to an EPO estimate, unless other cost-saving measures can be identified.

3. Making International Search Strategies Available

Right now, the offices where you enter the national phase can see the international patent classification number or numbers that have been applied to your application, but they cannot see the search terms and related logic that the ISA examiner has used to carry out the international search. Examiners uniformly prepare and use search terms and queries, and those search strategies are generally preserved in the application file. The USPTO and the IB have therefore proposed that the search strategies be made available so that other offices can rely on them in the national or regional phase. If national phase offices had access to international search strategies, national phase examiners would not need to repeat the search done in the international phase; they also would be able to verify that the international search had been done properly and that relevant search terms had not been overlooked. The greatest potential benefit of access to search strategies would be increased speed and efficiency in the national phase, but it would no doubt also lead to greater confidence in and reliance on the international search.

4. ePCT

The International Bureau of WIPO has reported that the ultimate goal of ePCT is to provide "a consistent service and electronic interface for all applicants across the entire PCT system, irrespective of which Office happens to carry out a particular function."[1] When fully implemented, every aspect of the PCT application process—from filing the international application until entry into the national phase—should be doable, searchable, and retrievable online on one common, secure, globally accessible portal. The result should be a far greater and more reliable source of usable information available to applicants, offices, and third parties.

For applicants, ePCT should approximate, and perhaps even surpass, the usefulness and benefits of the USPTO's Private Pair. The anticipated developments mean that applicants should be able to securely log into ePCT and:

- See the status of their applications at each office (RO, ISA, IPEA, IB), including outstanding requirements and estimates of when ISAs are likely to transmit ISRs and WOs;
- Use ePCT to communicate with ROs, ISAs, IPEAs, and the IB; and
- Directly request and effect changes in bibliographic information or the application body without having to submit clumsy letters of request and waiting for responses.

For all patent offices, from the RO to national and regional offices, ePCT should result in instant access to applications as well as to all other supporting documents and information. Accompanying that access will be the ability to communicate documents and information more efficiently among offices, which should help to speed up processing

1. PCT/WG/5/12, p. 8.

and examination. In a paper-based world, the international application had to exist in many copies: the RO needed to send the "search copy" of the examination to the ISA and the "record copy" to the IB, which also had to prepare a publication copy; and when applicants entered the national phase, the IB ultimately sent a copy of the application file to each national or regional phase office. With ePCT, only one copy of the application and one application file should be necessary, stored in a central database and accessible as appropriate to offices and applicants alike.

If ePCT achieves its goal of a seamless, reliable interface, we will all benefit from fewer delays and fewer mistakes, and a system that is not only much less complicated, but that also makes sense in today's electronic world.

5. PCT-PPH

With the increasing success of PCT-PPH to leverage the work products of ISAs, it is inevitable that PCT member countries will look for ways to expand the PPH system. A recent USPTO proposal would have PPH formally integrated into the PCT. The ability to take advantage of PCT-PPH would no longer depend on bilateral agreements between ISAs and national phase offices, but would be available across the board, regardless of the ISA that carried out the international search and the national phase office. If the proposal were to gain traction, applicants would be able (and also encouraged) to fast-track national phase applications that were presented with claims that the ISA determined to be patentable. The benefit for all applicants who wished to avail themselves of PCT-PPH would generally be faster national phase processing with fewer office actions per disposal, higher allowance rates, and reduced need for appeal.

6. Linking the International and National Phases

Somewhat related to the proposal to expand PCT-PPH is a USPTO and EPO proposal to require offices and applicants to give greater recognition to the results of the international phase when entering the national or regional phase. At its most basic level, the proposal would require the office that acted as the ISA to treat the ISR/WO as a first action on the merits when you entered the national phase in that office. In other words, when you selected an ISA (for example, the USPTO), you would effectively also be entering the national phase in that office. The IPRP that you received in the international phase would also be a first office action when you entered the national phase, and you would be required to respond to it within a given time limit (that is assuming that you actually do enter the national phase). The EPO instituted this procedure in 2010; it no longer carries out a supplementary European search when it was the ISA, and it gives you six months to respond to any negative indications in the ISR and WO once you have entered the regional phase. In addition to streamlining and speeding up prosecution, an important benefit of this proposal is that it would help ensure that the quality of the international search was at least the equivalent of the quality of the search at the national level. ISAs would no longer need to resist the temptation to disregard their international phase responsibilities under the guise that they could always perform "top-up" searches if and when applications came back to them in their capacity as DO/EOs. And you would have greater assurance that the basis for your national or regional phase prosecution was sound.

A more ambitious version of the proposal would require all designated national and regional offices (not just the office that acted as the ISA/IPEA) to recognize the IPRP as the first action on the merits in the national or regional phase. Under this version, national or regional phase entry anywhere would need to be followed by a response to any negative findings in the IPRP made by the ISA/IPEA.

7. Conclusion

The ultimate fate of the above plans and proposals will no doubt vary, and each will face particular challenges stemming from the fact that the PCT is a global, treaty-based system. The plan to expand ePCT, for example, will require implementation in the patent office of every PCT member state, many of which have only the most basic technological infrastructures. Devising electronic systems that respond to the needs of all offices regardless of their levels of activity is, as can be imagined, a daunting task. Moreover, most of the proposals will require amendment of the PCT regulations, which poses other significant challenges. The PCT system is governed by the principle of consensus, which means that any of the more than 146 PCT member countries can object and block the adoption of a proposed rule. Though all member countries share a common interest in improving the PCT, it is sometimes difficult to predict whether a particular country or group of countries may find that a proposed rule change would be contrary to its own needs or interests. It is therefore likely that some of the plans and proposals will never see the light of day, or they might emerge in a form very different from the way they were first envisaged.

Given all the challenges the PCT faces, what is most remarkable is how successful the system has been in reinventing itself to meet the needs of vastly expanded pools of applicants from an enormous number of member countries filing unanticipatedly large numbers of applications in technologies that did not exist when the PCT was created, and using electronic means of communication to do so. There is no doubt that the PCT system is complicated. But given its history, it seems clear that the PCT will continue to respond to the changing needs of its stakeholders (be they applicants, offices, or third parties). And even if the proposals outlined above are not implemented, others will be adopted that will allow the PCT to evolve and improve. The PCT is likely to continue to grow worldwide, and it is our job to take best advantage of it not only for the short-range interest of PCT applicants but also for the long-range benefit of our economic and technological well-being. As the PCT grows, so may our mastery of it. Here's to the future of the PCT!

APPENDIX

PCT Jargon

One of the complicating features of the PCT is that it has its own unique terminology. In order to maximize the benefits of the PCT, it is helpful to have a command of the language of the PCT. The following is a glossary of PCT terms.

1. Glossary of Terms

Chapter I of the PCT: The provisions in the PCT that regulate the filing of PCT applications, the establishment of international searches and written opinions by ISAs, and the international publication of PCT applications; provides for the communication of PCT applications and related documents to designated offices.

Chapter II of the PCT: The provisions in the PCT that regulate the optional international preliminary examination procedure.

Contracting State: A PCT member country.

Designated Office (DO): A national or regional office of or acting for a PCT member country designated in a PCT application under Chapter I of the PCT.

Designated State: A PCT member country in which protection for an invention is sought, as specified in the PCT application.

Elected Office: The national or regional office of or acting for a PCT member country elected by the applicant under Chapter II of the PCT.

International Authority: A national or regional patent office or international organization that fulfills specific search and examination tasks, as prescribed by the PCT.

International Bureau (IB): In the context of the PCT, the International Bureau of the World Intellectual Property Organization is the administrative arm of the PCT, responsible for PCT oversight. The IB acts as a receiving office for PCT applications from all PCT member countries. It also handles certain processing tasks with respect to all PCT applications filed with all receiving offices worldwide.

International Filing Date: The date on which a receiving office receives a PCT application (provided the application meets the treaty requirements).

International Patent Classification (IPC): An internationally recognized patent classification system. The IPC has a hierarchical structure of language-independent symbols that consists of sections, classes, subclasses, and groups. A patent office assigns IPC symbols according to technical features in the patent application. One patent application can be assigned multiple IPC symbols, as it may relate to multiple technical features.

International Phase of the PCT: The international phase consists of six main stages:

1. the filing of a PCT application by the applicant and its processing by the Receiving Office;
2. the establishment of an International Search Report and Written Opinion by an international searching authority;
3. the publication of the PCT application and related documents as well as their communication to designated and elected offices by the International Bureau;

4. the option for the applicant to file claim amendments or to seek international preliminary examination and file amendments to the claims and/or description and/or drawings ;
5. the optional establishment of a supplementary international search report by a supplementary international searching authority; and
6. the optional establishment of an international preliminary report on patentability (Chapter II of the PCT) by an international preliminary examining authority, or the communication of an international preliminary report on patentability (Chapter I of the PCT) by the international bureau.

International Preliminary Examining Authority (IPEA): A national or regional patent office appointed by the PCT Assembly to carry out international preliminary examination. Its task is to establish the international preliminary report on patentability (Chapter II of the PCT). There are currently 15 IPEAs, all of which also serve as international searching authorities (see below).

International Preliminary Report on Patentability (IPRP): There are two types of international preliminary reports on patentability: an IPRP (Chapter I of the PCT); and an IPRP (Chapter II of the PCT). An IPRP (Chapter I) is issued by the International Bureau when an applicant who has not requested international preliminary examination enters the national phase; it consists of the Written Opinion of the International Searching Authority to which a cover sheet (entitled IPRP (Chapter I)) is attached. An IPRP (Chapter II) is the Written Opinion of the International Preliminary Examining Authority (a preliminary, nonbinding opinion, established by the IPEA at the request of the applicant, on whether the claimed invention appears to be novel, to involve an inventive step (to be non-obvious), and to be industrially applicable), which is issued by the IPEA on the 28th month from priority. Prior to January 1, 2004, the IPRP (Chapter II) was known as the International Preliminary Examination Report (IPER).

International Search Report (ISR): A report established by the International Searching Authority containing citations of documents (prior art) considered to be relevant for determining, in particular, the novelty and inventive step (non-obviousness) of the invention as claimed. The ISR also includes the classification of the subject matter of the invention and an indication of the fields searched as well as any electronic databases searched.

International Searching Authority (ISA): A national or regional patent office appointed by the PCT Assembly to carry out international searches. ISAs establish International Search Reports and Written Opinions on PCT applications. There are currently 15 international searching authorities, all of which also serve as international preliminary examining authorities.

National Phase Entry: When the PCT applicant converts a PCT application into a national or regional application, it is referred to as entering the national phase before a national or regional patent office, or simply as national phase entry (it is also sometimes described as nationalizing a PCT application). National phase entry consists of the payment of fees and, where necessary, the submission of the translated PCT application. It must take place within 30 months from the priority date of the application (longer time periods are allowed by some offices). Entering the national phase in the United States is, in accordance with § 371 of the U.S. Patent Act (35 U.S.C. § 371), called entering the "national stage."

National Phase of the PCT: This phase follows the international phase of the PCT procedure and consists of the processing of the application before each national or regional patent office in which applicants seek protection for their inventions.

National Stage of the PCT: As provided in § 371 of the U.S. Patent Act (35 U.S.C. § 371), the term used to designate entering the national phase in the United States. The generic term for national stage is "national phase."

Paris Convention: An international treaty (The Paris Convention for the Protection of Industrial Property), signed in Paris, France, on March 20, 1883. It was the first, and remains one of the most important, multilateral intellectual property treaties. The Paris Convention establishes, among other provisions, the "right of priority," which enables a patent applicant, when filing an application in countries other than the original country of filing, to claim priority of up to 12 months for this filing. The PCT is a "special agreement" under the Paris Convention, and both are administered by the World Intellectual Property Organization (WIPO).

PATENTSCOPE Search Service: The PATENTSCOPE search service allows access, free of charge, to all published PCT applications. Since April 2006, the PATENTSCOPE search service has become the authentic publication source of PCT applications. Powerful, flexible search interfaces allow retrieval of relevant PCT applications and associated information.

Publication of PCT Applications: The International Bureau publishes PCT applications and related documents promptly after the expiration of 18 months from the priority date. If the PCT application is withdrawn or considered withdrawn, the application is not published. An applicant can request an early publication of the PCT application. An applicant can also request withdrawal of a PCT application to prevent publication.

Receiving Office (RO): The patent office or the International Bureau with which a PCT application is filed. The role of the receiving office is to check the application in accordance with the PCT and its regulations and to forward the application to the International Bureau for further processing and to the International Searching Authority for search.

Supplementary International Searching Authority (SISA): An international searching authority (ISA) that provides a supplementary international search service. Also known as "Authority specified for Supplementary International Search."

Supplementary International Search Report (SISR): A report, similar to the international search report, established during the supplementary international search. Supplementary international search permits the applicant to request, in addition to the main international search, one or more supplementary international searches, each to be carried out by an international authority other than the international searching authority that carries out the main international search. The supplementary international search primarily focuses on the patent documentation in the language in which the supplementary international searching authority specializes.

World Intellectual Property Organization (WIPO): WIPO is a specialized agency of the United Nations with a current membership of 185 countries. It serves as the international secretariat for both the Paris Convention and the PCT. WIPO was established in 1967 with a mandate from its member countries to promote the protection of intellectual property throughout the world through cooperation among countries and in collaboration with other international organizations.

Written Opinion of the ISA: For every PCT application filed on or after January 1, 2004, an international searching authority establishes, at the same time that it establishes the international search report, a preliminary and nonbinding written opinion on the questions whether the claimed invention appears to be novel, to involve an inventive step, and to be industrially applicable.

2. Glossary of Abbreviations

DAS: WIPO Digital Access Service for priority documents

DO: Designated Office

EO: Elected Office

EPO: European Patent Office (sometimes abbreviated just as EP)

IA: International Application (the formal name of a PCT application)

IB: International Bureau

INID: Internationally Agreed Numbers for the Identification of Bibliographic Data, used by patent offices to indicate bibliographic data on the cover pages of published patents and patent applications

IPC: International Patent Classification

IPEA: International Preliminary Examining Authority

ISA: International Searching Authority

ISR: International Search Report

IPRP: International Preliminary Report on Patentability (can be Chapter I or Chapter II)

JPO: Japan Patent Office

KIPO: Korean Intellectual Property Office

PDX: WIPO Priority Document Exchange

RO: Receiving Office (often designated as RO/US = Receiving Office at the USPTO; or RO/IB = Receiving Office at the International Bureau)

SIPO: State Intellectual Property Office of China

SISA: Supplementary International Searching Authority

SISR: Supplementary International Search Report

WO: Written Opinion (sometimes WOISA or WOSA)

WIPO: World Intellectual Property Organization

INDEX

NOTE: Page references in *italics* refer to figures.

About the ABA Section of Intellectual Property Law

From its strength within the American Bar Association, the ABA Section of Intellectual Property Law (ABA-IPL) advances the development and improvement of intellectual property laws and their fair and just administration. The Section furthers the goals of its members by sharing knowledge and balanced insight on the full spectrum of intellectual property law and practice, including patents, trademarks, copyright, industrial design, literary and artistic works, scientific works, and innovation. Providing a forum for rich perspectives and reasoned commentary, ABA-IPL serves as the ABA voice of intellectual property law within the profession, before policy makers, and with the public.